Review

Celia Martin's historical romance *Precarious Game of Hide and Seek* ranks as above average fare in this genre for a variety of reasons. One of the chief distinguishing factors setting it apart from other works of this ilk is its historical fidelity. It is clear Martin made a great effort to ground this work in its time, mid 1600's England during the time of Oliver Cromwell's rule over the isle, and it has the ring of truth. Other writers will adopt a historical setting in order to give their work an ultimately facile flavor but once you give their words a close reading, you discover their decision is window dressing alone.

The dialogue is another reason why this work rates as above average. The exchanges between Martin's characters advance the plot, develop character, and rarely strikes a false note. There's a musical quality to her best dialogue that never seems self-indulgent but rather a reflection of the high flown diction of the time. While she obeys many of the genre's conventions, she upends reader's conventions with her unfailing skill for assigning credible motivations for each of her characters rather than maneuvering her characters through the story like cardboard clichés present only to move the reader to the next scene.

The narrative moves at a swift clip without rushing things along in a dizzying manner. Her ability to develop each set piece in full without skimping on details is an outstanding aspect of the novel. The descriptive powers she exhibits throughout *Precarious Game of Hide and Seek* are impressive. Swaths of her language in this area may seem inflated to some readers, but her choice in this area is consistent with the novel's overall aesthetic and gives the novel a widescreen grandeur many readers, particularly those who enjoy historical fiction, will find quite fulfilling.

There are clear protagonists and antagonists throughout the novel. Many authors inexplicably fumble this, but Martin has a sure hand for this certain to grip many readers. Martin brings readers straight into the novel's action as it opens and she sets out the classical elements of what makes the form work from the start and throughout. The protagonists have clear goals they want to achieve, Martin throws a number of obstacles in their way, and she carries us towards an inevitable climax leaving each of the central characters forever changed since their initial introduction.

Precarious Game of Hide and Seek is the product of a fine writer working at or near the peak of her powers. Those who love historical romance will enjoy the book a great deal and even those who might disdain this genre will find themselves, if they bring an open mind to bear, entertained by this cinematic and well written piece of fiction. Evaluating works in specific genres must be by the standards constituting exceptional examples of the form and, by this test, Celia Martin's *Precarious Game of Hide and Seek* is a sparkling entry in the style that will likely endure for some time to come.

By Jason Hillenburg, themagicpen.com

Precarious Game of Hide and Seek

Celia Martin

KITSAP PUBLISHING

KITSAP PUBLISHING

Precarious Game of Hide and Seek
First edition, published 2020

By Celia Martin

Book Layout: Tim Meikle, Reprospace

Copyright ©2020, Celia Martin

ISBN-13 Softcover: 978-1-942661-22-1

This is a work of fiction. Names, characters, businesses, places, events and incidents are either the products of the author's imagination or used in a fictitious manner. Any resemblance to actual persons, living or dead, or actual events is purely coincidental.

All rights reserved. No part of this book may be reproduced or transmitted in any form or by any means, electronic or mechanical, including photocopying, recording or by any information storage and retrieval system, without written permission from the author, except for the inclusion of brief quotations in a review.

Published by Kitsap Publishing
P.O. Box 572
Poulsbo, WA 98370
www.KitsapPublishing.com

Also by Celia Martin

To Challenge Destiny

"Exquisite passion and breath-taking action! A historical romance feast!"

Curt Locklear - Laramie Award Winner

"Martin proves she has the vision and talent to make bygone times come alive for modern readers."

Anne Hollister, Professional Book Reviews

A Bewitching Dilemma

"A willful heroine cornered by a relentless foe and a dashing sea captain tormented by his past cast their lots against the tides of a history dark with treachery. A compelling read cover to cover."

Michael Donnelly - Author of False Harbor

With Every Breath I take

A love story laced with fun and surprises

Taking A Chance

"I've no hesitation to recommend this five-star read to new or old readers of historical fiction."

Trisha J. Kelly - multi-genre award-winning author of children and middle school books, and of cozy mysteries and crime thrillers.

"Celia Martin captures the complex landscape of people dealing with Puritanism which squelches the fun out of life for ordinary people. A great backdrop for the heroine to shine as she strives to marry the man she loves"

C.A. Asbrey - author of the 19th century murder mysteries, 'The Innocents' and of articles on history for magazines and periodicals.

cmartinbooks.kitsappublishing.com

I would like to thank my mother and father who taught me the joy of reading and the thrill of story telling.

A Collection of Romantic Adventures

Follow the romantic adventures of the D'Arcy, Hayward, and Lotterby families and their captivating friends in seventeenth century England and the American colonies. In Precarious Game of Hide and Seek Lady Rowena Crossly is willing to risk all to rescue her daughter from an unscrupulous Cromwellian. But can she contain her growing feelings for the highwayman, Nathaniel D'Arcy, who helps her save her daughter. And be sure to watch for Fate Takes A Hand when Amaryllis Bowdon, fearing her aunt means to kill her brother, two-year old Sir Charles, flees her home with her two young siblings. In her desperate flight, she never expected to be aided by Lady Selena D'Arcy, and her much too handsome brother, Reginald D'Arcy.

Chapter 1

Derbyshire England 1656

Rowena Plaisance Crossly, Lady Crossly, paced back and forth across her bedchamber wringing her hands and cursing in a most unladylike fashion. That her husband, Sir Lindell Crossly, Baronet of Crossly Oaks, had forcibly locked her in their bedchamber and placed a guard at the door had her rabid. Her fists ached from pounding on the door, and her throat was raw from yelling. Below her in the Crossly Oaks hall, her fourteen-year-old daughter, Cecily, was being compelled by her father to marry Orrin Haspel, a Puritan tax commissioner appointed by Cromwell's Major General in charge of Derbyshire.

A decimation tax being imposed on Royalists or merely suspected Royalists was meant to finance county militias. The zealous Haspel had been intent on assessing a massive tax on the Crossly Oaks manor whether the property income merited such a tax or not. Sir Lindell would have needed to sell off a portion of his land to pay the tax. Then Haspel had spotted Cecily. Just beginning to blossom, her figure still svelte and youthful, Cecily, though small for her age, was an undeniable beauty. She favored her father in her coloring, pale blond hair and vivid blue eyes, but she had her mother's straight, slim nose, sculpted jawline, and full, finely-molded lips. Being sweet-tempered, she perennially wore a smile and had a ready laugh.

Unbeknownst to Rowena, her husband made a bargain with Haspel – the tax assessment would be minimal in exchange for Cecily's hand in marriage. When told of the arrangement, Rowena had raged, "In no way will I allow Cecily to be married off to that Puritan ogre. First off, she is barely turned fourteen, but was she twenty, I would not consent to such a marriage."

Sir Lindell, his blue eyes sad, but his mouth set, responded, "She must marry him. Does she not, we stand to lose near half the manor. Besides, she is but a year younger than you were when you married me."

"I might have been but fifteen, Lindell, but you were our neighbor. I had known you all my life. With my grandmother's illness, and my mother's continual absences to care for her mother, I had been helping to care for my family from the time I was ten. My childhood was limited. By the time I was fifteen, I was already a woman. But Cecily is yet a child. And I intend she shall continue to enjoy her childhood for several years to come."

Shaking his head, Sir Lindell said, "That cannot be Rowena. I have already betrothed her to Haspel. The banns are being posted and read on the next three Sundays. A month from next Sunday, the local magistrate will perform the wedding ceremony here in our hall. I thought having the ceremony in our own home would make it easier for Cecily. You have a month to prepare her for her new duties as a wife."

As her husband spoke, Rowena stared at him in wide-eyed disbelief. "Never! Never!" she stormed. "Never will I let you marry Cecily off to that man. We have my dowry. We can use it to pay the higher tax assessment. We need not sell any of Crossly Oaks."

Sir Lindell reached out to take her hands, but she snatched her hands away and glared at him. Frowning, he said, "Would that we could use your dowry, but your grandfather tied it up in such a way we cannot touch it. It is in trust, and the monthly stipend is all we can ever have of it. I know you had planned to have a portion of that stipend transferred to Cecily as her dowry, but Haspel has asked for no dowry, so you will retain your full portion."

"My uncle controls the trust. Could he not release it to us?"

Twisting his mouth to one side, Sir Lindell shook his head. "Nay. I have already spoken with him. Before I consented to Haspel's request for Cecily's hand, I went to see Gaylord. He could find no way to break the trust. Nor could he offer us a loan. He, too, is being pressed financially. Due to a storm at sea, he lost a large cargo of woolen goods being shipped to Sweden. Right now he is barely able to make good on his debts besides keeping up with yours and your brother's stipends."

Rowena brightened. "What of Artus. Could he not loan us what we need?"

"Your brother will be lucky does he not lose more of Elkton Hall. He, too, has been assessed a massive tax, but he still has a good stand of woods he can sell off. That may save him. We had to sell off our timber to pay the fines and buy back Crossly Oaks after it was confiscated, so we have nothing more to sell.

"Had your mother willed Glenwood House to you instead of to Godwin, we could sell that land, but it is in trust to Godwin and cannot be sold until he turns twenty-one, does he then choose to sell it, which I would advise against."

"'Twas right Mother should will Glenwood House to Godwin. Milo will inherit Crossly Oaks, and Cecily will have a portion of my stipend for her dowry, plus the two-hundred pounds you have designated for her dowry. Besides, Godwin was named for Mother's father."

Rowena's two sons, Milo age ten and Godwin age seven, could not be more different. Milo looked like his mother, tall and slim with dark hair and brown eyes. Godwin looked like his father short and stocky with blond hair and blue eyes. Their personalities were also different. Both were cheerful boys, but Godwin was more serious and studious where Milo cared more for the outdoors and for horseback riding and hunting.

"Well then, Lindell, there is naught for it but to sell off some of Crossly Oaks to pay the tax assessment, for I will not have Cecily married to Orrin Haspel or anyone else at her young age. That you could even consider such a thing is a sad disappointment to me. And until you have informed Haspel that he will not be marrying Cecily, you will not be sharing my bed."

But her threats and her haranguing had not moved her husband, and Rowena had found herself sharing her daughter's bed instead of her husband's. She had given Cecily her word she would never let her be forced into marriage with Haspel, but here she was, locked in her bedchamber, unable to save Cecily from her fate.

Hearing a coach being brought around to the front of the house, Rowena hurried to her chamber window. Pushing open the casement frame with its diamond-paned glass, she leaned as far out as she could that she might see what was happening. She had been praying the magistrate would not sanction the marriage, Cecily being so young and Haspel being well into his middle years, but her prayers had not been answered. With a mournful gasp she watched Haspel lead Cecily to his coach. Lindell, following in their wake, was saying something to Cecily, but Rowena could not hear what he said. She but saw the hopeless look on her daughter's face. Then Cecily looked up, and her eyes met her mother's.

"Oh!" sobbed Rowena, stretching out an arm and leaning further out over the edge.

"My lady! Do have a care," cried her maid Liverna, tugging at Rowena's other arm in an attempt to pull her back into the room.

Her heart in her throat, Rowena watched the hated Haspel hand her daughter up into his coach. He clambered in after her, and Lindell shut the door. A footman swung up on the stand at the rear of the coach, the coachman flapped the reins, and the coach jolted forward, disappearing around the house and up the road. Eager to escape with his young bride, Haspel was not even staying for the wedding breakfast Lindell had ordered prepared. Rowena guessed Lindell would be sitting down to the elaborate breakfast with no one but the magistrate.

Frustrated and sickened that she had not been able to save her daughter, Rowena angrily plucked at the ivy climbing up the outside wall. Rage pummeling her soul, the small destructive action was not enough. Desperately needing to assuage her wrath, she tugged on a thick vine. She could not budge it. It clung to the weathered stone that had been its home for so many years. Straightening, she studied the vines. Whipping about, she demanded, "Liverna! Get me a pair of Lindell's breeches and be quick!"

Liverna eyed her mistress warily. "Rowena, what do you mean to do?" She had been Rowena's nurse when Rowena was young, and had come to Crossly Oaks as Rowena's maid when Rowena married the baronet. She knew her charge well, and Rowena knew better than to try to fool her maid.

"I mean to go after my daughter. I care not do I have to shoot Haspel, he will not take Cecily to his bed. Now, get me those breeches."

Casting a doubtful look at Rowena, Liverna nevertheless obeyed. Muttering loud enough for Rowena to hear that she wondered how

Rowena thought she would get a chance to shoot Haspel, she began digging into the large chest at the foot of the four-poster bed. Her brow creased in a frown, Liverna pulled out a pair of the baronet's breeches while Rowena, ignoring her maid's mutterings, yanked off her lappet cap, grabbed a garter from the chest, and tied her hair behind her at the nape of her neck. Snatching the breeches from Liverna's hands, she kicked off her shoes, jerked up her skirt and petticoat, and hastily donned the breeches.

"Get me my riding boots," she said, taking a sash from her gown and tying it about the waist of the breeches to hold them up.

Liverna found the boots in a corner, and handed them to Rowena. "Now how is it you plan to go after Cecily?" she asked, brushing a lock of her graying hair off her forehead.

"I intend to take Sir Lindell's gelding. He is the fastest horse in the stable."

"And how do plan to get out that door?" Liverna pointed to the locked door.

"I have no mind to go out the door," Rowena said, returning to the window. "I intend to go down this ivy."

Shaking her head, Liverna said, "I feared that was what you had in your head. Well, I cannot let you do that. You could fall. The vines could pull lose."

"I trust the vines will hold. And you cannot stop me." She caught her maid's hands in her own. "I must do this. You must see that, Liverna. Cecily is an innocent. Would you have me leave her in Haspel's evil hands?"

"No, my lady, but I fear for you."

"Have no fear for me, faithful friend. But know that I might be unable to return immediately. I might need hide out somewhere with Cecily." She thumped her forehead with her palm. "In my haste, I am near forgetting my pistol. And I will need something to fund us." Hurrying to her jewelry case, she pulled out everything in it, including her small six-inch flintlock, and stuffed first the jewelry then the pistol into her pockets.

"My lady!" Liverna cried. "You would not part with your dear mother's emeralds?"

"Mother would forgive me does it mean I use them to save Cecily." Returning to the window, she looked out. Seeing no one around, she dropped her boots out the window. Turning back to Liverna, she swallowed and said, "I will trust you to care for Milo and Godwin and make certain they understand why I must leave them for I know not how long."

"I will see to them, my lady. Like they were my own blood." She clutched Rowena's shoulders. "Oh, do have a care. Come home to us safe and well."

Wrapping her arms around the aging body of her beloved maid, Rowena gave her a quick hug and said, "I will. And with my daughter. I promise."

With that, she climbed onto the windowsill, and taking a deep breath, she placed first one stockinged foot and then the other onto thick vines in the ivy. Her footing secured, for a moment she clung to the windowsill. She looked up into Liverna's worried eyes then released one hand to grasp a vine. Not daring to look down, she moved one foot to a lower vine and released her hold on the windowsill. Totally supported by the vines, she slowly made her way down the wall.

When she touched the ground, she offered up a prayer then sat down to tug on her boots. Rising, she looked up at her maid. She offered Liverna a smile and a wave then turned and raced off to the stables. The musty smell of hay and muck assaulted her nostrils when she entered the stable, and the dim light made her halt until her eyes could adjust to the dark interior.

"Milady," a stable boy addressed her, obvious surprise in his voice. Standing with pitchfork in hand, he had been mucking out a stall.

"Where is the stableman?" she questioned.

"Why, milady, he be with the other members of the household having a bit of the cake and ale that Sir Lindell set out to celebrate Mistress Cecily's marriage. I was told to finish my work here afore I got any of the treat." He ducked his head then sheepishly looked back up. "I fear I was late rising this morning, so I be behind in me duties."

"Well, I am glad you are here. I need you to saddle Sir Lindell's horse."

"Saddle Sir Lindell's horse, milady?"

"That is what I said, and be quick about it."

Dropping the pitchfork, the boy said, "Aye, milady, and hurried to do her bidding."

Nervously grinding her teeth and knotting and unknotting her fists, Rowena willed the boy to hurry. The magistrate could choose to leave at any time and send the stableman to fetch his horse. How would she then explain her presence? At last the horse was saddled, and the boy asked if he should lead the horse out front.

"No," she snapped. "Go saddle my horse. I will lead Dalton out."

"Aye, milady." The boy looked at her a little warily. She had never been known to be cross with the servants. Feeling guilty, she gave the boy a smile but fluttered her hand at him. "Go ahead. Get my saddle onto Flyaway."

Nodding, the boy hurried to saddle the mare, and Rowena, after peeking outside and seeing no one around, led her husband's horse out the stable door. Having Flyaway saddled was but a diversion, though she wished she could take her mare with her for Cecily to ride after she rescued her. The mare, however, would never be able to keep up with Dalton, and Rowena meant to ride hard and fast. Leading the horse over to the stump her husband used when mounting his horse, she tossed the reins over the horse's head. She had never straddled a horse before, but she thought it looked like a far easier way to ride than on a sidesaddle as she had always ridden.

Before mounting, she reached into her pocket and fingered the small flintlock she had taken from her jewelry box. It was not a powerful pistol, but at close range, it would do the job. She hoped she would not have to shoot Haspel. She meant but to threaten him, but shoot him she would if she had no other way to save her daughter.

Fear returned as she heard voices coming from the back of the house. In an instant, she placed her foot in the stirrup and swung herself up onto the saddle. With no set plan in mind, but without a second thought, she shook the reins, dug her heels into the sides of the horse, and Dalton took off. As she raced past the side of the house, she saw Liverna in the window, but she dared not wave. She needed both hands on the reins to stay seated on the fast-moving horse.

She might have heard shouts as the horse thundered up the drive, but she paid them no heed. She had to catch Haspel's coach before it reached Derby.

Chapter 2

Nathaniel D'Arcy brandished his flintlock under the Puritan's nose. "Keep a civil tongue in your mouth do you not wish to lose it."

Jowls wobbling, dark eyes narrowed to slits, the Puritan had been cursing D'Arcy and swearing the law would catch him and his gang of highwaymen, and he would see them all hanged. Having noted the fear on the Puritan's young daughter's face, D'Arcy, peeved at the Puritan's language, had threatened him. Too late, he realized his threat to the girl's father probably frightened the child more than her father's swearing scared her. Apologizing, he tipped his hat to the child and started to close the door to the coach.

He was one of the few highwaymen who had no fear of robbing coaches or riders in broad daylight. He and his men laid their plans well. And they chose their targets well – only Puritans or supporters of the Cromwellian regime. They particularly liked to rob tax collectors or men who had bought confiscated Royalists', church, or the King's lands.

"Rider coming and riding hard!" one of his men said.

"Ye gads! Looks to be a woman," another said.

"Mother!" the girl cried, rising from the corner where she had been cowering.

Her father shoved her back into the corner, and looking at D'Arcy, said, "You have what you want. Let us be on our way."

D'Arcy cared not for the way the man treated the child. Knitting his brow, he asked, "Have you taken this child from her mother?"

One of D'Arcy's henchmen, Caleb Hayward, said, "The woman is hollering for us to hold the coach. Why not ask her. Even now she is sliding off her horse."

"Let us go! Let us go!" the Puritan demanded, but D'Arcy looked at the girl. She was again sitting forward, her hands clasped together in an obvious plea or prayer.

A dark-haired woman pushed past D'Arcy's men to the open door of the coach. Stopping at D'Arcy's side and looking up into his eyes, she said, "I want my child."

"Nay! She is now my wife!" the Puritan snarled.

"Wife!" D'Arcy said, shocked upon learning the child was not the Puritan's daughter. Revulsion knotted his stomach.

"She will never be your wife, Haspel," the woman spat out, pulling a small pistol from her pocket. "I will kill you before I ever let you have her."

"Hold," D'Arcy said, reaching for the gun, but the woman jerked away and pointed the gun at him.

"Sir. I will have my daughter. Cecily is barely turned fourteen. She is yet a child. My husband forced her to marry this Puritan swine this morning against my pleas. I mean to take my daughter with me. I see you all wear kerchiefs covering your faces. I would hazard you are highwaymen. I care not if you rob Haspel. But I mean to take my daughter."

Under his kerchief, D'Arcy's mouth twitched. He liked the woman's spirit. And he found her most attractive. Her dark brown eyes were riveting, and her full lips, set in a firm line, looked delicious. Glancing back into the coach, he asked, "Child, do you stay with your new husband or go with your mother?"

Starting to rise, the girl said, "I go with Mother."

"No!" the Puritan said, jerking the girl back down. "She is my wife."

Angered by Haspel's rough treatment of the child, D'Arcy pointed his pistol in Haspel's face. "Not any longer." He reached out to the girl. "Come. You may go with your mother."

As the girl clambered out and fell tearfully into her mother's arms, Haspel looked out at the woman and snarled, "You will regret this Lady Crossly, as will your husband. I will ..." but his words were lost because D'Arcy slammed the door shut, and another of his henchman, Torrance Madigan, hitting the rump of one of the coach horses, told the coachman, "Get going."

The coach drove away with Haspel still yelling and cursing in a most unsaintly way.

"Thank you. Thank you so much," Lady Crossly said, looking at

D'Arcy over the head of her small daughter still clutched in her arms.

Pulling down his kerchief, D'Arcy bared his face. "What are your plans, Lady Crossly? Do you return to Crossly Oaks?"

She looked startled. "How do you know of my home."

"'Tis our business to know where our prey travels are we to catch them unaware. We learned Haspel, one of Cromwell's tax assessors as well as tax collector, was staying the night with the local magistrate. Unbeknownst to Haspel, one of my men followed him and the magistrate to your home. We had no knowledge of the marriage taking place there, but we knew Haspel was due back in Derby to meet with the sheriff today and turn over his tax collections for safe keeping. So, we arranged to wait for him."

Her eyes wide, Lady Crossly shook her head. "I would never have guessed highwaymen to be so clever. I would think they but laid in wait for whomever might pass."

Chuckling, D'Arcy said, "Not many are clever. 'Tis why they are caught. Many are but desperate men. Men who have lost their homes yet have families in need. However, my question remains unanswered, Lady Crossly. Where do you go from here? Do you return to your home, Haspel will, by legal right, again take your daughter from you."

"That I know, and I have no intention of returning to Crossly Oaks. I will have to find a place my daughter and I can hide."

"In that case, you had best come with us. And we must be leaving this area quickly. As soon as Haspel reaches Derby, he will have the militia after us – and you."

Lady Crossly eyed him warily. "Nay. We shall go on our own."

"Then you will soon be caught. You are easily recognizable. In no time, the militia will learn where you hide. We are bound for Cheshire. We have many who give us aid along the way. Do you truly wish to keep your daughter out of Haspel's hands, you had best come with us."

"Why would you want to help us?"

"Your husband is a Royalist. Haspel is Cromwellian. 'Tis the only reason we need." He looked around at his men. "Is that not the truth, my friends."

Several chuckled and nodded, and all agreed he spoke the truth.

Giving Lady Crossly a moment to think, D'Arcy inwardly smiled when she sighed and said, "We go with you." She had little choice but to trust her fate to him and his highwaymen.

Giving her a slight bow, D'Arcy said, "Men, meet Lady Crossly and her daughter, Mistress Crossly. They will travel with us until we can find them a safe place to hide."

His men pulled their kerchiefs off their faces, saluted the two women, and sprang up on their horses. For the time being, D'Arcy had no intention of introducing himself or his men to Lady Crossly. Too risky when they still had far to go before they could shake the militia that would soon be after them.

D'Arcy's second in command, Jack Chapman, said, "The lady's horse is sadly winded." His gray-blue eyes thoughtful, he added, "I cannot think the horse can carry both the ladies. Or even one right now. Fact is, he will need his strength just to keep up with us."

"Hmmm." D'Arcy scratched his chin then brightened. "I will take Lady Crossly up with me." He looked over at Deverette Preston, only son and heir of Sir Lionel Preston of Britteridge Hall, and in D'Arcy's sister's opinion, entirely too well-favored for the safety of any woman. "Dev, you take her daughter up with you."

His handsome mouth spread in a cheery grin, and his light hazel eyes dancing merrily, he held out a hand to Cecily. "Come young miss, up you go."

Cecily looked at her mother. "Seems we have no choice, dear," Rowena said. "We must trust these highwaymen with our safety. Give the man your hand."

Leaving her mother's arms, Cecily held out her hand, and in an instant, she was pulled up onto Preston's lap. He settled her in front of him and gave her a pat. "Have no fear little one. We may take some fences and hedges, but Galantyne will ne'er even feel your light weight. He will fly right over any obstacle."

Mounting his horse, D'Arcy held out his hand to Lady Crossly. Removing his foot from his stirrup, he said, "Place your foot in the stirrup, and I will pull you the rest of the way up. I fear I cannot swing you up as Dev did your daughter."

For the first time, Lady Crossly smiled, and he liked her smile. Giving him her hand and placing her booted foot in the stirrup, she laughed and said, "Sir, you are tall and look strong, but I would not expect you could lift me as your man did Cecily."

With Lady Crossly putting her weight onto the stirrup, D'Arcy, with a gentle tug, was able to pull his unexpected encumbrance up and plop her down on his lap. She squiggled around a bit until she made herself comfortable then said, "I am ready, sir."

"Let us go, men," D'Arcy said, and with Chapman taking Lady Crossly's horse in tow and setting out in the lead, they raced off across the field bordering the road.

The militia would be able to follow their tracks across the fields, but when they hit another hard-packed road, their tracks would disappear or meld with other tracks. Later, he and his men would split into three groups, each group taking a different route to their chosen destination. D'Arcy was not sure he should have burdened his men with Lady Crossly and her daughter. Yet, the two women desperately needed help. He could not have left them to fall into Haspel's hands. And, he had to admit, he was drawn to Lady Crossly. She was a beauty with her dark hair and eyes, sensuous full lips, and classic straight nose. She was tall and slim, yet her figure was every bit that of a nicely endowed woman. Most appealing, though, was her courage. She had been intent on rescuing her daughter. Even did she have to kill Haspel and face the gallows. That kind of love and devotion for one's child deserved to be rewarded.

※ ※ ※ ※

Rowena admitted to being tired. She had kept herself erect, not giving in to her body's wish to relax against the highwayman's strong chest until finally, shortly before they stopped to give the horses a breather, she reluctantly settled back against him. She thought she heard him chuckle but could not be sure.

They made a brief stop to rest and bait the horses, and for one of the men to pull bread and cheese from a pack on the back of his horse and distribute portions to all the men and to her and Cecily. Their drink, for them and the horses, was water from a swift flowing stream. They were a little way off the highway, but hidden from the road by a clump of trees. During the rest, the men talked quietly, and though they were friendly to her and Cecily, Rowena realized she was not to learn their names, at least not their surnames. What she did determine, though, was that they seemed to be gentlemen. She wondered if they had been Royalists who had lost their lands to confiscation and had not been able to compound, pay their fines, and buy back their land as her husband and father had done. Well, it mattered not. Once she and Cecily were safe in Cheshire, she would most likely never see any of these men again.

She was relieved to learn Dalton was rested, and she could again ride him, but Cecily was transferred to a different highwayman. "Not good to have any horse carry extra weight for too long at the speed we are traveling," the highway said. "We have many a mile to go yet."

With that brief respite, they resumed their trek. Rowena had learned her dubious savior's given name was Nate, and he was the leader of the highwaymen. She knew naught else about him. Naught except he was tall, she guessed well over six feet, had a strong build, was well-spoken, and decidedly handsome in a rugged sort of way. His skin was bronze, his hair dark brown, his eyes a melting blue-green. He had high cheekbones, a firm chin, and a straight nose. His features all worked well together.

His horse was powerfully built, and even when carrying her added weight, the horse took fences and hedges, streams and gullies effortlessly. Horse and rider seemed melded into one entity, and when they rose to fly over an obstacle, they moved as one. Rowena had marveled that she moved with them. Nate's strong arm held her securely on his hard-muscled legs, and when Nate rose with his horse, she rose. After the first leap over a fence, she never had another fear that she might fall and be crushed under the horse's hoofs. At least she had no fears as long the fences and hedges were low and the streams and gullies narrow. Had they been higher or wider, she might well have felt differently.

She had been relieved to see the man named, Dev, was equally at home on his horse, and her worry for Cecily's safety eased. The fear that had covered Cecily's face had been replaced by her lovely smile. She had been enjoying the ride, and apparently, also, the handsome man carrying her so effortlessly on his lap.

Rowena was surprised when a short time after their rest, they reached a crossroad, and two of the highwaymen left and headed off in a different direction. Then later, after again resting and baiting the horses, and after transferring Cecily to the man named Jack who had been the one to lead Dalton, two other highwaymen separated from the group. With their departure, only three of the gang remained, Nate, her highwayman, the man named Dev who had first carried Cecily, and Jack, now carrying Cecily.

"A fortnight?" the first departing men had confirmed with Nate, and he had answered, "Aye." The two men had then ridden off. When the second two highwaymen left, one of the men said, "My place?" and again Nate answered, "Aye." And those two rode off. That they had plans to meet up again was a given. That must mean they would take to the highways and rob more people. They seemed so nice. She would hate to see them caught and hanged. Yet – they were highwaymen. What they were doing was wrong. Still, they helped her save Cecily from Haspel. For that, she was most grateful. So, she had to wish them well, even if they were bandits.

But for the present, after this long day of traveling over rivers and streams and up and down hills, and keeping off the highways whenever possible, she but wished they would reach their night's destination.

Chapter 3

D'Arcy patted his horse's rump when the horse gave a little whinny and hastened his step. The horse knew he would soon be ending the day's long journey, and he would be treated to some hay and oats and a nice long rest. Many a time over the past five years D'Arcy and all or some of his men had stayed with the Taverses. Ethelinda Harmon Tavers was D'Arcy's cousin, daughter of his great aunt, Alfreda D'Arcy Harmon. The Taverses lived in a tiny hamlet outside Burslem, a small village in Staffordshire. Herman Tavers owned a large pottery manufacturing business in Burslem, but he and Ethelinda preferred life in the country to life in the bustling village. Their hamlet was small, consisting of several other families of varying wealth, plus an ale house, a goose farm, and a blacksmith shop.

The Tavers family had been in pottery production for several generations, mostly to supplement their farm income, but in 1607 Herman's grandfather, with income he made from the sale of coal mined on his freehold, expanded his shop, built two large kilns, contracted with local miners to provide his fuel, and hired and trained several new people. Herman presently employed twenty potters. Though much of his trade was in storage jars, butter pots, and earthenware dishes, he also produced decorative slipware vases, loving cups, candlesticks, and bowls. The availability of many types of clay as well as a source of coal and of lead ore in the vicinity was giving rise to pottery manufacturing in the region. That Herman's business provided his family with a substantial income was evident in their sizable home and comfortable furnishings.

"Jack." D'Arcy called to Chapman, and his second in command dropped back to ride alongside D'Arcy on the pathway leading to the Taverses' hamlet. "You need ride ahead and let Mistress Tavers know our situation."

"Aye, and have Lady Crossly and her daughter new names?"

D'Arcy pulled up, as did Chapman, and Lady Crossly rode up beside them. When Preston, again carrying Cecily, joined them, D'Arcy said, "Lady Crossly, as Jack reminds me, I think 'tis best for your safety do we keep your identity secret." At Lady Crossly's nod, he continued, "I think you, Lady Crossly, will be Mistress Anna Hall, and Cecily will be Agnes." He looked from Lady Crossly to her daughter. "Are both of you comfortable with that?"

Cecily bobbed her head up and down. "Oh, yes sir. 'Twill be easy for me, I but have to respond to being addressed as Agnes. And Mother will still be Mother."

Lady Crossly smiled. "I on the other hand must remember to address my daughter as Agnes and to respond to the name Mistress Hall. However, I do believe I shall manage it."

"Good," D'Arcy said. "Now, I am Nate Drummer. Dev is Devon Mills. Jack is Jack Chapman." D'Arcy chose not to tell Lady Crossly that Chapman went by his real surname. For many years Chapman and his father had tramped the shires of Cheshire, Stafford, Derby, Shropshire, Nottingham, and parts of Lancashire with packs on their backs taking trade goods to towns, villages, and hamlets. Too many people knew Chapman for him to be able to disguise himself. But due to his nomad days, Chapman knew isolated farmsteads where the inhabitants would offer shelter and a place to hide. He knew where to find fords for streams and rivers, and he seemed to know every backroad, trail, and path through woods, up and down hills, and across moorland in all those shires. Indeed, Chapman was an invaluable asset to their gang.

"What is our story for why the women are with us?" Chapman asked.

Giving some thought to a fabrication, D'Arcy pursed his lips and cocked his head to one side before answering. "Mistress Hall and her daughter were on their way to Mistress Hall's sister in Chester when the two men Mistress Hall hired to take them to Chester made off with their horses and goods and left them stranded by the side of the highway where we found them. Per usual, we were returning from delivering our cattle to a buyer in Birmingham."

Looking from Lady Crossly to Cecily and back to Lady Crossly, he said "You are from Walsall, Staffordshire, a good-sized market town. You, Mistress Hall, are a widow of ten years. Your husband was a saddle maker. He left you with a small, though comfortable income, but when your sister's husband died, she invited you to come live with her in Chester – combine your incomes. For your daughter's sake, you thought the idea a good one so you made arrangements to move to Chester. You get sick when traveling by coach, hence you chose to travel by pillion to Chester. You being headed for Chester gives you reason to continue with us."

Shaking her head, Lady Crossly chuckled. "You are creative."

"'Tis a necessity in our line of work, Lady Crossly, or rather, Mistress Hall. From now on we will address each other in our character names. That way you can adjust to the names for us and for each other." At his questioning glance, they both nodded. "The Taverses," he continued, "the people we will be staying with for a couple of days, believe we are cattle merchants. They know nothing of our true occupation. They are but friends. Now, do you have questions?"

"Will we not be imposing on your friends?" Lady Crossly asked.

Reading the concern on her face, D'Arcy smiled. "Nay, their home will easily accommodate all of us. Any other questions?"

Lady Crossly shook her head as did Cecily, and both said no.

"Good. All right, Jack. Ride ahead."

As Chapman took off, D'Arcy told Lady Crossly, "By the by, for the present, your horse will be our horse. An extra. 'Tis not unusual for us to have an extra horse when we travel. In case of emergency. For example, should one horse become injured and unable to travel fast enough."

"I understand," Lady Crossly said, and when D'Arcy nudged his horse with his heels, and they set off after Chapman, she followed suit.

For the Taverses' safety, D'Arcy hid the fact from Lady Crossly that Ethelinda and Herman knew full well what he and his men were doing. But their two children, nineteen-year-old Aiden and sixteen-year-old Marissa, were not privy to their secret. Aiden and Marissa knew D'Arcy was their cousin, but they believed they could not call him such because he had warrant on his head. D'Arcy had been granted a parole after fighting for Charles I, but he had broken it by fighting for Charles II. Three of the Taverses' servants who had been in the Taverses' employ for many years, Herman's valet, Ethelinda's personal maid, and the coachman, knew D'Arcy's true identity, but they were loyal to the

Taverses, and like the Taverses, they were loyal to their King. They would not betray a Royalist. The other servants, being newer to the Taverses' household, simply knew D'Arcy and his men by their fake names and occupation. They were dispossessed gentlemen forced to earn their bread in the cattle trade.

The Taverses' house was old, but had been remodeled primarily in brick. The front entrance, though, had not been changed. Dating back to Elizabethan days, it was a timber-framed white stucco with decorative timbers and plasterwork. The heavy dark oak front door opened as D'Arcy rode up, and the house steward hurried out and down the front steps to greet him.

D'Arcy's cousin, Ethelinda, arriving in the doorway, gave D'Arcy a wave. "Welcome, Mister Drummer, welcome." Advancing down the steps, she said, "Do allow Myron to help Mistress Hall and her daughter down. Mister Chapman has told me all about their ordeal. How fortunate they are that you happened upon them."

Her smile bright and welcoming, she exuded good cheer. Though in her early forties, she was still an attractive woman. Only a few strands of gray showed in her dark hair, and her hereditary blue-green eyes, so like D'Arcy's own, danced with merriment. The color of her eyes was the only D'Arcy family feature similar to his. She had a small nose, rounded face, and long, swan like neck which she kept adorned with necklaces or high frilly collars.

Ethelinda's daughter Marissa trailed out behind her mother. Marissa had her mother's coloring, but her father's features, a pointed chin, thin lips, and a slim nose. She was a pretty girl, if not beautiful, and at sixteen, she was developing a pleasing figure. D'Arcy imagined she would soon have any number of suitors.

While the house steward helped Lady Crossly down, D'Arcy dismounted, and once Cecily was lifted down, Preston swung gracefully off his horse. A couple of stable boys arrived to take their mounts, so D'Arcy and Preston pulled their weapons from the leather holsters at the front of their saddles and their packs from behind their saddles. Their belongings taken by two footmen, D'Arcy turned to introduce Mistress Hall and her daughter.

Gracious as ever, Ethelinda welcomed her guests into her house.

"Herman is not yet home," she said, ushering them into her bright parlor. Though the last rays of the sun shone in from the windows, candles on the mantle had been lit. "I sent Herman word we were having guests. He always enjoys your visits, Mister Drummer. I have no doubt he will want you to ride out with him tomorrow to see the new bull his sister's husband recently purchased."

"And how is Mister Tavers's sister – and her husband? Both well, I hope," D'Arcy said.

"Mable and Enos are both well, but their younger son…" She shook her head. "Well, I will not go into that. Do be seated here next me, Mistress Hall," Ethelinda said, seating herself on a couch of floral printed damask and patting the cushion beside her. "We will have a little refreshment, then I will show you and your daughter to your room. I know you must be exhausted."

Sitting as directed, Lady Crossly acknowledged she was very tired. "It has indeed been a frightening experience. I know not what would have happened to us had Mister Drummer not kindly offered to take us on to Chester. I gave some thought to trying to get back to Walsall, but other than our personal goods, which were stolen, everything else we owned has been sold or shipped to my sister's. And as Mister Drummer is going to Chester anyway – and we could hardly afford to buy new horses…" She raised her hands in a hopeless gesture. "I could see no other way of getting to Chester than to accept his kind offer of transport."

D'Arcy was pleased with how well Lady Crossly elaborated on his concocted story. She was a born actress. Of course, Ethelinda had already been told the true story by Chapman, but Marissa or any servants listening would be completely fooled.

Ethelinda was shaking her head sympathetically. "Shocking. Truly shocking. At least you will have a day or two to rest here while Mister Drummer and his men relax after their long cattle drive. Such an exhausting occupation for a gentleman. These confiscations of men's property – so wrong. I admit to being glad Herman, my husband," she explained to Lady Crossly, "I am so glad he chose not to join in the fighting. Oh, he did give funds to the King's cause, unbeknownst to his father who was still alive at that time. Not that his father was not loyal to the King, but he was wary, very wary. And that was a good thing because as the Puritans ended up winning and taking over the government, we have had no worry that our business or our home would be subject to confiscation. Nor have we yet been subjected to the decimation tax which is proving such a hardship to so many Royalists."

"That is most fortunate, Mistress Tavers. And what is your husband's business?" Lady Crossly asked.

D'Arcy was enjoying Ethelinda's chatter. She was as good an actress as Lady Crossly.

"My husband owns a rather large pottery manufacturing shop," Ethelinda said, pride in her voice. "Many of his pieces are highly prized. Even the Queen once placed an order for a set of candlesticks. I have no doubt she would have ordered more pieces had not the trouble started, and she had to flee to France."

"Mistress Tavers." Myron, the house steward, stood in the doorway. "We have the refreshments you requested."

"Oh, splendid," Ethelinda said and directed Myron to serve them.

Two maids carrying trays entered the room behind Myron. As the women were served a light sherry, and D'Arcy and Preston, seated in heavy leather chairs across from the women, received brimming mugs of ale, D'Arcy noted that Marissa and Cecily, seated on a tufted felt settee, seemed to be enjoying a friendly chat. He hoped Cecily would be able to engage in conversation without giving away her true identity. The daughter of a baronet would have different experiences than the daughter of a saddle maker.

"Will there be ought else, Mistress Tavers," Myron asked as the two maids exited.

"Yes, do tell Cook to hold supper a bit. Mister Tavers is late returning home and our guests need time to refresh themselves."

"Yes, Mistress," Myron said, and with a slight head bow, he exited.

Returning her attention to her guests, Ethelinda said, "Herman tends to work longer hours with these summer days staying light for so long. Especially if he has a big order to fill."

As Lady Crossly nodded understandingly, Chapman entered, a mug of ale in his hand. "Noting I was late, I stopped by the buttery for my ale," he said, raising his mug in salute. Shaved, his unruly hair combed off his forehead, and changed out of his riding breeches and coat into buff colored breeches and a dark green coat and waistcoat with gold trim, he looked clean and relaxed. He looked a gentleman.

"Ah, Mister Chapman, you found all you needed in your chamber?"

"Indeed, Mistress Tavers. All and more. 'Tis a wonder your staff managed to accommodate my needs so rapidly."

"I am pleased. I must tell Myron how well they performed their duties." She looked at Lady Crossly. "I believe when a job is well done, it should be noted."

"Yes, Mistress Tavers, I think that most wise."

"How is Aiden?" D'Arcy asked after the Taverses' son.

"He is still up at Oxford. He complains of the Puritan strictness, but he knows, does he wish to be an astute businessman as is his father, he must continue his education. Then he must go on to one of the Inns of Court for at least a year that he will know enough law to be aware if someone is trying to cheat or bamboozle him."

"Good for him," D'Arcy said. "And what do you hear from your mother?"

"Mother is well. Father suffered the gout, but Mother made him stop drinking the red wine he so loves, and made him eat lamb, fish, and fowls instead of beef, and he is improved." Ethelinda turned to Lady Crossly. "My parents, and a couple of siblings, live in Chester. Before you leave, I will give you a letter of introduction to them. My mother is quite a remarkable woman. I know you will like her."

"I am sure I would, but I would hate to impose on her. And I am not sure what transport my sister will have."

Ethelinda waved her hand and glanced at D'Arcy. "You know, do you not, Mister Drummer, my mother would welcome Mistress Hall with open arms." She looked again at Lady Crossly. "Mother will find your adventure most interesting. And your daughter will need to meet young people. My brother, Alfgar, has a daughter, Jebelle, Marissa's age. I know she would be happy to introduce your Agnes to the youth of the city."

"That is most kind of you to think of Agnes. Thank you."

D'Arcy knew Lady Crossly meant to remain in hiding, but how she meant to pay her way, he had no idea. His great aunt, Lady Alfreda

Harmon, might be able to assist her. He would give that some consideration.

"Well, I would think by now your rooms will be ready," Ethelinda said, rising. "Mister Drummer, you and Mister Mills will have the chambers you normally occupy. Mistress Hall, do you and Agnes accompany me, I will show you to your room."

D'Arcy saw the relieved look on Lady Crossly's face. He doubted not she hoped for a brief rest before coming down to supper. Ethelinda led her guests up the stairs to the landing looking out over the Elizabethan hall. When the house was remodeled a narrow corridor had been cut down the center of the upstairs portion of the house. Bedchambers now opened off the corridor. No longer did one room open into another and into another. The bedchambers were smaller, but they offered privacy.

Striding down the corridor to his chamber, he left Lady Crossly in Ethelinda's hands. Both women had played their parts well. No one should suspect Lady Crossly and her daughter were fleeing a greatly disgruntled Puritan.

Chapter 4

When Mistress Tavers opened the door to the chamber Rowena was to share with her daughter, Rowena was surprised to find a young maid awaiting them. The skinny girl with large gray eyes and blond curls peeking out from under a white day cap curtsied and said, "I have laid out the gowns as you directed, Mistress Tavers, and the water is still nice and hot. And Cook not only warmed the towels, but she had me bring up a bowl of nuts, are Mistress Hall and her daughter hungry, what with supper being later than 'tis norm."

Spotting two gowns draped across a large decorative cedar chest, Rowena turned to Mistress Tavers. "What are these gowns?"

"Well, you and Agnes can hardly travel all the way to Chester with naught but the gowns you are wearing," Mistress Tavers said. "I have no doubt my gown will fit you. We are much the same size, but I know nothing of Marissa's would fit Agnes, so I had Charlotte," she nodded to the maid, "donate one of her gowns, and then I added one of Marissa's aprons and a collar. Should work for tonight, but I can have my mantua maker here in the morning to fashion Agnes a more suitable gown."

"Mistress Tavers. You are too kind. We cannot possibly accept such generosity. We are complete strangers to you."

"You need but remember the 'Good Samaritan'. I know I could do no more for you than I would wish someone would do for me was I in a dire situation. Allow me to enjoy the delightful feeling I get when doing a good deed." She glanced over at the maid. "And Charlotte, too. She is greatly pleased to be able to help."

The maid bobbed another curtsy. "Indeed, I am, Mistress Hall. And the gown is clean. 'Tis my Sunday church gown," she assured Cecily.

"You are both so kind. We thank you."

"Yes, thank you so much," Cecily said, beaming her lovely smile.

"Well, we will leave you to wash up and rest a bit. Charlotte will come up to help you dress for supper when my husband returns." With that, Mistress Tavers and Charlotte exited.

"Oh, Mother," Cecily cried, giving her mother a hug. "They are so kind. To think how this morning started. I thought I would sooner kill myself than be married to Orrin Haspel. I should have known you would keep your promise and would save me."

"I am not sure how I would have saved you had Mister Drummer and his highwaymen not held up Haspel's coach." She took her daughter's face in her hands. "But I would have saved you did I have to shoot Haspel."

"Well, I am so thankful for Mister Drummer and Mister Mills. And I do like Marissa. She agrees with me that Mister Mills is the most handsome man either of us has ever known. She says he comes through here ever so often with Mister Drummer and Mister Chapman, and that they never know when they will come, but they are always made welcome. I believe Mister Drummer must be a very good friend to the Taverses."

"Yes," Rowena said thoughtfully. A very good friend indeed. Mayhap more than a friend. She could not help but notice the similarity of Mistress Tavers's and Marissa's eyes to Nate's eyes. That vibrant blue-green color was most distinctive.

"But, Mother," Cecily said, looking down at her hand. "I forgot to take off the ring Haspel put on my finger, and Marissa noticed it. I told her it was my grandmother's ring, and I wore it like a wedding ring to keep my grandmother's memory close to my heart."

"Very smart." Rowena was proud of her daughter's ingenuity.

"Yes, but I have no wish to continue wearing this ring. I suppose now I must until we leave here."

Rowena nodded. "I suppose you must. But I see no reason we cannot give it to Mister Drummer once we leave. It can be a form of payment for all their help."

Cecily's lovely smile brightened her face. "That is a wonderful idea. But now, Mother, I would like to wash away some of the dust and mayhap lie down for a bit before we must dress for supper."

"I would like to do the same," Rowena said, and going over to the wash stand, she poured warm water from a white porcelain pitcher into a matching bowl. She told Cecily to wash first. While awaiting her turn, Rowena looked around the room. It was not large, but it had all the comforts – a four poster bed with down quilts and thick brocade curtains, the cedar chest upon which their gowns had been laid out, two tall floor tripod candle holders with beeswax candles giving off a bright but delicate light to the room, a maple table next to the bed with a comb and a candle atop it, a maple chair set at a small writing table, a gilded looking glass hung over the washstand, and a closed stool was behind a screen in the far corner of the room.

The walls were wainscoted halfway up, and the upper half of the walls were a creamy, swirling plaster. Several rag rugs decorated the floor, and gold curtains covered beveled windows. A small brick hearth was laid with wood ready to be lit come morning to take away the early chill did the summer weather turn cooler.

When she had climbed down the ivy and gone in pursuit of her daughter, never had she dreamed she would be spending the night in a gracious home, treated to every kindness. And never could she have imagined she would be so intrigued by a handsome highwayman. She was a married woman. She should not be having heart palpitations each time Nate looked at her with those incredible eyes of his. His strength and masculinity were unlike anything she had ever experienced. Her husband had never exuded such virility. And when Nate smiled, which he did too often, he took her breath away. Somehow she needed to regain control of her emotions before they set off for Chester. At least they would have a couple of days rest with the Taverses before they took to the road. She believed Nate would not be stopping here unless he had no fear they might be found and arrested. She could not say why, but she trusted him.

After taking her turn at the washstand, Rowena helped Cecily out of her gown. Neither Cecily nor Rowena had given in to Cecily's father's pleas to have a new gown made for Cecily's wedding. When Rowena had been locked in her bedchamber, and Cecily forced downstairs to the Crossly Oaks Hall, Cecily had worn naught but an everyday gown. She had at first refused to deliver her wedding vow, but at her father's threat to send her off with Haspel to be wed to Haspel when she came to her senses, she had tearfully acquiesced.

Upon learning of her husband's threat to her daughter, Rowena was even more enraged. She could not believe the man she had known as her husband for the past sixteen years had behaved in such a despicable manner. Any love she had for him vanished when she heard Cecily's woeful tale. Tightly embracing her daughter, she declared, "Never will he ever be part of our lives again. As of now, he is no longer my husband, no longer your father."

Pulling her jewelry and her pistol from her pockets, she placed them on the bed. "We have enough here to pay our way, be it humble, for several years. And must I find some type of work, mayhap as a companion or some such, so will I do. Then once you are twenty-one, we will seek an annulment. Or could be Haspel will be the one to seek an annulment. Certainly, does a year or two pass, I would think he would."

"Mother, that is all your jewelry. Even Grandmother's emeralds."

"Yes, dear, and they are our most valuable possessions. We will part with the emeralds last, but part with them we will to keep ourselves in hiding." She cocked her head thoughtfully. "I would think Mister Drummer would be able to help us find the best place to pawn these jewels."

Cecily sighed, "Think you there is no other way?"

"Not for the present. Mayhap in the future I could arrange with Uncle Gaylord to receive my stipend. But that is a long chance. Now, we must see can we grab a wee rest before supper. I know neither of us slept a wink last night," Rowena said, gathering up her jewelry and the pistol and stuffing them back in her pockets.

"Now, dear child, help me out of my gown, and these boots and breeches."

Cecily obliged and after snuffing out the candles, they were both soon stretched out on the bed with the top quilt resting softly over them. Ever so weary, Rowena drifted into sleep. Too soon, she was startled awake by the maid's light tap on the door.

Entering the room with a candle, Charlotte said, "Mistress Hall, Miss Agnes, I have come to help you dress for supper. Mister Tavers has returned home and is readying himself."

Rubbing her eyes, Rowena rose and nudged Cecily. The child was so tired she had not heard Charlotte's tap and light speech.

After lighting the room's candles with the candle she carried, Charlotte said, "Mistress Tavers sent you clean hose and a pair of shoes." Holding up a pair of black shoes with low heels, she added, "Mistress Tavers says are they a tad large, I can stuff some linen in the toes. She thought you might not want to be wearing your boots."

"Again, your mistress is too kind," Rowena said taking the items from the maid.

"Might I help you do your hair, Mistress Hall?"

"Do Agnes's first. I wish to wash the sleep from my eyes, then I will don the clean hose and try on the shoes."

As Cecily scrambled from the bed and took a seat on the chair to have her hair combed out, Rowena washed her face, and for the first time looked at herself in the looking glass. She was a sight. Her thick dark hair was an unruly mess, strands sticking out in all directions. Charlotte would have a much more difficult time doing something with her hair than with Cecily's silken blond tresses. And her eyes – bloodshot and with dark circles under them. She sighed. Naught she could do about her eyes, but by biting her lips and pinching her cheeks, she was able to bring a little color to her face.

A light tap sounded at the door, and a wizened maid entered the room. "I have come to replace the candles, Mistress Hall," she said in a raspy voice.

"Thank you," Rowena answered as the old woman, shoulders hunched, went around the room snuffing out the candles and cutting the wicks on the used candles before placing them in a basket on the crook of her arm. She then put new candles in the holders, and lit them from a candle she had set on the hearth.

Her job finished, the old woman smiled a near toothless smile and said in her grating voice, "Mistress Tavers says to tell you they will await you in the parlor."

Rowena thanked the woman who nodded and hobbled out.

With the door's closing, Charlotte said, "That is Laudie. Poor dear was dismissed when she got too old to do the work in a gentleman's house in Burslem. Mister Tavers found her sitting on a church step crying and clutching her little bag of belongings. She not knowing what would become of her. So Mister Tavers brought her home with him, and she does what jobs she can manage around the house."

"How very kind of the Taverses," exclaimed Cecily, and Rowena agreed. The Taverses were some of the most selfless people she had ever known.

"Aye. The Taverses be good people right enough," Charlotte agreed then said, "I am ready to do your hair, Mistress Hall."

Rowena looked at her daughter. Cecily was so lovely. Her light blond hair glistened in the candlelight, and her pale skin glowed. Her eyes looked a little tired, but they were also alight with an eagerness to experience life. She was a happy soul.

After much yanking and pulling, Charlotte managed to comb out Rowena's hair, twist it in a bun, and pin it atop her head. Soon she and Cecily, with Charlotte's help, were dressed and ready to go down to supper. Rowena was pleased that the gown Mistress Tavers had given her fit near perfectly. It was a bit lose in the waist and a bit low over the bosom, but a shear scarf had been provided, and Rowena tucked it in around the neckline. The shoes fit also, and they were sturdily made. They would be good practical walking shoes. Cecily's gown was simple and a tad long. She would have to hold it up so not to trip on the skirt, but with the clean apron and flat lace collar, she looked perfectly presentable.

"While you are at supper, I will have your gowns brushed," Charlotte said. She held up the breeches. "Should I also have these brushed."

Rowena nodded. "I may yet have need of them, so I suppose 'twould be best."

Charlotte chuckled, more a happy little chirping, as Rowena and Cecily left the room.

※ ※ ※ ※

Upon entering the parlor, Rowena and Cecily found Mistress Tavers and Marissa, and Mister Tavers, and the three highwaymen awaiting them. "I fear we have delayed your supper," Rowena said after she and Cecily were introduced to Mister Tavers.

"Nonsense," he said. "You gave me a chance to greet our three dear friends here. As we have not enjoyed their company for near six months, we are more than a little pleased to have them again with us."

Rowena immediately liked Herman Tavers. A robust man with a vigorous personality, he had, if not a booming voice, a lusty voice full of good cheer. He had twinkling hazel eyes, and so jovial was his laughter, he made the room seem brighter just by being in it.

"Well, I know you all must be starved, so let us go into supper," Mistress Tavers said, and taking Nate's arm, she let him lead her into the dining chamber. Mister Tavers took Rowena's arm, Jack Chapman followed with Marissa, and Dev with Cecily. Rowena guessed her daughter could not be happier than to be seated next to the handsome highwayman. She hoped the girl would not form a tender for the youth, but she could understand how both Cecily and Marissa would be attracted to Dev Mills, or whatever his true name might be.

Like Chapman, Nate and Dev had shaved and changed into gentleman's apparel. If she had thought the two men handsome in their rough and dusty clothing, seeing them scrubbed and clean gave them a most unfair advantage. Though very different in appearance, they were each more attractive than they had any need to be. That they were gentlemen, she had no doubt. So sad they had obviously been forced by circumstances into a life of crime.

The table was set with porcelain dishes on a white linen tablecloth and white napkins were at each place setting as were spoons as well as knives. That was most considerate, Rowena thought, considering she and Cecily were without the knives they normally carried if they were to dine away from home. Having eaten nothing since the night before but the bread and cheese Chapman provided when they had stopped to rest, Rowena was starved. She soon realized she would not be going hungry at the Taverses' table. Though it was but supper, three courses were being served, and wine, not ale, was the drink.

For the first time since Rowena had been shocked by her husband to learn he meant to sell their daughter to the lecher, Haspel, Rowena was able to relax and enjoy her meal. Her soul had been in turmoil for so long, now she could be at peace. Cecily was safe. And somehow, she would keep her safe, no matter the cost. She absently reached into one pocket and fingered her jewelry. She would have to guard their treasure carefully. Even sleep with it. She could not let it off her person. For the time being, she could trust no one. Not even the Taverses. No one must know about the jewelry.

She glanced at Nate and wondered whether he would take the jewels from her did he know about them. He was, after all, a thief. She trusted him to get her and Cecily to Chester, but that was as far as her trust extended.

Taking another sip of wine, she let the feeling of relief wash over her. A full stomach and good company. Sitting around the table enjoying the laughter and the conversation, she thought it seemed ludicrous to think that three of the men sharing the meal were highwaymen. Yet they were. Well, for this moment in time, she meant to forget who they were and just enjoy being alive and having her daughter safe.

Chapter 5

D'Arcy lay with his hands behind his head and stared out into the dark room. He had pulled the heavy curtains completely closed. Not a scrap of moonlight peeked in from the windows. He liked the dark, liked to test his senses. What could he hear? What could he smell? What might his body sense? 'Twas important to always be alert when awaiting a prey's arrival. Or when hiding from a militia unit or other entities in pursuit of him and his men. Only once had he been slightly careless, and one of his men had been shot. Caleb Hayward might have died if not for his wife. In their desperate flight, Sidonie Hayward, despite her pregnancy, had insisted upon accompanying her husband. Her courage had saved Caleb's life. And D'Arcy had vowed he would never again let his men's lives be placed at risk.

Lady Crossly had shown the same kind courage in her quest to save her daughter. He learned from her that she had climbed down ivy vines outside her window to make good her escape from her husband and go after her daughter. He had been both pleased and sorry that she wore breeches under her skirt. Having her positioned on his lap while her horse was given a breather had been a challenge, especially if she squiggled even the least little bit. The breeches helped protect them both. Lady Crossly was a shapely woman, and the gown she had worn at supper had been cut low enough to reveal the mounds of her breasts. A sheer scarf had partially covered them, but not enough that he, being seated beside her at the table, could not enjoy them.

Lady Crossly's husband might be a lout, but she was still a married woman, and he needed to mind his thoughts about her. Problem was, not thinking about Lady Crossly was proving difficult. He could not remember when he had been so attracted to a woman. And he yet had a long way to go in her company. At least she would not be riding on his lap. She would ride her own horse, and they could borrow a pillion for

Cecily. From Burslem to Nantwich, their next destination, they would not be needing to cut across fields and jump fences. They would go sedately down the highway. The trek could be managed in one day if they left early enough.

He forcibly turned his thoughts away from Lady Crossly – Rowena, he had learned was her given name. The morrow would be a busy day for him. He would ride with Herman to Burslem where his first stop would be with the goldsmith, Winnlock Measure. Herman had alerted Measure that D'Arcy would be coming. Measure was an ardent Royalist, and one of the few individuals D'Arcy trusted to hold their plunder until he could meet with his brother, Ranulf, who would transport the treasure to their King in exile.

Measure's hatred of the Puritans was understandable. His brother had been killed fighting for Charles I at Naseby in 1645 leaving his childless wife dependent upon Measure. Measure's son was captured at the same battle and due to overcrowding of the prisons in London was imprisoned on a ship in the Thames. At news of her husband's imprisonment, the son's wife went into early labor and lost her baby, a boy child. Measure sent an agent to buy his son's parole from the prison, but his son died of a fever before he could be freed. The news of her son's death caused Measure's wife to go into decline, and she had remained bedridden ever since. His son-in-law, Meldon Tremont, returned in such poor health from prison and the poor treatment of his battle injuries, he could do little to maintain his family. Tremont's manor had been confiscated, and Measure had been forced to pay his son-in-law's fines to save the manor.

At present, Measure's household consisted of his sick wife, his teary-eyed sister-in-law, his daughter-in-law, and his granddaughter, Elmira, who gave him the only pleasure he found in his home. The little girl was all that remained to him of his son. Measure now had no son or grandson bearing his family name to carry on his business. He could but hope his daughter's son, Willard Tremont, or his son's daughter, Elmira, would someday be able to keep the business going, but it would no longer bare his surname. The business had been founded by Measure's grandfather, a goldsmith, but it had been a number of years since any smith work was done on the premises, not since Measure's father died. Still, Measure kept a good supply of gold along with many other valuables in his brick vault, and he issued promissory notes and made loans. He would keep the moneys D'Arcy had taken from Haspel and other prey until D'Arcy retrieved it.

D'Arcy's second bit of business would be to visit the Hare Lair, an inn with a dubious reputation. Cambern Tapscott liked to keep the Cromwellians guessing, liked having the militia search his establishment – they afterwards stayed and drank. He had friends he could count on to spread tales. Such tales kept godly patrons out and brought more sinful patrons in – they drank more. Truth was though, he ran an orderly public house. Well over six feet, broad shouldered and with massive arms, he seldom had trouble keeping the peace in his establishment. But did he have any trouble, his handsome wife appeared with a pistol in each hand. And everyone understood she well knew how to use those poppers.

Both Cambern Tapscott and his wife, Barilia, were fervent Royalists. They used the frequent visits from the militia to learn the various plans the militia had for raids on unsuspecting businesses, households, or Royalists. The militiamen drank, ate, and boasted. And the Tapscotts listened. And passed on what they learned. Often times they also learned when some wealthy Puritan would be passing through town, or when the tax collector had amassed much of his tax moneys. A couple of times D'Arcy had captured a goodly sum for King Charles II thanks to the tips given him by Tapscott. He had to be careful, though. He preferred not to plan many raids in or near Cheshire. He wanted the militia to think he and his men were based in Derby, Shropshire, or Nottingham. Occasionally he even conducted a couple of raids in Northampton and Lincoln, just to keep the militia guessing.

In the morning, he would visit Tapscott and drink an ale with him. At present his gang was dispersed, and he was not looking to go on any raids. Particularly not with Lady Crossly and her daughter traveling with him. But 'twas always best to stay informed.

His final stop, before meeting up with Herman to visit Herman's brother-in-law and see the new bull, would be a visit to the church cemetery. He would pay his respects to a friend who had died of the wounds he received at Worcester fighting for Charles II. David Pettigrew had not served in D'Arcy's unit, but he and David had known each other from their days at Oxford, and the two had carried on a constant correspondence after their schooling ended. D'Arcy felt a deep loss. He missed his friend's humor, his quick wit, and his thoughtful musings. Yet one more reason to hate the Puritans.

Saddened by thoughts of his lost friend, he turned his thoughts back to Lady Crossly. In some ways, he wished she was less attractive. At the same time, he had to admit he was looking forward to spending more time with her. And he was looking forward to getting to know her better. He had a feeling, though, he had best stay on his guard. 'Twould be too easy to find himself enmeshed with that woman. Much too easy.

※ ※ ※ ※

Liverna tossed in her bed. How could she sleep when she could not stop worrying about Rowena? She had been hired as Rowena's nurse when Rowena was but a year old. And she loved Rowena as she would a child of her own. A willful child, Rowena had been, but a loving child, devoted to her family. When Rowena's mother had been needed to care for her mother, Rowena had, without complaint, and at the early age of ten, taken over the management of Elkton Hall, the Plaisance home. Liverna had helped Rowena, but the actual burden of directing the serving staff in everything from keeping meals on the table that would satisfy her father and her brother, keeping the linens and clothes washed and a guest room ever ready should it be needed, as it often was for her father's numerous friends, and keeping an accounting of supply expenditures had rested on Rowena's young shoulders.

Rowena had shouldered the burden with an easy grace. Seldom needing to raise her youthful voice to any of the servants, she kept the Plaisance home running smoothly. She had a knack of making the servants want to please her. Ever ready with praise, yet not afraid to confront any servant that might have thought to trespass on her youth and either steal supplies or fail to perform their tasks, she was just and competent. At the same time, she continued with her studies, sharing her brother's tutor, and eagerly reading any books she could find in her father's small library.

Barely turned fifteen when her grandmother died, and her mother returned home to Elkton Hall, Rowena was given in marriage to the fifty-year-old widower, Sir Lindell Crossly. Rowena's mother allowed Rowena could refuse the proposed marriage, but Rowena accepted her parents' counsel. Lindell Crossly had no children by his previous marriage and no close kin. Everything he owned would someday go to Rowena and her issue.

Crossly Oaks was a more substantial manor than was Elkton Hall. The manor house, though old like Elkton Hall, portions dating back to the twelfth century, had been remodeled, and the grounds and stables were well maintained. Crossly Oaks and Elkton Hall bordered on each other, and Rowena's father had ever been interested in acquiring a wooded section of Crossly Oaks with a stream known for its good fishing running through it. When Rowena consented to the marriage, the contract was drawn up. Rowena's father got the section of land he wanted, and Rowena brought naught to the marriage but her youth and a stipend her mother's father had set up for her. But Sir Lindell was satisfied.

Sir Lindell was very happy with his young bride. She knew how to manage his hall, and though young, she was well-read enough to be conversant on dark cold winter nights before they climbed into the large four-poster bed. Liverna believed Rowena was also happy, especially once she found she was with child. She sang a lot and whistled, and her voice was filled with joy and laughter. Sir Lindell fairly beamed when he gazed upon his wife, and he was beyond exuberant when he learned she was to bear him a child, an heir, someone to carry on his name and to leave his manor to. He had not even been disappointed when the first child was a girl, but his joy knew no bounds when Rowena gave him first one son and then another.

Robust enough for his age, he was, if not a particularly handsome man, a good companion for Rowena. Having spent five years of her youth tending Elkton Hall's needs, Rowena had had little time for fun or companionship. With Sir Lindell, she had both. He had a house steward to tend to many of the details that Rowena had needed to manage at Elkton Hall, and he had a larger staff, so Rowena had more free time. Sir Lindell liked to take Rowena riding, and she became more and more accomplished on horseback. He liked to take her shopping in Derby, and unless Liverna guessed wrong, he liked to show Rowena off.

Despite the war raging around them, Sir Lindell and Rowena seemed happy. Most likely would still be happy had Sir Lindell not sided with the King. He never went off to battle as did Rowena's father, but he helped financially, sending money with Rowena's father to help buy supplies for the King's forces. When the war ended with the beheading of King Charles I, the trouble came to Crossly Oaks – in the way of confiscation, fines, and most recently, the decimation tax assessments culminating in the sale of Cecily to Haspel.

Liverna had done her best to explain to Rowena's sons, Milo and Godwin, why their mother had left them, and why she might be gone for a very long time. The boys, despite their youth, seemed to understand. They knew their mother was against their sister's marriage to Haspel, and because they loved their sister, they were against it, too.

When Haspel and the militia had arrived at the Crossly Oaks door that evening with news that Rowena, in conjunction with a number of highwaymen, had spirited Cecily away from Haspel, the boys, along with Liverna, had rejoiced. Sir Lindell, however, was devastated. He had lost his wife, and knew not when, if ever, he might see her again, and Haspel, with the loss of his bride, was threatening to increase Sir Lindell's taxes beyond their settlement. The boys had been excited about the highwaymen, but Liverna could only wonder how Rowena and Cecily came to be in the company of such men and pray they would be safe.

Chapter 6

D'Arcy was up early to see Jack Chapman off. Chapman would take to the road with his pack on his back. A tradesman or peddler on foot attracted little attention from the militia or other government officials. Chapman's job was to reach the Preston home, Britteridge Hall, near the thriving town of Nantwich and determine if the area was safe or was it being watched. Like D'Arcy, Deverette Preston was a fugitive, wanted for having fought with King Charles II at Worcester. They and the others in D'Arcy's gang had decided to become highwaymen, robbing from the Puritans and Cromwellians to send money to their exiled King in Europe rather than surrender and face imprisonment or even transportation and enslavement in the Indies as had happened to other Royalists or, as they later learned had happened to many, impressment into Cromwell's army to fight in Ireland.

Having arrived on horseback as a drover, Chapman would depart on horseback so none of the Taverses' servants would suspect he meant to change his identity. He indicated he was parting company with his fellow drovers because he meant to visit a friend before continuing on to his home in Cheshire. He would, however, leave the horse at a designated spot, and Herman Tavers's brother-in-law, Enos Saticoy, would collect the horse and hold the animal until the following day when D'Arcy would retrieve the horse as his group set off for Nantwich.

With Chapman on his way, D'Arcy joined Herman and broke his fast before the two men left for Burslem. D'Arcy had hoped to see Lady Crossly, but neither she nor her daughter appeared before he left. Riding into town with Herman, D'Arcy said, "I hope we have not put you in any danger by bringing Lady Crossly and her daughter to your home."

"What else could you have done. As you said, you could not leave them to the Puritan's mercy. Besides, my wife is enjoying helping them. She sent a message to her mantua maker last evening requesting she come out to the house this morning with several bolts of cloth to fashion a couple of gowns for a young girl." He chuckled. "My wife spends enough with the woman; she will be happy to comply. We could well pass the woman on her way to our house."

As Herman had prophesied, a cart soon came into view. It was being driven by a grizzled man in a slouch hat, and the seamstress was perched beside him on the cart seat. Herman greeted the woman, and D'Arcy nodded to her. He noted that besides several bolts of fabric in the back of the cart, two young girls, most likely the seamstress's assistants, sat on the back of the cart, their legs dangling off the end.

Upon entering town, D'Arcy made his way to Winnlock Measure's shop. He was greeted differentially at the door by one of Measure's scriveners. "Mister Drummer, welcome. We have not seen you in any number of months."

"Aye, I take my trade where I may find it," D'Arcy answered. "Is Mister Measure free?"

"Yes, sir, go right into his office. He has no one with him at present."

Passing through the brightly lit front room of the goldsmith shop to the back room, D'Arcy wagered Measure was doing well. The goldsmith had three scriveners perched atop stools and busily working at their desks. Lanterns hanging above the desks and wide windows gave good lighting for the scriveners. A guard with a blunderbuss resting across his lap sat on a high stool in the far corner of the room. His large brimmed hat partially shielding his alert eyes, he gave D'Arcy a nod, and D'Arcy returned the nod before ascending the four steps up into Measure's office.

Measure, his gray-streaked russet hair disheveled, his waistcoat buttons skewed, and his coat cuffs rolled up, rose from his paper-strewn heavy oaken desk. Extending his hand, he said in a hushed voice. "Welcome, Nate, it has been too long."

"Winn, good to see you again." Grasping the hand extended to him, D'Arcy also used a lowered voice. No reason the scriveners or the guard should know of their friendship.

Returning to his normal voice, Measure said, "Sit down, sit down," and indicated a tufted armchair in front of his desk. "Did your cattle sales prosper? Have you a deposit to make with me?" he asked.

Measure knew full well that D'Arcy's deposit had nothing to do with cattle sales, but none of Measure's employees knew D'Arcy's true occupation. Business would be conducted with the understanding that Measure's employees might ease drop at any time. Caution need always be the keystone in their dealings.

Pulling two bags out from his pockets, D'Arcy deposited his take from Haspel and other of his prey onto Measure's desk. Opening the bags, Measure peered into them. His squinting eyes behind his spectacles lit up, and he smiled, but he said, "Looks like you did little more than break even, though should be enough for you to buy your next herd. But Mister Drummer, you are not getting wealthy."

"Nay," D'Arcy said, grinning and enjoying the play-acting, "but we have expenses, and my drovers must be paid."

"Well, I shall put your gain in my vault then give you a letter of credit."

"Thank you," D'Arcy said as Measure closed the two sacks and rose from his desk.

D'Arcy could think of few places his treasure would be safer. The building was of brick with a slate roof so the probability of fire was low. Plus, the building stood alone, no walls from other buildings were connected to the two-story building. At night, iron shutters covered the windows and iron gates were closed over the heavy oak front and back doors. The guard, presently sitting in the front room, slept upstairs, and according to Measure, the man was a light sleeper. But what gave D'Arcy the most confidence was the double iron vault, a vault within a vault, and the doors on the vaults were locked with three heavy iron locks. No one but Measure had the keys to those locks.

During business hours, the first door stood open, but the second door remained locked and Measure had to open each lock before he could put D'Arcy's treasure into his safe. Each morning and each evening, Measure was escorted to and from his home by two armed footmen. Having been attacked once in his younger days, he and his keys had only been saved when several of the town citizens fell upon the would-be robbers. After that, Measure took no more chances. He never went anywhere without a guard. He said he missed his freedom, but he had a duty to protect the treasures entrusted to his care. Measure's father and grandfather had lived above the shop where the watchman now lived, but Winnlock had wanted a house for his family.

With their business completed, D'Arcy wished Measure well and headed over to the Hare Lair Inn. The day yet being early, few people were in the public room. That was good. Fewer people to notice him. Once his eyes adjusted to the dark interior from the bright outdoors, D'Arcy spotted Tapscott.

Greeting D'Arcy with a welcoming smile, Tapscott said, "Now what can I be getting you, Mister Drummer? You have not been in our parts of late."

"An ale would do me good, and mayhap some news of the area. Anyone looking to part with some of their livestock?"

Tapscott poured ale into two mugs, and coming out from behind the cage where he kept his kegs, he joined D'Arcy at a table. "I cannot say I have heard of anyone in these parts wanting to be parting with their cattle, but late last evening we had a visit from the militia."

"Did you?" D'Arcy's eyes sought Tapscott's.

"Aye, seems they are after some highwaymen who not only robbed a Cromwellian tax commissioner, but they abducted his young wife. Said to be a flaxen-haired beauty. They say the girl's mother was in league with the highwaymen and planned the robbery and abduction."

"Do they now?"

"Aye. And the Cromwellian, name of Haspel, is offering a hefty reward for the return of his bride. She must be a comely wench. Those militiamen, what came through here, are hoping they will be the lucky ones to escort the girl back to her husband. Unmolested, of course."

"And did they say where they mean to search for this girl? Where they think she might be headed?"

"They feel certain the highwaymen headed west. Followed their tracks across a field, but lost them when they met up with a hard-packed highway." Tapscott rubbed his chin and added, "Oh, and they say the girl's mother is riding a fine horse, black with a white blaze on his nose and one white foreleg. They say the mother is fair to look upon, too. She might not reach Derby and jail unmolested."

"Hmmm." D'Arcy pushed his hat back on his forehead and narrowed his eyes. In a low voice he asked, "Would you be knowing anyone who would like to make a tidy profit on the sale of a horse, did they take that horse south and east of here?"

His lips pursed, Tapscott nodded. "Aye," he said, "I am thinking Barilia's brother, Druce, may be wanting to visit their sister in Leicester. Seems he says he was thinking about leaving early tomorrow. Set out before the sun is up to be getting a ways down the road."

D'Arcy shook his head. "Nay, the horse cannot be moved until tomorrow evening."

"Hmmm. So, where might Druce be finding this horse that will bring him a tidy profit?"

Twisting his mouth sideways, D'Arcy inhaled thoughtfully then in a low voice said, "I would think at Meldon Tremont's. Measure's son-in-law's manor just a ways north of town."

"I know it well," Tapscott said.

D'Arcy nodded. "I will affirm it with Measure. Is there a problem, I will get back to you, but if all is well, then the horse will be in Tremont's stable. Evening, once the moon is up, might be a good time to get the horse. Tremont keeps only two horses now. Since his illness, he cannot ride. His son, Willard, is away at school so his horse will be in the field. Only other horse would be an old cart horse. The stableman is a wizened old fellow, been with the family for years. Meldon will but tell the old man that Druce will be picking the horse up sometime in the evening, and the old man will have the horse saddled and waiting."

"Good. I will tell Druce to ready himself. He has been helping Iola in the kitchen today. Iola needed help cutting up portions of a butchered hog I purchased yesterday. 'Tis not work Druce much cares to do, but Iola twisted her wrist, and strong as she may be, she has been needing help from both Barilia and Druce."

D'Arcy knew the widowed Iola Pickworth, Barilia's sister, and Druce Howell, Barilia's younger brother owed much to Tapscott. Iola's husband died at Worcester, and with his death, Iola lost her tenancy on a manor south of Burslem. The farm had been in the Pickworth family for numerous generations, and as Pickworth's wife and heir, Iola could have kept the farm had she been willing to marry another farmer who could work the land. But Iola had no wish to remarry, so the Tapscotts offered her a home at their inn.

According to Tapscott, the Roundhead who purchased the confiscated Royalist manor had raised all the rents, so Iola was just as happy to leave the tenancy behind. Tapscott loved having Iola at the inn. She was the best cook his inn had ever had. Barilia's younger brother, Druce, had inherited the Howell tenancy on the same manor after his older brother died at Naseby in 1645, but being young – Druce had but recently reached his majority – and then with his father's death, he had been unable to pay the raised rents so had lost the tenancy three years back. Since then he had been working for Tapscott and taking any odd jobs he could find when Tapscott had no work for him.

"Druce is a bright lad," Tapscott said, "and he can tell a tale that no one will doubt 'tis the truth. But do you have ought you would have him say, is he stopped by the militia before he sells the horse?"

"Aye, and he should tell the same tale when he sells the horse. He will say he met a dark-haired lady on the road to Leicester, though he thought she might be headed to London. She said she needed money and would sell her horse for three pounds plus his horse would he trade. He had but two pounds, but she was still willing to trade. His horse being old and having seen better days, he knew he was getting the better deal. What surprised him was she gave up the saddle as well, and it was a fine saddle. Much better than anything he had ever known."

"Is it a fine saddle?" Tapscott asked.

D'Arcy chuckled. "Aye. Druce will enjoy it. Padded, good stirrups. A gentleman's saddle. Do the militia stop Druce, they will ask him if the woman had a blond girl with her. He should say he saw no girl, but she could have been in a nearby farm house."

"All good. Druce is yet that young, he will enjoy the adventure."

"D'Arcy pulled his purse from his pocket and drew out several coins. Placing them on the table, he said, "Tell the boy to put these coins in his boot. Is he stopped before reaching Leicester or after selling the horse, he can pay his coach fare home."

Pocketing the coins, Tapscott asked, "Any notion when you will be back in these parts. Should I be keeping me ears open?"

"'Tis not likely we will be back here soon. Always risky to visit any place too often."

"Aye, well, I wish you safe travels."

"Thanks, and give my best to Mistress Tapscott and Mistress Pickworth."

"That I will do."

Upon leaving the inn, D'Arcy retraced his steps to the goldsmith shop. Again, he was greeted cordially, and he asked, "Is Mister Measure still free?"

"Aye. He is," the scrivener answered, and D'Arcy went quickly back to Measure's office.

Measure looked surprised to see him, but when D'Arcy indicated with a hand signal that they should move into the vault that they would not be overheard, Measure nodded in understanding. In short order, D'Arcy told Measure of the situation with the Crossly horse being too recognizable, and Measure immediately fell in with the plan.

"I will send a footman with a note to Meldon. There should be no problem. But should anyone notice the horse, Meldon will say he is keeping him for a friend."

Thanking Measure, D'Arcy left, but his thoughts were awhirl. Cecily Crossly was too recognizable. If he took the Crosslys with him, he was putting himself and his men at risk. But if he left them here, he was putting his cousin and her family at risk. Well, naught he could do at the moment. He would swing by the cemetery and pay his respects to his old friend David Pettigrew, then he would meet Herman and go see his brother-in-law's new bull before he and Herman went home to dinner. He would get Ethelinda's thoughts on the situation. A woman's perspective could well be helpful. His mother's always were.

Upon entering the cemetery grounds, D'Arcy spotted a figure he knew, Maura Pettigrew, David's widow. She was sitting on the ground beside David's grave. Though they had only met twice, D'Arcy feared the widow would recognize him, and that would not be good. He pitied the widow and would like to have offered her his most sincere condolences, but he dared not. To the people of Burslem, he was Drummer not D'Arcy. One slip could cost him his life. That Maura still mourned her husband was obvious. She was an attractive woman and no doubt could remarry did she so choose. Such devotion was laudable.

After silently paying his respects to his deceased friend from a distance, D'Arcy headed for his rendezvous with Herman Tavers.

Chapter 7

Ethelinda nodded her head thoughtfully. She was not surprised the militia was searching for Cecily Crossly, or that they had a good description of the girl. Cecily was a little beauty. Nor was Ethelinda surprised that Nate came to her with his dilemma. Already concerned for the girl and her mother, she had been deliberating various ideas.

Herman and Nate had returned from her in-law's in time to wash and ready themselves for dinner, but after dinner when everyone adjourned to the parlor, Nate had caught Ethelinda and told her he needed her advice. He needed to talk privately. Suggesting they take a stroll in the garden, he announced in a louder voice, "Mistress Tavers, do me the honor of showing me the rose you were telling me of last night. You did say 'twas blood red and an early bloomer. I would like to tell my mother about it. She does love roses."

"Ah, Mister Drummer, you have often mentioned how much your mother loves the roses. I would be happy to show you my prize." And so, they had wandered into the garden and strolled slowly toward the roses while Nate told her of the new development.

He had solved the problem of ridding himself of the recognizable horse, but the Crosslys were another matter. "I feared something like this, Nate," Ethelinda said, "and have been considering what might be the best solution. You must rid yourself of the girl."

"What!" Nate stopped and looked down at her, surprise in his eyes.

She smiled. "Yes, there is naught for it but to turn her into a young page boy. Though our nephew, Ovid Saticoy, is but ten, I feel certain his clothes will fit Agnes, or rather, Cecily. She is so tiny. It will hurt the child to do so, but you will have to chop her hair off, and she will have to ride astride while her mother rides on the pillion."

Catching Ethelinda's hands Nate said, "Brilliant, but do you think 'twill work?"

"If Caleb Hayward could masquerade as a woman while suffering from a gunshot wound, Cecily Crossly can be turned into a boy. But not here. Though I trust most of our servants, a reward can turn heads. She must leave here as a girl, then when you reach a safe area, you must transform her into a young page."

Grabbing Ethelinda and giving her a hug, Nate said, "You are a genius, Cousin."

Chuckling Ethelinda returned the hug then said, "I will tell Mistress Hall, or Lady Crossly, that I wish to show her the garden. I will then explain all to her. She will be frightened, but no doubt she will see the wisdom of the plan. In the meantime, you and Herman must again visit the Saticoys and collect two sets of clothes from Ovid. His mother will know what might work best. Remember, Cecily will be a humble page so the clothing should not be fancy."

"I understand. I will fetch Herman, and we will pay another visit to his sister and brother-in-law. I will say that I decided I must see that bull once more to see if I might try to buy it. Naturally, Enos will not want to sell, and I will return a disappointed man."

Ethelinda put her hand on Nate's arm. "Oh, and shoes or better, boots. Cecily must have a boy's footwear."

"You have a good head, Ethelinda. Any chance you want to join my little gang. Attention to detail is important to our survival."

Smiling, she gave Nate a swat on the shoulder. "You would not now be a free man did you not plan out everything you do in complete detail. 'Twas just you were not expecting to have to see to the safety of two desperate women. Were you not ever vigilant, had you not visited Tapscott, we would not know we need to take these new precautions. But do have a care, Nate. Did anything happen to you or your brother, your mother would be devastated."

"Aye. For Mother's sake, I will make certain nothing happens to me or Ranulf."

"Give Ranulf our love when next you see him. And tell him to assure the King that he still has many supporters here in England."

"That I will do. Now I will collect Herman, and you have your stroll with Mistress Hall."

Hoping they had settled on the best plan, Ethelinda went to find Lady

Crossly. Poor woman. She must have thought herself safe. She was so enjoying having the two new gowns made for Cecily. She felt bad she could not pay for the gowns, but she had promised Ethelinda that once she reached her sister's she would send what she could.

Ethelinda had told her she need not worry, that she was happy to help furnish the girl with a wardrobe. But now, with the seamstress and her assistants hastily working on the gowns to finish them by evening so they would be ready for the Crosslys's departure on the morrow, the gowns would not be of any use to the girl. At least not until the Crosslys were someplace safe. Pray God they did make it to safety.

❀ ❀ ❀ ❀

"Your garden is truly lovely," Rowena said after she and Mistress Tavers had strolled out into the middle of the garden where a small fountain of two cupids spurting water up from their mouths made a pretty gurgling sound. Flagstones formed an oval court around the fountain and decorative benches were on either side of the fountain.

"Let us sit, Mistress Hall," Mistress Tavers said. "'Tis so pleasant here, and 'tis one place I can always be certain no one can overhear my conversation."

Rowena sat, but she was immediately wary. What did Mistress Tavers want to tell her that no one else should hear? Looking expectantly at the woman beside her, she said, "Have you something you wish to ask me or tell me?"

Mistress Tavers took Rowena's hand. "Yes, I am afraid we have a problem. Mister Drummer has had to tell me the truth about you and your daughter, Lady Crossly."

Rowena sighed and her shoulders slumped, but before she could say anything, Mistress Tavers said, "Please, be not alarmed. Your secret is safe with me and my husband. The problem lies not with who you are, Lady Crossly, but with how recognizable your daughter is."

"What!" Rowena frowned, her gaze meeting Mistress Tavers's.

"In town today," Mistress Tavers continued, "Mister Drummer learned the militia have a description of you and your daughter and your horse, and a large reward is being offered by your daughter's husband for the return of your daughter."

Gasping Rowena clutched at her throat. For such a short time she had believed she and Cecily were safe. She had let down her guard. She had laughed and enjoyed being free from fear. Now everything was collapsing around her.

Mistress Tavers tightened her grip on Rowena's hand. "Have no fear, Lady Crossly. We have a plan to keep you and your daughter safe, but you must be willing to accept our plan."

Breath rushing back into her lungs, Rowena said, "A plan?"

"Yes, dear. I am sorry to have frightened you so, but I could think of no other way than to blurt it out. Now, while you are here, you will continue as the Halls. Once you leave here, you will be assuming new names and appearances. And I am sorry to tell you, but Mister Drummer is having to get rid of your lovely horse."

"My horse? Dalton? He is getting rid of my horse? What will I ride?"

"You will ride on a pillion behind Mister Drummer or your young page."

"My page? What page?"

"Why your daughter, of course. You will have to cut off her lovely hair. Darken her hair and face with a walnut stain I will give you. And even now, my husband and Mister Drummer are going back to the Saticoy's to collect boy's clothing for your daughter. All these things will be done after you leave here tomorrow. My servants must see you leave as you arrived. Until then, you are Mistress Hall and Agnes. Even to my own daughter."

Cocking her head, Rowena stared at Mistress Tavers then she slowly smiled. "Yes, I do believe that could work. Cecily can handle a horse, is the horse not too spirited. Oh, but what will we do for a horse if we cannot use my horse?"

"Mister Chapman's horse is at present in the Saticoy stables. Mister Mills will collect him tomorrow after you leave here. He and Mister Drummer know of a safe place where your daughter can be transformed into your page."

"But where is Mister Chapman? I thought he left. Does he not need his horse?"

Mistress Tavers chuckled. "Mister Chapman travels as fast on foot as on horse, does he so choose. He left here as he arrived, as you will do tomorrow, but he left his horse with the Saticoys. My husband's brother-in-law, saying he bought the horse and saddle for a good price, will in turn say he sold the horse to Mister Mills for a better price."

"And the pillion? Where do we get that?"

"It is mine. I intended it for your daughter, but 'twill serve you. It has served me for many a year, but now, I prefer to travel in our coach. I have not used the pillion in years and Marissa, does she not ride in the coach, prefers to ride her own horse."

"You are so kind. And how well you and Mister Drummer have seen to the details of keeping me and my daughter safe. I cannot think how I will ever be able to thank you enough."

"Tut, tut, dear." Mistress Tavers smiled then became serious again. "I must tell you one other troubling thing, Lady Crossly. The man your daughter was forced to marry, I do believe Mister Drummer said his name is Haspel, he is saying you were in league with the highwaymen. He says you planned the whole robbery and abduction. Mister Drummer says he cannot credit that. He says you and your daughter were quite on your own when he came upon you."

Rowena looked at Mistress Tavers in surprise. Could she not know Nate was a highwayman? "I assure you, I had nothing to do with that robbery. 'Twas but luck that the highwaymen stopped Haspel, and that they allowed me to free my daughter from Haspel. But what did Mister Drummer tell you?"

Mistress Tavers widened her eyes and said, "Why, naught but that he came upon you on the highway, and after learning you were escaping with your daughter, he thought 'twould be best you use a name other than your real name. Fearful if others knew you were spiriting your daughter away from an unwanted marriage you might be apprehended, he came up with the tale he told us." She narrowed her eyes. "'Tis a good tale and 'twill serve you well until you leave. Now, I think 'twould be best do we continue our stroll around the garden. We cannot want any of the servants to become suspicious."

"Yes," Rowena said, her head in a spin. Could Mistress Tavers truly not know about Nate and his nefarious deeds? Could she not know his surname was not Drummer or that he was not a cattle drover? Well, it mattered not. What mattered was Nate was still willing to help her and Cecily escape. And at a risk to himself. That had her confused but grateful to Nate and to Dev, whatever their true names might be.

※ ※ ※ ※

Once in bed with the candles out and moonlight peeping in the window, Rowena finally had a chance to tell her daughter of the danger they were facing and the plans Nate and Mistress Tavers had made to keep them safe. To her relief, Cecily had no trouble with the plans. Yes, she had been excited about the new gowns made for her, especially the pink fustian, a cotton and flax blend with a silky finish, but she accepted that she would be a young boy for a while.

She giggled. "Could be fun. 'Twill be interesting to be treated as a boy and not a girl."

Rowena gave her daughter a hug. "You are very brave, my dear child."

"Not as brave as you, Mother. To think what you did to save me. To be here with you and not with Haspel makes any and all trials seem trivial."

"That is certainly the way we must view our upcoming adventure. Well, we had best get to sleep. Mister Drummer says he wants us on our way as early as possible."

"Yes, Mother, good-night."

"Good-night, dear." Rowena would not tell her daughter, but she believed Nate feared that at any time the militia might learn of their presence at the Taverses' home. That fact kept Rowena's heart skipping beats, and she began a slow count to one hundred in the hopes she could calm herself enough to get some sleep. She could not afford a sleepless night. She needed to be alert come morning.

Mistress Tavers had provided her with panniers to carry hers and Cecily's clothing. How diligently the seamstress and her two assistants had worked to ready the gowns for Cecily, barely taking time for their dinner before returning to their sewing. But the seamstress declared herself most proud of their work when Cecily tried on each gown, and they fit her sweet young figure so perfectly. "Worth all the effort the seamstress declared." And Mistress Tavers had seen her well compensated for all her effort. Mistress Tavers gave small bonuses to the two assistants as well, and they were sent back to Burslem in the Taverses' coach.

Rowena heard Mistress Tavers telling the seamstress in a loud whisper, "I would not want Mistress Hall embarrassed by my charity on her next visit here. So, I would not expect to hear of this being gossiped about."

"Oh, no, Mistress Tavers," the seamstress said. "My girls and I will not breathe a word." She glanced back at Rowena, and smiling, gave a little wave.

Rowena acknowledged the seamstress who was then escorted out by Mistress Tavers. When Mistress Tavers returned, she whispered, "That should at least keep them quiet for a while, but do they hear of the reward, one of them may talk."

Concerned, Rowena said, "I am so sorry we may be putting you and your family in danger."

Mistress Tavers shrugged. "Do we help keep your daughter safe and help thwart the evil designs of a Roundhead, 'tis well worth it."

Rowena had no idea how, but she hoped someday she would be able to repay the kind people who were doing so much for her and Cecily.

Listening to her daughter's soft, steady breathing, Rowena made herself resume her counting. Somehow she had to get to sleep or come morning she would be worthless. Slowing her own breathing as she watched the moon drift higher in the sky, she began to nod, and never knew when she drifted into sleep.

Chapter 8

With the early morning light seeping in through the window, Rowena and Cecily were up and dressed before Charlotte arrived to light their candles. Rowena knew Nate was determined to get an early start. Their gowns, Cecily's two new ones and two of Mistress Tavers's that the kind woman insisted Rowena take, were already packed in the panniers, but Charlotte helped pack the toiletries Mistress Tavers had given them.

"Mister and Mistress Tavers await you in the dining chamber where you may break your fast before you leave," Charlotte said. "Mister Drummer and Mister Mills have already eaten and are readying the horses."

"And I thought we were up early," Rowena said.

Charlotte chuckled. "Oh, you are. 'Tis just Mister and Mistress Tavers know Mister Drummer always leaves early, so they were up to bid him a farewell. Now you go on down, and I will take the panniers out to Mister Drummer."

"Thank you, Charlotte, and thank you for all you have done for us. I am so sorry I have no way to give you a gratuity."

"Oh, never you mind that, Mistress Hall. You are kind, and I enjoyed serving you and Miss Agnes." She smiled at Cecily. "May you have a safe trip and find your sister well."

Rowena and Cecily found a sleepy-eyed Marissa had joined her parents in the dining chamber. "Could not let you leave without telling you how much I enjoyed meeting you, Agnes," Marissa said. "And I will write my cousin in Chester and tell her how lovely you are, and that she will love you as I do."

"Oh, Marissa, you are so kind," Cecily said. "I am so pleased to have met you."

"Nice you girls have enjoyed each other," Mistress Tavers said, "but

Agnes, you and your mother must eat. No telling when Mister Drummer will stop to eat a nuncheon does he get in a hurry."

Rowena glanced at the sideboard. Platters of hot buns, warm sausages, several kinds of cheese, and fresh berries in a clotted cream awaited them. She had not expected to have an appetite but she did, and she insisted Cecily eat well. Did they run into any trouble, 'twas better to face it on a full stomach than an empty, gnawing stomach.

They had just finished eating and were washing it down with warm cider when Nate arrived. "We are ready are you ready, Mistress Hall," he said.

"We are ready," Rowena said, rising.

Hugs and well wishes were exchanged, and before she knew it, Rowena was up on Dalton, the panniers attached on his rump, and Cecily was perched on a pillion behind Nate. Rowena knew this arrangement would soon end, and she gave Dalton a pat on his neck. What would be his fate she could not know, but she hoped he would have a kind master wherever he might end up.

With many waves and shouts of good-bye, Nate took the lead, and they set off on their journey – to where, Rowena had no idea.

※ ※ ※ ※

D'Arcy hoped his cousin and her family would not have any problems with the authorities. He had little doubt but that the militia would visit them. Someone would hear of the reward and hope to claim it by telling about the girl the Taverses had hosted. The Taverses were not known as Royalists, but they were known not to support the Puritan creed. That could make them suspect, but 'twas unlikely any case could be made against them. Even was the girl they housed the one the militia sought, how could the Taverses have known it. Ethelinda was not worried, nor was Herman, so D'Arcy did his best to tamp down his concern. He had enough to worry about in keeping the Crosslys safe. And now he had to keep them safe – they knew too much. Not that they would willingly divulge anything, but Cecily could be made to talk was her mother threatened with hanging. He needed to keep the Crosslys out of the Cromwellians' hands.

They had not traveled far when Preston took off for the Saticoys to retrieve Chapman's horse, and D'Arcy turned down a winding lane leading to a sheltered stream where Cecily could be transformed into a young page. Their freedom would depend on her ability to act the part of a boy. Hopefully, staining her skin – it would have to be her face, hands, and neck – and dying her hair would give them an added edge.

Relief flooding him, he slowly let his breath out and pulled up on his reins. They had reached their first destination and had encountered nary a soul on the way. No one would be able to describe them or tell tales. Turning to look back at Rowena, he told her and Cecily that they would need to dismount and walk the horses into the wooded niche.

Swinging off his saddle, he lifted Cecily down from the pillion and turned to help Rowena off her horse only to find she had already dismounted. She had donned her husband's breeches under her skirt again to ride her horse astride, but once Cecily became her page, she would need to tuck the breeches into a pannier and settle onto the pillion. D'Arcy had a feeling she would not like the change. Not that she would complain. She knew the necessity of their disguises, but she would not be happy that she was unable to control her own mount. She rode well. He but hoped Cecily would be able to ride half as well.

Ducking under low hanging branches, he led his horse down a narrow deer path partially overgrown with stiff grasses and brambles. Cecily followed behind him, and Rowena, leading her horse, brought up the rear. Branches tore at his hat and he removed it, only to have his hair grabbed. Bending lower, he glanced back at Cecily. She was daintily picking her way through the brambles that snatched at her skirt, but she was so small, she barely needed to bow her head. Her mother, though, was fighting the same tree branches he fought, but was also struggling with her skirt getting caught in the brambles while having to lead a distraught looking horse. The horse, eyes rolling, head bobbing, snorted his irritation. D'Arcy's horse had no such problem. He was used to such maneuvers. Many the time he had plowed his way through worse entanglements.

D'Arcy's admiration for Rowena Crossly continued to grow. She would do whatever was necessary to keep her daughter safe. That was good. All their lives could well depend upon her courage and stamina.

Hers and Cecily's.

When they finally broke into the tiny clearing, Cecily cried, "Oh, how pretty it is!"

D'Arcy looked around. He had never made note of the beauty of this secret sanctuary, but the girl was right. What to him seemed naught but a perfect place to hide was truly a lovely bower. Blue and yellow flowers dotted the soft green grass, and a pebble-strewn stream gurgled its way out of the woods and back into the woods.

After tying the horses at the edge of the clearing so they would not be in the way, yet giving them enough lead to graze, D'Arcy turned to Cecily. "Well, young mistress, are you ready to become a page?"

To his surprise, her face brightened. "Oh, yes, Mister Drummer. Very ready. 'Twill be great fun. I have always thought how lucky boys are in their freedom. Now I shall have a chance to experience that freedom."

"I admire your spirit," he said before looking at Rowena. "You have the scissors and the stain?" he asked.

"Aye," Rowena answered, pulling scissors and a corked bottle of brown liquid from her pocket. "Mistress Tavers says this is a walnut stain mixed with a flaxseed oil. She says does it soak in good, then even with washing, it should last on the skin for several days. It will stain clothes, so we must apply it carefully. In the panniers, I have a towel I can wrap around Cecily before I set to work on her." She frowned and shrugged. "I suppose I must first go ahead and cut her hair."

"Might as well start on it," D'Arcy said, thinking 'twas a shame to cut off that beautiful pale blond hair, but they had no choice.

"Sit here on this log, Cecily," Rowena directed, and Cecily obeyed. Slowly Rowena undid the little topknot bun at the back of Cecily's head and combed the hair out with her fingers. Cecily's hair was so fine and silky, and though her hair had been slightly curled on the sides, the curls had not held well, and the strands were easily straightened when Rowena dampened them with water from the stream.

D'Arcy saw Rowena swallow before grasping a section of her daughter's hair. Holding up a strand, she asked, "Does this look right? Should I cut it here?"

"Yes, I would say it should fall mid-point between her shoulders and her ears."

Swallowing again, Rowena began cutting. The lovely strands of hair fell on the ground around the log, blending prettily with the yellow and blue flowers. When she finished, Rowena stepped back and looked at her daughter. Shaking her head, she pulled some strands on the top of Cecily's hair forward and cut a fringe across her forehead. Once again stepping back, she looked at D'Arcy. "What say you?"

"I say you still have a lovely daughter. 'Twill take that stain and the boy's clothing to hopefully turn her into a page."

Cecily smiled. "Never fear, Mister Drummer. I shall make you a very good page."

D'Arcy returned her smile, but hearing noises coming from the path, he drew his pistol. As first one brown horse and then another wandered into the clearing, D'Arcy put his gun away. Preston soon followed after the horses.

Preston was chuckling. "I knew Boffin and Galantyne would stay on the path, so I let them head on in while I stayed back to brush away some horse tracks and footprints, and to cover over the entrance where some of the grasses were mashed and branches broken."

"Good thinking," D'Arcy said. "All went well at Saticoy's?"

"Aye, when I was leaving, Enos was making a good showing of the nice profit he made on the horse and saddle I bought from him."

"Well, by the by, what think you?" D'Arcy pointed to Cecily, still seated on the log.

Preston's handsome face broke into a broad smile. "I would say she looks like one of the wee pixies I have heard tell of since I was a youth and had an Irish nurse."

Cecily giggled, and D'Arcy said, "Now that is one thing you must not do, Cecily. You must guffaw, guffaw instead. That giggle is too sweet and feminine."

With a mischievous glance at D'Arcy, Cecily brought forth a, "chirrup, chirrup," from the back of her throat, and D'Arcy burst out in a fit of laughter. "Excellent, excellent," he said.

Joining in the approval with a hearty chuckle, Preston set his pack on the ground then pulled out a set of boy's clothing and a pair of boots. Handing the clothing and boots to D'Arcy, he turned to tie up his horses beside the other horses.

Rowena pulled a towel from her pannier then asked, "Where am I to disrobe my daughter?"

"Oh," D'Arcy said, looking about the crowded clearing. With the addition of Preston and the other two horses, the tiny bower had become much more compact. "I suppose Dev and I will sit over at the edge of the woods with our backs to you until you have Cecily changed into her boy's duds. I am thinking you will not be needing our help."

"You are correct," Rowena said, and with a nod, D'Arcy slapped Preston on the shoulder, and the two stretched out on a blanket D'Arcy took off his horse and spread on the grass.

With their backs to the two women, D'Arcy said, "No reason we cannot get a few winks," and Preston happily agreed with him.

※ ※ ※ ※

Having slept poorly the past two nights, his mind busy with how to keep everyone from his men, to his cousin and her family, to the Crosslys safe, D'Arcy had also been tormented by thoughts of Rowena Crossly, so he was not surprised he had slept soundly in their little hideaway. He awoke to Preston's low chuckling. It annoyed him that he had so let down his guard, but when he sat up and looked where Preston looked, his annoyance evaporated.

"Gads, if you have not worked a miracle, Lady Crossly," he said.

"Think you so? Will Cecily now make a good page?"

D'Arcy could do little more than nod. The child who stood before him looked nothing like the pretty young girl she had been when he closed his eyes to nap. Her slender legs were encased in floppy boots, brown trunk hose, and brown gathered breeches fastened below the knees. A reddish-brown loose-fitting leather jerkin fell to mid-thigh, and the sleeves of a white linen shirt with a falling collar poked out from under the jerkin. A brown narrow brimmed cap was perched on a head of short brown hair, and pale blue eyes peered out from a lightly tanned face sporting a wide grin.

"Now we must decide on names," Preston said. "To me, she looks like a Peter."

"Do you like that name?" D'Arcy asked Cecily. "'Twould be simple and easy to remember."

"'Twill do. But what will be my surname?"

"Do you have a preference?" D'Arcy asked her, thinking the girl should have some say in her name this time around.

"I think it should be something simple. How about Morse?"

D'Arcy frowned. "Why Morse?"

Cecily smiled a little wistfully. "'Tis the name of a boy I once knew and liked."

"Aye, a nice boy, from a nice family," Rowena said with the same little smile. D'Arcy guessed both women were thinking they would never see the boy again.

"Sounds fine to me," Preston said.

"Then Peter Morse you are," D'Arcy said with a firm nod to his head. "I am now John Blucher. And you, Lady Crossly, are now Mistress Mary Blucher, my wife."

Rowena's eyes widened in surprise. "We have little choice, I fear," he said. "We will not make our destination tonight. This delay has cost us, and we yet have to get rid of your black horse. We will have no choice but to stay the night in an inn. But have no fear, you and Cecily will take the bed, and I will take the cot provided for your page. Preston, who will now be Will Jamieson, a stranger we met along the way who travels with us for safety, will sleep in the men's dormitory."

"Had we not best be on our way?" Preston asked. "And I think mayhap I alone should take the horse to his temporary stable. Does anyone see me with a black horse, they will be able to describe but me. I shall don a different coat and pull my hat low, so there will be little to describe."

"Good thinking, Dev, I mean Jamieson." He looked at Rowena and Cecily. "Again, we must stay in our roles so the names come naturally, and we answer to them when addressed." Turning back to Preston, he said, "You go first. Be certain all is clear. We will follow more slowly then cut over to the highway by way of the Hampton Lane. Catch up to us as you can."

Preston nodded, and after watering his horse and the too identifiable black horse, he started to make his way back along the deer path they had followed into their shelter. As he exited, Rowena ran over to her horse, and taking the horse's nose in her arms, she rubbed her cheek against his soft muzzle.

"Poor Dalton," she said. "I am sorry this is to be your fate. May you have a good home."

The horse bobbed his head up and down as if he understood, and when she stepped back, and Preston gave a tug to his bridle, the horse looked back at Rowena before following after the horse in front of him.

When Rowena turned back around, D'Arcy saw she had tears in her eyes.

Chapter 9

Rowena took a deep breath and brought her emotions under control. Offering Nate a smile, she said, "I would guess we need tidy up here. Hide any evidence of what we have done. Besides the towel, I had to cut a portion of Cecily's shift into rags and use them to keep the stain from staining her clothing and to apply the stain to her hair and skin. I did her hair first so it could be drying while I did her face, neck, ears, hands, and wrists. The stain soaks into the skin very quickly, but you will see I have yet to remove the rags protecting her clothing from her wrists and neck. Is there any stain on her cap, it will not be noticeable."

She held out her hands. "I have also stained my hands. I will try scrubbing them in the stream with some of the smaller pebbles and sand, but I wish I had some vinegar or my cook's soap. For now, I will wear the gloves Mistress Tavers gave me. What a gracious lady she is."

"Indeed, she is," Nate said. "You go ahead and see can you clean some of the stain from your hands. I will dig a hole in the woods and bury the towel, Cecily's curls, and the rags. As soon as possible, we need be on our way."

Rowena nodded, and after carefully removing the protective rags from Cecily's neck and wrists, she handed them to Nate and went to the stream to scrub her hands. After scrubbing them, she wiped them on the grass to dry them. Holding her hands up to inspection, she saw the scrubbing had done little to help. With a wry twist to her mouth, she rose and retrieved a drinking cup from the panniers. Another gift from Mistress Tavers.

"You cannot be lying on your belly scooping water from a stream," Mistress Tavers had said. "Now, here is a cup for you and your daughter to share, and a knife and spoon. You will be traveling as a lady. A lady will be expected to have such things."

A multitude of other items Mistress Tavers considered necessities were stuffed into the panniers; a comb, a small hand looking-glass, some lotion and some perfume, hair pins and a hair ribbon, practical as well as lace handkerchiefs, an extra pair of hose, a night shift, a warm wrap for cooler evenings, and a large floppy brim hat for protection from the sun. Rowena doubted she would ever be able to fully repay Mistress Tavers's numerous kindnesses.

After giving Cecily and herself a drink, she dried the cup on the hem of her skirt, and put it back into a pannier. She then donned the gloves. She would not put on the hat until they were back out on the lane.

※ ※ ※ ※

Rowena was pleased Cecily was having no trouble controlling the horse she rode. Her daughter had never ridden astride before, but she seemed to be adjusting remarkably well.

"'Tis really easier than riding on the sidesaddle," Cecily said. "Feels more secure. I feel I could even take a jump if I had to."

"There will be no jumping, Peter," Nate said. "We will ride sedately down the highway."

Rowena was pleased to hear that. She felt rather insecure on the pillion and would not be in favor of taking any jumps over hedges or fences as they had done on their desperate ride to the Taverses'. They had not been long on the highway when Dev caught up with them.

"All went well?" Nate asked him.

"Could not have gone better," Dev answered with his bright smile. "The master himself was awaiting me where his property joins the lane. He said he would have the horse hidden in his stable until nightfall, and the rider comes to collect him."

"What is to be done with Dalton," Rowena asked, but Nate shook his head.

"'Tis best you not know. The less you know, the less you can tell are we apprehended."

Rowena noted Dev had mentioned no names. The highwaymen could not be too careful. She liked that they were so concerned about protecting those who helped them.

"You are not thinking we will be caught, are you, Mister Drummer?"

Cecily asked, concern obvious in her voice.

Nate looked over at her. "I am Mister Blucher now, Peter. You must remember that."

"I am sorry, sir. I will not forget again."

"Good. And I am not expecting we will be caught, but we may be questioned. The militia are ever out prowling." He twisted to glance back at Rowena. "I am John Blucher, recently returned from Virginia, headed to visit my brother in Whitby in Cheshire. You are my wife, Mary. You were born in Virginia. Your last name before marrying me was Smith."

"Should they ask me about Virginia," Rowena said, "I know nothing of the colonies."

Nate chuckled. "Tell them anything you want. They know nothing about the colonies either. Especially not Virginia. Just tell them there are lots of trees and lots of Indians and 'tis sweltering hot in the summer."

"Is that what you say if questioned?" Rowena asked, wondering if his descriptions of the colony were accurate.

"I have yet had the need. I trust we will not have the need now either, but do we, I have confidence in you, my wife. Your fabrications when talking with Mistress Tavers could not have been better. You will do fine. By the by, neither of you are to know the Taverses."

"What of me, Mister Blucher? Am I also from Virginia?" Cecily asked.

"Hmmm. I think that would be best. You are an orphan. Your family died of the recurring fever. However, I am hopeful no one will scrutinize you."

Cecily smiled, and lowering the timbre of her voice, said, "I am not afraid. They will never guess I am not a boy."

"Bravo!" Dev said. "I trust you completely."

And so, the remainder of the morning disappeared as they traveled sedately along the highway leading to Nantwich in Cheshire. They stopped beside a stream to bait the horses and eat bread and cheese and sausages Mistress Tavers had packed for them. Rowena and Cecily were able to relieve themselves behind some bushes near the stream and Cecily giggled at trying to squat and manage her breeches.

"No giggling," Rowena hissed. "You must remember that. 'Twill give you away."

"I am sorry," Cecily said, "but these breeches make relieving myself difficult."

"I know, dear. I wore both breeches and my skirt all the way to the Taverses' house."

"Yes, I remember, Mother."

"Mistress Blucher to you, Peter."

"Yes, Mistress Blucher," Cecily said, choking on a giggle and turning it into an unladylike snort.

Nothing else broke up the dull ride other than Rowena's various fears. Her heart had thudded in her chest anytime they met a rider or coach or wagon on the highway. And once when a couple of riders had come thundering up behind them, she had feared they were to be caught, but the riders, barely slowing their mounts, had raced past them. She wondered that Nate and Dev could be so calm but guessed they were more than used to being in disguise and acting completely natural. Why should anyone think they were highwaymen?

When at last they reached an inn that Nate thought acceptable, Rowena was ready to drop. She believed she was near as tired as she had been when they reached the Taverses'. Riding on the pillion and jostling about on the horse's rump was not in the least bit comfortable. At least not to her. She pitied the many women who had traveled in such a fashion over the centuries. She knew she would be more comfortable if she would scoot closer to Nate and wrap an arm around his waist instead of clinging to the rim of his saddle, but he already had her head in a whirl. To be in bodily contact with him could well jeopardize her senses.

The inn Nate chose was old, but semi-clean, and the innkeeper's wife was hospitable. She escorted Rowena up to what she called their married couples' room. "We are respectable here," she said, climbing the stairs ahead of Rowena. "I know a gentleman and a lady right enough. Now are you certain you are wanting your page in your room? We have a nice chamber for the single men, and not that many guests."

Nate had told the innkeeper they would need a cot in their room for their young page, and the innkeeper, after a glance at Cecily, had assured Nate they had a trundle bed that should suit the youth. "Him being slight like he is. He will not be needing much padding."

Nate had agreed and Rowena had been forced to hide a smile knowing Nate would be the one sleeping on the poorly padded bed.

In answer to the innkeeper's wife, Rowena said, "Peter is young and only recently lost his parents to the fevers. He is near like a son to us. I know he will feel more secure is he close by."

The wife looked around Rowena at Cecily who was struggling up the steps with the panniers slung over her shoulders. "Right. He is but a mite. Sorry he lost his folks."

Opening a door at the top of the stairs, the wife said, "Well, here it is. Best room we got."

Rowena was pleased with the room. It had a large four poster bed with curtains that could be drawn. There was no hearth, but it had a brazier already laid with coal should the evening turn cool. A tin water pitcher sat in a red crockery bowl and both looked clean as did the towels hanging on pegs above the basin. Best of all was a table with two slat-back chairs pushed back into a corner of the room.

"Oh," Rowena said, "I see the table here in the room. Might we take our supper here?"

"Does your page fetch it for you, that you may." the innkeeper's wife smirked a little. "Many a time does the wife prefer to have her meal here rather than in the public room. 'Tis why we squeeze the table in here." She looked at Cecily. "Guess your page can serve you, too."

"Yes, he is still learning his duties, but serving he does fine."

"Well, are you wanting hot water to wash, send him to the kitchen. Cook will see he gets it. Otherwise, there is a pump behind the inn. 'Tis where most of the men guests wash up." She started to leave, but turned back. "There is a charge for each candle. How many more would you be wanting?"

The innkeeper's wife had left but the one lighted candle in the center of the table, but Rowena, having no idea what Nate's finances were like, shook her head. "I will have to consult my husband."

"As it should be, as it should be," the wife said, and looking at Cecily added, "Do you bring the pitcher, I am going to the kitchen. You can follow me."

Cecily looked to Rowena and Rowena nodded. "Yes, Peter. Do take the pitcher and get the warm water. I am longing to wash up after today's ride."

"Yes, Mistress Blucher," Cecily said, and grabbing the pitcher scurried after the innkeeper's wife.

Rowena stood in the middle of the room and tried to calm her heart. Having Cecily out of her sight in the inn, not knowing who might accost her kept Rowena's nerves frayed. She would not be able to relax until Cecily returned.

※ ※ ※ ※

After leaving Rowena and Cecily with the innkeeper's wife, D'Arcy had gone back out to see to the horses. The inn had an ostler, but D'Arcy preferred to see to the care of his horses. His and his men's lives were dependent upon the speed and well-being of their horses. Any little thing from a bruise to a sneeze was carefully monitored. He found Preston in the stable caring for his horse. The ostler had gone out to see to the horses of a dilapidated coach that had just drawn up, so D'Arcy had a chance to talk to his comrade.

"What do you think, will young Peter pull it off?"

Preston nodded but said, "'Twas hard to watch him struggling with those panniers and not offer to help. For us, they weigh nothing, but to Peter…"

"Aye. There will be some rough men in the inn. Do you keep an eye out do any of them attempt to take advantage of Peter."

With a half-smile and slightly narrowed eyes, Preston said, "I will be on the alert. But you, you must be watchful. A lovely woman is your wife."

"Humph! Do I not know it? 'Twill not be easy being in the same room with her."

Preston but chuckled and turned back to currying his horse.

Chapter 10

Cecily smiled and, using her disguised voice, thanked the cook for the warm water. The cook, a burly woman with thick white hair and a little mustache over her upper lip, had a wispy voice that was at odds with her appearance. "You sure you can manage that pitcher, lad? You look like you could use some fattening up."

"'Twas the fever I had, left me weak," Cecily said. "Same what killed my folks."

Turning over a slab of dough and whapping it onto her work table, the cook peered out of squinted eyes at Cecily. "Lost your folks? Shame. Lost mine when I was not much older than you. Lucky I was to learn to be a cook." She whacked the dough again. "Got to get my bread ready to rise am I to bake it tomorrow. Need a good stock on hand afore Saturday evening. The mistress be strict in observing the Sabbath. Come Saturday evening all work must stop until Sunday evening. Pity does any guest not observe the Sabbath. They will not find a warm meal nor changed sheets here."

"I suppose that means more work for you," Cecily said. "Readying up and all?"

"More work tomorrow, but then come Sunday, I just sit on my fat arse all day. Got no church near enough to attend. Vicar from Sidell comes round once a month and holds services here in the public room." She chuckled. "Oft times, I find myself under the weather on those Sundays. Mistress complains but is not apt to let me go. Hard to find another cook who would work for as little as I get paid. But I got my room and board so I cannot complain."

Cecily liked the cook, and the smells emanating from the kitchen. She was hungry and knew her mother was hungry. "When should I return to get my master and mistress's supper?"

"Any time. I got a pork stew on the fire, ready to eat. Morty over there, is frying up some sausages." She pointed to a youth with a shock of red hair and a mass of freckles. Squatting before the hearth, he hovered over a huge black skillet. "And I got a dandelion sallet dressed in some bacon drippings and topped with some blackberries. So after you take up that water, you come back when your mistress wants her supper."

Cecily again thanked the cook, and hefting the pitcher filled with warm water from a kettle hanging over the fire in the large stone hearth, she left the kitchen. The kitchen being out behind the inn, she had to set the pitcher down on the step at the back door in order to open the door. After making her way inside and shutting the door, Cecily decided being a page was not going to be easy. How she was to manage bringing the food in was beyond her, but for the moment, she needed to concentrate on getting the heavy pitcher back to her mother's room.

Engrossed in her struggle, she failed to notice two men staggering into the public room. They arrived at the stairs at the same time she did. She had to stop short to keep from bumping into them. Some water from her pitcher spilled out and a few drops landed on one man's shoe.

"Hey! Look what you done!" the man snapped. He was being held up by the second man, and Cecily could smell the alcohol on his breath when he leaned forward to snarl in her face.

Adopting her lower voice, she said, "I am that sorry, sir. Please do be forgiving me." Still struggling with the pitcher, it was getting heavier and heavier, she hoped the men would let her pass up the stairs ahead of them.

To her surprise, the man grabbed her shirt collar, making more water spill onto the floor. "Down on your knees. I want you to clean my shoes. Do you hear me!"

With his face in hers, she could hear him very clearly, but she knew not what to do. What would a page do in such a situation? Do as the man demanded, or call for help. Her dilemma was solved for her. Her assailant, grabbed by his coat collar, found himself looking up into Dev's angry face.

"Do you release the youth ere I shove my fist down your throat," Dev growled.

The man's unshaven face blanched, and he immediately released Cecily.

"Go on up to your mistress, Peter" Dev said. "I will make sure this lout ne'er troubles you again."

"Th…thank you, Mister Jamieson," Cecily said, barely managing to remember to call Dev by his new name. Balancing the pitcher the best she could, she made her way up the stairs. She had no idea what Dev was saying to the two men for his voice was a low growl, but in glancing back she saw both men looked sheepish and seemed eager to escape their tormentor.

Upon reaching the door to their chamber, she knocked on the door with her toe. Her mother opened the door almost before she regained her balance. Taking the heavy pitcher and backing up into the room, her mother said, "I was beginning to worry. Did all go well?"

"Mostly," Cecily answered. "The cook is very nice and said I may return to get our supper whenever you say. But at the stairs two drunken men accosted me. Thankfully, Dev, I mean Mister Jamieson, arrived and saved me."

Setting the pitcher down, Rowena whipped back around. "Two men accosted you! What did they do? Did they harm you?"

"Nay, Moth…, I mean Mistress Blucher. One grabbed me by the shirt collar but before he could do aught else, Mister Jamieson grabbed him and said did he not release me, he would shove his fist down his throat." Turning a giggle into a guffaw, she said, "You should have seen that man's face. I know he must have looked much more afraid than did I."

Her mother let out a deep breath. "I will not in the future let you go off alone. 'Tis not safe. We will have to come up with some excuse that I or Mister Blucher or Mister Jamieson should always be near to hand."

Cecily frowned. "I suppose that might be best, but I hate do I not fulfill my role."

Bending over, her mother gave her a kiss on the cheek. "You are doing wonderfully well. I am so proud of you. You are being so brave. But you cannot help that you are small. However, at present, that works to our advantage. Just so long as we do a better job of watching over you."

"How shall we manage my going to the kitchen to get supper?"

"We will discuss that with Nate, I mean Mister Blucher, when he arrives, but for now, I intend to wash up and see if I cannot get some of this stain off my hands." Pouring some of the water from the pitcher into the crockery bowl, her mother added, "You, Peter, must be as careful as you can when you wash. No scrubbing. Wash just enough to get the dust off your hands. I'll see to washing your face."

"Yes, Mistress Blucher. I will be careful," Cecily said in her gruff little voice. She rather liked the playacting they were doing, but she hoped she would not again encounter any men like the two drunkards who had accosted her. She had not been terribly frightened of the men, just more afraid of having her identity revealed, and that would have put them all in jeopardy.

※ ※ ※ ※

D'Arcy arrived in the bedchamber with three extra candles. He was playing the part of a respectably, if not overly, well-off gentleman. That meant no skimping on candles or gratuities. Paying for the Crosslys was going to cost his purse, that was for certain, but upon entering the chamber to find Rowena and Cecily eagerly awaiting him, both with bright smiles, he decided the cost might well be worth it.

Upon learning what had happened when Cecily was bringing back the water, he decided on a plan. "I will wait outside behind the inn. When Peter comes from the kitchen with our supper, I will open the door for him. You, my wife, will keep a watch out for Peter from the room here. I will shortly follow Peter inside. He should not be out of our sight except while he is in the kitchen. We will not again let him be accosted. I give you my word."

The smile Rowena gave him near took his breath away. Gads but she was a beautiful woman. What a fool her husband had been to sell his daughter to Haspel and end up losing his wife in the bargain. He knew he should be on his guard, but for this evening, he intended to enjoy the company of a beautiful woman. For this evening, she would be his wife. At least until time for them to go to bed.

※ ※ ※ ※

Preston had finished his supper and was sipping on a mug of ale when two militiamen swaggered into the public room. They were easily recognizable. Arrogant in the power they believed they wielded or the fear they believed they caused in the breast of any Royalist, they loudly called for the innkeeper.

When the innkeeper hurried forward, they asked him how many guests he had. The worried innkeeper described his guests from the Crosslys and D'Arcy, to the two drunkards, to other more respectable travelers. Finally, he pointed to Preston. "And there is Mister Jamieson."

"Jamieson." The taller of the two men strutted over to Preston. "Where do you travel from?" he growled.

"Biddulph," Preston answered, keeping his voice congenial.

"Where do you go?"

"Nantwich, then Wrexham."

"Wrexham! What business have you in Wales?"

"Sheep."

"Sheep?" The man glared at him. "You a sheep merchant?"

"More a cheese merchant."

"Cheese merchant!"

"Aye. The profit on ewes' milk cheese is close to double that of some cheeses. Not all, of course, but enough to make it worth my while to travel into Wales."

Again narrowing his eyes, the man asked, "On your travel today or yesterday, did you see a dark-haired woman traveling with a lovey fair-haired chit?"

"Nay. The only woman I saw was Mistress Blucher. She and her husband gave me company on a most tedious ride."

The man turned back to the innkeeper. "These Bluchers he speaks of, 'tis but the two of them and their page?"

"Aye. Devoted couple," the innkeeper said with a snicker. "Considering their age."

"Elderly are they?"

"Elderly enough they should not still be looking at each other as they do." He chuckled again. "My wife ne'er looks at me like that anymore."

Preston screwed up his mouth. So he had not imagined the looks D'Arcy and Lady Crossly exchanged. The innkeeper had also seen their mutual gazes of admiration.

"Humph!" the militiaman said. "Well, let me tell you this. Do you see a dark-haired woman traveling with a fair-haired chit, there be a reward for them. You keep yourn eyes peeled, and that reward might be yours." He looked from the innkeeper back to Preston.

"I could do with a reward," the innkeeper said. "Do I see them, who do I summon?"

The militiaman smirked. "Me. You just hold them. Lock them in a shed or some such. We will be back in a couple of days. We are visiting all the inns between Lyme, Nantwich, and Whitechurch. We are making a circle. Did they come this way, someone will have seen them. Also, the women may be traveling in the company of six or seven highwaymen. We have no description of the men, but be alert. Now, tonight, we need supper and bed."

Squinting his eyes, the innkeeper asked, "You have the coin?"

The militiaman glared at him, but snarled, "Yeah, we got the coin."

Fearing the militiamen might attempt to join him and question him more, Preston gulped down his ale, rose, and headed for the men's dormitory, located off the public room. Not trusting his pack to the men occupying the beds in the dormitory, he had the pack looped over his arm.

"What do you carry there?" the second militiaman demanded.

"My pack. I would not leave it to be riffled ere I went to my bed."

"I will have a look at it," the man said, beckoning Preston with his hand.

Smiling inwardly, Preston rejoined the two militiamen and slapped his pack down on the table he had just left. He knew he had nothing incriminating in his pack. His better coat and waistcoat, even the kerchief he wore when committing the robberies were in D'Arcy's pack, D'Arcy being a gentleman in this particular masquerade. His better shoes and breeches were in his pack along with his knife and spoon, some stockings, an extra shirt, some bread and cheese, enough coin to cover his travel needs, and his pistol and shot. Everything an ordinary man might be expected to have when he traveled any distance. He also had a letter of credit from a London goldsmith. The letter was worthless, but it looked real, and that was all that mattered.

He resented the militiamen pawing through his things, and he watched them carefully as they handled his coins. He would not trust them not to take a coin or two. The man who had called him over tried to read the letter of credit. He waved it around. "What is this for?"

"The sheep cheese," Preston answered.

"Fancy breeches and shoes here," the larger militiaman said.

"Aye, I make a better bargain do I look prosperous."

"I say here," interrupted the innkeeper. "Mister Jamieson is a good paying customer. He means to seek his bed. As do I. Do you want your supper, you best let him be and sit yourselves down. Here comes me wife with your feed."

The larger man pushed Preston's pack at him and said, "Good night to you. And do be alert do you see those two women."

"I will," Preston said, stuffing his items back into his pack. As the two militiamen settled down to eat, he made his way to the dormitory. The room was dark except for the moonlight peeking in through a partially open shutter on the window. Loud snores and snorts emanating from the two drunkards he had chastised for accosting Cecily reverberated around the room, but Preston had learned from his days at Oxford to put his mind on another plane and to shut out obtrusive noises. Spying an empty cot under the window, he stripped off his coat, waistcoat, and boots, and using his pack for a pillow, he was soon able to drift into an untroubled sleep.

Chapter 11

Sitting back in his chair, D'Arcy looked across the table at the beautiful woman posing as his wife. Gads, but he would not mind were she truly his wife. That thought surprised him. Not that he had never expected to marry. He had just never met any woman who had moved his thoughts in that direction. Not until now.

'Twas not just her beauty he admired. She was an intelligent, well-read woman. She was a brave and loving mother. He had learned she had two young sons. Being parted from them tore at her heart, but saving Cecily was paramount. She left her sons in the care of her maid who had helped raise her, but she prayed her sons would forgive her for deserting them.

D'Arcy had been enjoying the evening so much, he was surprised by a knock at the door. Cecily, acting as the page, answered the door. A maid had been sent to collect their dishes. "Morty, Cook's help, asks if you be done, could I bring down the dishes so he could wash up and go to his bed," the girl said.

D'Arcy looked at Rowena. "I would say we are finished, would you not, my dear?"

Smiling, Rowena nodded. "Aye, I have eaten my fill."

"Might be your page could light my way down?" the girl asked.

Rowena turned frightened eyes to D'Arcy, but he rose, saying, "Aye, that he can. I mean to find the necessary out back. I will follow the two of you down."

As Cecily gathered up the remains of their dinner and put them on the tray, Rowena gave D'Arcy a smile of thanks. She knew he would escort Cecily safely down to the kitchen and back.

The maid, considerably larger than Cecily, took the heavy tray that Cecily had somehow managed to carry up to their room, and Cecily carried the empty wine jug D'Arcy had provided and a candle to help light their way. All went smoothly. Cecily returned the wine jug to the innkeeper, then continued to light the way for the maid to return to the kitchen.

Outside the kitchen door, D'Arcy said, "I will go to the necessary. You light my way."

"Yes, sir, Mister Blucher," Cecily said, opening the door to the kitchen for the maid.

They found the necessary, and D'Arcy took the candle from Cecily. "Stay close to the door," he said. "Does anyone come, you are but awaiting your turn."

After quickly relieving himself, he found Cecily safe and ready to take her turn in the privy. Handing her the candle, he said, "I will be right out here. Take your time do you need to."

"'Tis not at all clean," Cecily said when she emerged. "I wonder, is that the norm?"

"Shhhh," he cautioned, but whispered, "too often, yes." Yet more experiences the girl is being subjected to, he thought. She was braving it all well.

Crossing through the public room, D'Arcy noted two men with their backs to him and Cecily. They had been bent over and shoveling in their supper when they had passed through earlier. They had not even looked up when Cecily left the empty wine jug with the innkeeper. They were now calling for another round of ale. The innkeeper looked annoyed. No doubt he was wanting his bed, but he brought them their ale as D'Arcy herded Cecily up the stairs. He mistrusted something about the men. Having arrived late, they could be militiamen. Dev might know. But no matter, he had no wish to have Cecily exposed to them.

Safely back in their room, D'Arcy found Rowena had let down her hair and was combing it out. She had pulled the trundle bed out and pushed it over near the table. Her shift was laid out on the bed, as well as a night shirt for Cecily. Likely she had taken care of her other needs while he and Cecily were out of the room, for she indicated a dilapidated looking close stool tucked back in the corner near the far side of the bed. Cecily had to tell her about using the privy.

"'Twas quite disgusting," the girl said, and Rowena proclaimed in the morning Cecily should see to her business by using the close stool, as poor a unit as it was.

"I suppose we must now retire, Mister Blucher, are we to rise early tomorrow," Rowena said, her face flushing a pretty pink, no doubt at the thought of sharing a room with him.

D'Arcy would have liked to spend more time getting to know Rowena better. He had enjoyed sharing his supper with her. Cecily had taken her bowl of stew and cup of wine and had gracefully positioned herself on the floor. She had seemed content to let him and her mother converse. Lost in her thoughts and new experiences, he guessed.

The evening at an end, he regrettably agreed, "You are right. I will step outside while you and Peter ready for bed. I will be close to hand, so tap on the door when you are done."

"Very well, Mister Blucher, and thank you so much for all you are doing for us."

Giving her a nod and a smile, he exited.

※ ※ ※ ※

Rowena again had trouble getting to sleep. Once Cecily was in bed with the sheets pulled up to her chin, Rowena had tapped on the door then scurried under the quilts as Nate returned. The candles had burned low and were sputtering, but she could still watch Nate, admire his strength, his broad shoulders, and his near cat-like movements. He seemed ever alert. She saw him bolt the door and test it. He next propped one of the chairs under the latch.

Seeing her watching him, he said, "Cannot be too careful."

She gave him no answer, and he seemed not to expect one.

He next tried the single window in the room, a leaded diamond-paned window. He pushed it open, looked out and down, then securely closed it. He put his pistol and sword close to his cot, took off his coat and waistcoat and placed them on the table. Pulling off his boots and padding over to the washstand in his stocking feet, he washed his face, neck and hands. Finally, he went around and put out all the candles, the last one on the table next to his cot.

Darkness engulfed the room until her eyes adjusted, and in the dim moonlight peeking in the window, she could just make out Nate on his cot. His feet stuck out over the little trundle bed. She hoped he would not be too uncomfortable. Not that the bed she and Cecily were sharing was anything wonderful. It sagged in the middle, and the ticking smelled. She would not be surprised did she and Cecily arise with some unwanted traveling companions. Well, that was a minimal worry. Keeping Cecily safe was all that truly mattered.

For a while during their supper, Rowena had pushed her worries aside. She had enjoyed talking to Nate. Intelligent, well-educated, he had read many of the books she had read, and they had enjoyed a lively discussion. He was easy to talk to, and she had found herself telling him much about herself. Yet, he had divulged nothing about himself. At times, she completely forgot he was a highwayman.

She feared she was immensely attracted to Nate, but she knew, too, that nothing could come of it. She was married, and he was a highwayman, and for all she knew, he, too, was married. He might have children. Mayhap he had lost his land due to confiscation or Cromwell's taxes, and he had no other way to support his family than to commit highway robberies. Scoffing at herself, she acknowledged this was but one of several scenarios she had made up about Nate.

What troubled her most, though, was how she kept wondering what it would be like to kiss Nate. She had kissed her husband, her parents, her children, but somehow, she believed kissing Nate would be very different. She touched her fingertips to her lips. What would she do if he tried to kiss her? She believed he was attracted to her as she was to him. How would she respond? Would she let him kiss her? She was afraid that yes, yes she would.

She had never regretted her marriage to Lindell Crossly. At least not until he had sold Cecily to Haspel. Before then, she had been happy. She loved her children, and she had been glad she could live on a manor next to her parents and had been able to visit them often. When they died, at least her brother and his wife were still there. She felt sorry for her brother. He and his wife, Dorisande, had thus far been unable to have children. Did they never have children, it would mean after five hundred years and twenty-five generations, the Plaisance name would die out at Elkton Hall.

The manor was not entailed, so at present, Rowena's older son, Milo, was named as Artus's heir. They had a distant cousin who bore the Plaisance name living somewhere in Yorkshire. His grandfather was her great grandfather's younger brother. That younger brother had gone into the law and had prospered as had his son. Did Artus have no sons, the distant cousin or his son would be the principal bearer of the Plaisance coat of arms as the surviving male head of the senior line of the family, but he would not inherit the manor.

Rowena was close with her brother, and prayed he would understand her need to save Cecily from Haspel. He was a good uncle to her children, and she hoped in her absence, he and Dorisande would give comfort to her sons. Did she ever find a way to visit her sons, she believed she could trust her brother not to give her away. But she would never trust Lindell again. He had destroyed what love she bore him. Not that she could say she had ever loved him as a lover. At least not the Romeo and Juliet kind of love. But she had been immensely fond of him and had enjoyed his company.

Their bedding had offered her no thrill. Her mother had warned her the first time could be unpleasant but had promised the coupling would improve. Rowena, however, had found none of their sexual relations pleasant, and it had often been painful until after Cecily was born. After the birthing, the bedding had merely been a matter of performing her duty as a wife. The past couple of years, they had had less and less coupling. They shared the same bed, but more often than not, Lindell's need for her in a sexual way had dwindled. For her that had been a blessing. But now, as she looked over at Nate, she wondered if bedding him might be a very different experience.

Chapter 12

When Nate lifted Rowena onto the pillion, she determined she would not again force herself to be so uncomfortable. Today she would slip an arm around Nate's waist and lean against his strong back. After all, they had spent the night in the same room. They had shared a cozy supper and good conversation. He had made no impolite suggestions or even hinted at anything improper, so she saw no reason she could not trust him to accept her closeness and not feel she was being immodest.

Nate had insisted on a very early start. They had not even taken the time to break their fast, but the innkeeper's wife had provided them with bread and cheese that they could eat later. Rowena learned the reason for the hasty departure had to do with the two militiamen staying at the inn. Nate and Dev thought 'twould be best did they not see Cecily. The two men were too inquisitive for Dev to like. And, because Dev knew the men would be headed to Nantwich, they had been forced to leave the highway and take rough trails so not to be overtaken by the two men along the highway.

The morning had been cloudy and cool, and Rowena worried Cecily might not be warm enough, but from his pack, Nate produced a small coat for her. It was almost too small.

"'Twas the best Mistress Saticoy could manage for us," Dev said, his hazel eyes thoughtful. "The good thing is, all the other clothing fits. A youth outgrowing his coat is to be expected. Should not cause questions to be asked."

It was mid-morning before they stopped to break their fast, and Rowena's stomach had been growling for some time. The morning clouds had danced away and a bright sun shone down on them. They stopped by a stream with a goodly number of trees to hide their presence yet with enough grass along the edge of the stream for the horses to graze after being watered. Taking a small blanket off the back of his horse,

Dev threw it over a rough log to make a seat for Rowena, but he, Nate, and Cecily took seats on the ground. Rowena was so proud of Cecily. She had done everything asked of her and with no complaining. She even seemed to be enjoying herself.

"Having to take these back trails has slowed us some, but I am still thinking we will reach Britteridge Hall by mid-afternoon," Nate said.

"These are more friends of yours at this Britteridge Hall?" Rowena questioned.

"They are." Nate said with a nod of his head.

"Will we be putting them in danger as we did the Tavers?"

"No, you and Peter, will not be putting the Prestons in any danger. Fact is, you may help keep any danger away."

Confused, Rowena asked, "How is that?"

"No need for you to know. Just know that in this case, you will be a help."

Cecily made her little guffaw, and said, "Such an adventure as we are having. Am I to continue as a page?"

"You are, and you will find you have two pretty girls to flirt with," Dev said.

Cecily burst out in another guffaw, and said, "Mister Jamieson, you had best give me some advice. I fear I will not know how to flirt with girls."

"Nay, you will not be flirting with the girls," Nate said. "You are a page. They are ladies of the family. You will be servile." He chuckled. "However, as you make a rather handsome lad, you may find the girls staring at you. And certainly, are any younger serving maids in the house, they could well want to flirt with you. So, could be you could use some pointers."

Nodding, Dev said, "I think it might be best, do any of the maids flirt with you, you should but duck you head and pretend to be shy and tongue-tied."

"Where will Peter sleep?" Rowena asked, feeling some concern.

With a tiny smile, Nate said, "I would think, do we have a closet off our room, she will sleep with you and I will have the closet. If not, we will have a cot in the room, and I will have the cot."

"You cannot have been very comfortable last night, Mister Blucher,"

Rowena said, then asked, "Are we still the Bluchers?"

"We are, and Dev is still Will Jamieson. Now, 'tis time we get back on the road."

🌱 🌱 🌱 🌱

Rowena was amazed at all the back paths and trails Nate and Dev seemed to know. "Have you traveled this way often?" she asked.

"From time to time we have found it necessary," Nate said. "We normally skirt Nantwich, it having supported the roundheads. Never know when we might encounter the militia."

Rowena had a feeling Nate had other reasons for not going into Nantwich. Mayhap his home was near here, and he feared he might be recognized. That might be why she and Cecily would cause his friends less danger than he would himself.

As they failed to stop for a mid-day meal, she guessed Nate was in a hurry to get to his friends' home. Must be he wanted to get there before dark. On the back pathways they were traveling, they passed few other travelers, just the occasional farmer, and once a couple of youths trotting home with their day's catch from a nearby stream. She was not particularly surprised when she saw a man sitting on a fence stile whittling. As they drew closer, she thought the man looked familiar. Then she realized the man was Jack Chapman, the highwayman whose horse Cecily was riding.

Pulling up in front of Chapman, Nate said, "All look clear?"

Chapman nodded. "Aye," he said, but his eyes were on Cecily. "You are a day late, and I see you have made a slight change in the plans."

"'Twas necessary," Nate said. "Large reward is being offered for the return of two women, one with dark hair, one a young fair-haired beauty. Militia abound. So, Jack, allow me to introduce Peter Morse. My wife's page. He, too, is from Virginia and is an orphan. Lost his parents to the fevers."

"Sorry to hear that, Peter," Chapman said. "Kind of the Bluchers' to take you in. Nice horse they have provided for you."

"He is a fine horse, Mister Chapman. He does whatever I ask of him."

"The black horse was too recognizable," Nate said. "Had to give him up."

"Figures," Chapman said, "but 'tis a shame. He was an impressive horse. However, Tourney has our spare for us, so all is well. With this change, I will need to let the Prestons know of it before you arrive. They were expecting your wife and daughter, not a page. Guess I had best set out. I will go through Nantwich. Will get me there quicker. Mayhap you should go by Tourney's first, leave off Jamieson then circle around to the Prestons'."

"Sound plan," Nate said.

With a nod of his head, Chapman put away his knife and the stick he had been whittling, settled his pack on his back, and set off across a field.

"Where does he go?" Cecily asked.

"He will pick up the highway leading into Nantwich and go directly on to the Prestons'," Nate said. "We will take a long way around. We will do as Jack suggested and visit the Tourneys first. Jamieson will be staying with them." He glanced at Rowena. "Nice young couple. They have their first babe on the way."

Rowena gave a hesitant smile. "We are putting you to so much trouble. But we thank you so much. I fear had you not helped us, we would have been apprehended by now."

"'Twould be a good likelihood," Nate admitted, "but to keep Cecily safe has become important to us, also. Not just to frustrate a Puritan fanatic, but because no young woman should be forced into an unwanted marriage. Now, let us resume our journey."

As they again started off down the barely visible trail, Rowena mulled over Nate's words. He believed no woman should be forced into marriage. But most women were. Or, at least, their marriages were arranged for them, and they had little choice in the matter. Yes, her mother had told her that she would not be forced to marry Lindell, but she knew both her parents thought the arrangement a good one despite the difference in her age and Lindell's. Trusting her parents, she had married Lindell.

Her mother was a strong-willed woman, yet when her father wanted her to marry Thierry Plaisance, Esquire, she married him, as her father did bid her. At least her mother and father had been close in age, and her father had been a handsome man and generally easy going, if not particularly wealthy. But the Plaisance family was old, dating back to Henry II. Rowena's grandfather wanted to gain access into the world of the landed gentry. Plaisance gave him his entry. The Plaisance fortunes had been going downhill for many a generation. The Doggett money Rowena's mother brought to Elkton Hall revived it. It even allowed Rowena's father, once he was released from the Cromwellian prison, to pay his assessed fines and buy back his estate without having to resort to selling off large portions of his forest as Lindell had to do.

Thoughts of her father saddened her. He had come back from prison a shell of himself. And he had been restricted to his parish. Not that he had had any wish to go anywhere. Mostly he had but wanted to sit in his chair and stare out the window or sometimes seemingly stare at nothing at all. Rowena's mother had pampered him and had occasionally been able to get him out for rides or walks, but any activity seemed to be a major effort for him, and in mid-summer of the year fifty-one, shortly before Charles II came marching down from Scotland in hopes of reclaiming his crown, her father died. Her mother died a year later of what a physician said was a cancer. Ampora Doggett Plaisance had spent five years caring for her invalid mother, and then five years caring for her ailing husband. Rowena wondered just how much joy had ever been a part of her mother's life.

Turning away from her morbid memories, Rowena pondered her own future. Eventually Haspel would have his marriage to Cecily annulled. And when Cecily turned twenty-one, she could no longer be forced into a marriage not of her choosing. She would be free and safe. She could return to her home and be welcomed by her brothers. But what of me, Rowena wondered? Had she been branded an outlaw? Would she ever have to remain in hiding? That thought gave Rowena a shiver, and she gave her head a shake. She could not dwell on such fears. All that was important at the moment was keeping Cecily safe. Future worries would have to wait their turn.

Chapter 13

D'Arcy inwardly sighed when the Tourney house came into view. Staying off the highway and circumventing Nantwich had made for a long day, but they were now safely reaching their destination. The Tourney house was a pretty two-story red brick house with a slate roof, numerous chimneys, and a vaulted ceiling in the roomy kitchen. New by most standards, Errol Tourney's father had built the house not twenty years past. Tourney's ancestors made their money in the tannery business, invested well, and those investments allowed Errol's father to buy the Tourney estate and build Reverie Manor.

Trotting over the pretty stone bridge built over the small placid stream that gave the estate its name, D'Arcy glanced at Rowena. "We can expect a royal welcome here. The Tourneys are very fond of Jamieson. However, we will not be staying long as we will not wish to hold up the Prestons' supper."

"Will my page be eating his supper in the kitchen with the other servants?" Rowena asked.

He could hear the concern in Rowena's voice. "When we arrive at Britteridge, I will inform Lady Preston that we have not had anything to eat but bread and cheese since mid-morning, though I would guess Mistress Tourney will offer us something. However, I will ask Lady Preston to see Peter receives something to eat forthwith."

"Thank you," Rowena said then asked, "After he eats, what will he do?"

"Go up to our room. It may be boring for him, but he will await us there."

"Poor, dear," she said. "At this point, did I have a sword, I would feel like running it through my husband. To think what he is putting his daughter through."

D'Arcy chuckled. "Cannot blame you, but keep in mind, we have no daughter."

"Yes, Mister Blucher, so I will."

As they rode up through the brick gates with its two-room gate house, they were greeted by the skinny young gatekeeper. "Welcome, Mister Blucher, Mistress Blucher, Mister and Mistress Tourney have been expecting you. And welcome to you Mister Jamieson. 'Tis good to see you again, sir."

Preston drew up. "Thank you, Brock. All is well with you I trust."

"Yes, sir, Mister Jamieson. 'Tis kind you are for asking."

Continuing up the well-maintained lane leading to the house, D'Arcy again glanced back at Rowena. "Does Peter need to tend his business, he will need use the privy behind the house. Mistress Tourney will see you are accommodated. We will stay long enough to drink a sherry or some such, then we must be on our way."

"I understand," Rowena said.

They had barely reached the wide steps leading down from the front entrance when two young groomsmen ran up to take the horses. "You may stable my horse, and take my pack and weapons to my room," Preston said, "but you need but tie up the Bluchers' and their page's horses. They will be leaving soon."

"Yes, Mister Jamieson," one youth said as Preston dismounted. D'Arcy swung down and reached up to help Rowena off the pillion. Cecily had to manage her own dismount which D'Arcy was pleased to see she did quite well. She might be a slight little thing, but she was not lacking in mettle.

The door opened and the Tourneys' butler stepped aside as a young woman, her wide hazel eyes glowing, her generous mouth curved in a beaming smile, rushed down the steps to fling her arms around Preston's neck. "Oh, Mister Jamieson, you are here at last. When you failed to arrive yesterday, I began to fear something had happened."

Returning the hug and then drawing free, Preston said, "Mistress Tourney, you must allow me to introduce Mistress Blucher."

D'Arcy had been watching Rowena's face. Hestia Preston Tourney had not done a good job of disguising her love for her brother, and D'Arcy knew Rowena made note of it. She had to assume some sort of relationship existed between the two. However, she said nothing and graciously accepted Hestia's invitation to come inside the house.

"Mistress Tourney," D'Arcy said, "we have not stopped since mid-morning. I wonder might you have someone show our page where he might find the necessary."

"Oh, of course," she said in her honeyed tones. D'Arcy had always thought Hestia had the sweetest voice. Turning to the remaining groomsman, she said, "Lanny, do you please show the Bluchers' page where he needs go."

Hestia had barely glanced at the page, but D'Arcy saw Lanny eye Cecily strangely as he said, "Follow me."

Rowena gave her daughter a worried look as Cecily followed after the footman, but she turned back to Hestia and said, "You have a lovely home and grounds."

"Thank you," Hestia said. "My husband is most proud of it. I must credit his mother with the garden. She planned it and for many years directed its care. Sadly, she is an invalid now and can do little more than sit in her room and look out the window at the grounds or on a nice day, sit in the garden." In a conspiratorial whisper, Hestia added, "'Tis her heart, poor dear. It leaves her breathless. Errol and I both hope she will live to see her grandchild born." She patted her stomach and smiled sweetly.

"When is your babe due?" Rowena asked.

"The mid-wife says early fall. So not too long. Oh, and here is our housekeeper." Hestia indicated a young woman with her hair tucked neatly under a lappet cap and a courteous smile on her round face. "Mistress Lord, do you show Mistress Blucher upstairs that she may wash away the dust and refresh herself."

"You come with me, Mistress Blucher. I know you must be exhausted," Mistress Lord said, extending an arm toward the stairs.

"When you come back down, Mistress Blucher," Hestia said, "we will be in the parlor." She motioned to an open door off the wide elegant hall with its pale yellow carved inlaid paneling and cloud studded mural on the ceiling.

No question, the Tourneys had designed and decorated their home exquisitely, D'Arcy thought as he watched Rowena follow the housekeeper up the curved staircase leading to the landing overlooking the hall. Everything about Reverie Manor was appealing.

"Do you join us, Mister Blucher," Hestia said from the entrance to the parlor. "Errol will be home shortly. He had a meeting with our steward and a cattle buyer. I am afraid it could not be postponed."

D'Arcy nodded and joined Hestia and Preston in the graciously furnished parlor with its glazed windows and white stucco walls and ceiling. Hestia, turning to her house steward, directed him to pour the sherry then bring some biscuits from the kitchen.

"I know 'tis not long until you must head over to Mother and Father's, but 'tis right you should have some refreshment first. Oh, and your young page, he should have a biscuit." She told the steward when he finished pouring the sherry into four crystal goblets to tell the cook to make sure the page had an ale and a biscuit.

When the steward exited the room, Hestia jumped up to again hug her brother. "Oh, Deverette, we were so worried when you failed to arrive yesterday. But Father sent over a message that Mister Chapman was not concerned. He would have had some word had anything gone amiss. But what did keep you?"

"'Tis a bit of a tale, Hestia, and I will tell all later, but not now. You need but follow Jack's direction and treat me and Nate as friends and treat the woman traveling with us as Nate's new wife. Now, tell me, when will I see the rest of the family?"

"Mother and the girls are coming over tomorrow morning. Father will come in the afternoon and then the following day," she looked at D'Arcy, "all the family and the Blucher's will come to dinner."

"Jack seemed to think all was clear," D'Arcy said. "No one has been nosing about recently? Mayhap they believe Dev is with the King in Europe."

"I think that may be the case," Hestia answered, "but Father warns us we must be ever cautious. He will not trust his staff though most of them have served him for many years."

"Rightfully so," D'Arcy agreed. "You are so close to Nantwich, you must need be more watchful. At my sister's, either Harp's Ridge or Knightswood, the distance to a town sizable enough to keep any militia to hand is great enough we have little to fear. And, when we are at either abode, Berold keeps guards posted day and night to alert us should any large number of men approach the manor. We would be long gone ere they ever reached the grounds."

"Aye," Preston agreed. "And the staff knows did any of them dare breathe a word about D'Arcy visiting, they would face Berold's wrath. That, they would not like."

A tap on the door interrupted their conversation, and the footman opened the door for Rowena. Her face washed, her hair neatly done up in a bun at the back of her head, the dust brushed from her clothing, she took a seat next to D'Arcy. Smiling brightly, she said, "I must tell you, Mistress Tourney, your housekeeper is a wonder. Especially for such a young woman. Most competent. When I showed her I had stain on my hands from foolishly handling green walnut husks when we stopped along the road yesterday, she knew just what I needed. First a little oil to seep into the skin, then salt and vinegar, and finishing off with a lovely rose scented soap, so the smell of vinegar is near gone and the stain is greatly faded."

"Oh, I hope you got no walnut stain on your clothing," Hestia said.

Rowena shook her head. "Nay, but I should have known better. 'Twas too early for the nuts to be ready to eat. I think my brain is a tad befuddled."

"And rightfully so. How different England must be to you after Virginia."

D'Arcy noted the smile Rowena gave Hestia. She knew that Hestia knew she was not really from Virginia, but she played the part and answered, "Yes, 'tis quite different."

They sipped their sherry and ate the biscuits the steward served off a silver tray then D'Arcy said, "We must need be on our way, Mistress Tourney. I have no wish to hold up your Father's supper. Your parents are being most kind to again offer me, and now, also, my wife, their hospitality."

At his words, Rowena looked at him in surprise, then she looked at Hestia. "Are the Prestons, the people we are staying with, your parents?"

"Why, yes," Hestia said. "Did you not know that?"

"I suppose I neglected to tell her," D'Arcy said. "I thought I must have mentioned it, but I guess I failed to do so." He looked at Rowena.

"Sorry, dear."

"Well, mayhap you did tell me, and I forgot," Rowena said with a slight smile. "As I have mentioned, my brain is terribly addled."

She rose as D'Arcy rose and Hestia and Preston also rose. "So nice to have met you, Mistress Blucher," Hestia said, glancing at D'Arcy before looking back at Rowena. "By the by, you will be coming back here for dinner in a couple of days, and we will have a chance to get better acquainted."

Hestia and Preston escorted them to the door, and the butler opened it. Cecily, chatting brightly with the young groomsman, awaited them by their horses. Using the gruff little voice she had adopted so easily, she was telling the wide-eyed groomsman, Lanny, all about Virginia.

※ ※ ※ ※

They had not gone far when Rowena said, "Mister Blucher, could you not have trusted me enough to have told me the Tourneys and the Prestons were related?"

Though her voice was quiet, D'Arcy could hear the anger in it. "'Tis not that I fail to trust you, or Peter, 'tis as always, the less you know, the less you could reveal are we apprehended."

"You think we would tell tales on you?"

"I think did anyone threaten Peter, yes, you would talk. Or did anyone threaten you, yes, Peter would talk. You would say as little as you could, but did you need to sacrifice someone else to keep your loved one safe, yes, you would. So, until 'tis necessary for you to know any details, I fear I must keep as much from you as I deem prudent for all concerned."

For some time, Rowena was silent, then she said, "I am sorry. You are correct that you must need protect your friends. And yes, did anyone threaten my child, I would tell them whatever I needed to tell them to keep her from harm. But rest assured, we would tell as little as possible."

"I have no doubt about that. Now, as to your host and hostess, you will find Lady Preston gracious, but quiet. Sir Lionel, however, though in his mid-fifties is yet a man to be reckoned with. Mistress Tourney is their elder daughter, their two younger daughters are Amethyst and Camrielle."

"And Will Jamieson is their son?" Rowena said. "You may deny it, but I can see Mister Jamieson's resemblance to Mistress Tourney, from the hair, the eyes, the mouth. And Mistress Tourney's joy at Jamieson's arrival was more than just joy at seeing a friend."

Rowena was no fool. He was not surprised she had seen the resemblance, all the same, he said, "I do deny it, my good wife. Will Jamieson is but a very dear friend. He was a close friend of Hestia's brother, Myles, who died any number of years ago, but the bond was strong. Do you wish to see Myles's grave, he is buried on the Preston estate in their private cemetery."

He doubted he was fooling her, but she would accept his word. Eventually, she said, "I must have been mistaken. But tell me, Mister Blucher, now that you have a wife, are you needing to stop here again, what will you do with no wife?"

He chuckled. "I will still have a wife. Just my wife will be home caring for the children."

She snorted then said, "I suppose the Prestons have no idea, any more than do the Tavers, what you really do for a living. Do they also think you are a cattle buyer?"

"No, they know me to be a friend of Mister Jamieson. They know he and I do, from time to time, travel together. Mister Jamieson is a cheese merchant. I am a lawyer. I travel on various assignments for various Chester merchants. And as I once had business with Sir Lionel, he has ever offered me his home's hospitality."

"I wonder might you truly be a lawyer, Mister Blucher?"

"I studied at Lincoln's Inn."

"Did you now? And did you plan to become a barrister?"

"I might have had some thoughts along those lines." He had intended to be a lawyer with hopes of being called to the bar, but in August of forty-two when the King Charles I raised his standard at Nottingham, he had joined his older brother Kenrick to fight for their King. He had been at Oxford when the city surrendered in forty-six. Once he had his parole pass, he had considered going back to school, but first he had wanted to see his home, Wealdburh, on the Wirral Peninsula. He had wanted to see his family.

Having visited his home, instead of going back to study the law, to help his father, he had taken over as steward for all his father's manors other than Wealdburh and Tyneford. Though his father had not fought in the war, he had helped finance the King, and the sequestration committee had assessed a delinquency on each of his manors. D'Arcy's job was to buy them back, and to sell off what portions of the manors or timber on the manors were needed to cover the fines. Traveling from the Wallingford manor in Oxfordshire to the Wynn Alawn in Wales to the two manors in Derbyshire, the two in Northampton, and the smallest, but one of the loveliest, in Somerset, he had made a yearly circuit.

Consequently, in his near five years of traveling about England before he again took up arms to go back to war for his new King, Charles II, he had learned many a short cut, and had made numerous friends. Royalist friends that he could count on in an emergency. Loyalty to King Charles was not dead just because the Parliamentarians were at present ruling the country.

"Might you not have returned to Lincoln Inn after the war?" Rowena broke in on his thoughts.

Shrugging, he said, "I had other more pressing matters that needed my attention."

"'Tis a shame," she said. "'Twould seem to be a safer way of making a living."

Chuckling, he agreed, then looked over his shoulder at Cecily. "Young Peter, whatever were you telling that groomsman at the Tourneys'?"

Giving a shake of the reins to urge her horse up beside his, Cecily said, "You said I might make up whatever I wanted about Virginia. So, I was telling him about the Indians, and all the bears and wolves, and about the growing of tobacco."

"Good heavens. What do you know about growing tobacco?" he asked.

"Why nothing. But I know about growing wheat and barley. At least I know a little about it since we grow both at Crossly Oaks. I have seen the tenants ploughing, and I see the harvesting every year. I just turned the wheat into tobacco. But 'twas the Indians the groomsman was most interested in. I once saw a picture of some Indians in a book in Father's library. The men wore almost no clothing but had drawings all over their bodies. They wore feathers in their hair instead of hats on their heads. And they lived in what looked like straw huts. Lanny asked if the women and girls wore clothing, and I told him, of course they do."

Chuckling, D'Arcy said, "The drawings on their bodies are tattoos." He decided not to tell her that many of the women were often also scantily dressed. "Their houses," he continued, "are wood framed with woven reeds or branches and are then plastered over with mud. But they can look like grass houses because often the roofs are of grasses or reeds and they flow almost to the ground."

"How do you know this, Mister Blucher?" Cecily asked, awe in her voice.

"I have met people who have traveled to the colonies. Another thing, the forests in the colonies are so vast and thick, they make our largest forests seem puny. Oh, and they have an animal 'tis a cross between a dog and a cat. It has black rings on its tail and a black mask across its eyes. It can climb trees, and it has hands and likes to wash its food. 'Tis called a raccoon."

"You are making that up," Rowena said with a laugh.

He shook his head. "Nay, 'tis true. So, Peter, do you tell any more tales, you may tell about the raccoons. I understand some people have tried to keep them as pets."

"Oh, thank you. I wish I had known about the raccoon sooner," Cecily said. "That groomsman wanted to know all about Virginia."

"Ah, here we are," D'Arcy said as they rounded a stand of beech trees, and a large Jacobean house came into view – a two-story red sandstone house with decorative pilasters, turreted wings with mullioned windows, and a central porch with a terrace extending on either side. A well-maintained lane lined with shrubs led up to the entrance before circling behind the house to the stables and coach house.

Turrets matching the ones on the house were on either side of the gate, and as they entered the grounds, a woman stepped out from one of the turrets. Bobbing a curtsy, she said, "Welcome back, Mister Blucher. We was told you would be coming. My man is up to the stables helping ready things for you, the head groomsman being down with the ague. Poor soul is getting old. No doubt Sir Lionel will soon be giving him his pension."

Knowing the gateman's wife to be a wealth of gossip, D'Arcy had cultivated her natural loquacity. She knew more about what went on in the neighboring farms and manors and the town of Nantwich than did the Prestons, and knowing about the most recent happenings was important to his and his men's safety.

Her eyes sharp, the woman glanced at Rowena and Cecily. "Mister Chapman did tell me you had your new wife with you." She bobbed another curtsy to Rowena. "A welcome to you, Mistress Blucher."

"Thank you," Rowena said, giving the woman a bright smile.

Cocking her head, the woman said, "Be but you and Mister Chapman visiting this time, huh?"

"That is correct, Hilda," D'Arcy said. "But tell me, all is well with you and yours? Any new births I should congratulate you on?"

She chuckled. "You be a good one to be asking, Mister Blucher. Yes, my middle daughter had her first. She is the one, do you recall, what married the baker's son in Nantwich."

"I do recall it. I congratulate you and her. I suppose all is well in Nantwich?"

Hilda snorted. "Humph! Well as can be expected what with the property taxes and the Puritan Justice of the Peace poking his nose into everyone's business. Low-born he be and my son-in-law says he is apt to call up the militia at the least little rumor."

"That so? Not well liked by the citizens of Nantwich?" How ironic that Nantwich had held for Parliament, but now there was no Parliament, just Cromwellian rule. The people of property disliked having a levy on their property that was not passed by Parliament. They also disliked being under military rule.

"Not liked by any what has any sense," Hilda said. "But here I am yammering in your ear, and your Mistress is no doubt eager to be getting off that horse."

Laughing, D'Arcy said, "Always a pleasure talking with you, Hilda, but yes, I do believe my wife is more than ready to get off this horse." Tipping his hat to the woman and lightly touching his heels to his horse, and with Cecily right behind him, he headed up the lane to the house.

Chapter 14

Welcomed into the Britteridge spacious hall by Sir Lionel and Lady Preston, Rowena, exhausted by the long day, appreciated her host's and hostess's graciousness. She could also see where Dev and Hestia got their good looks. Their mother, despite the fact she must be in her fifties, was beautiful. Lovely hazel eyes with thick lashes, a sweet generous mouth curving in a genuine smile, an exquisite nose, high cheekbones, and perfectly coiffured silver hair with but a tiny net cap resting atop her head. Sir Lionel, though in his late fifties, was a tall, broad-shouldered, robust man with a booming voice, and searching eyes under heavy eyebrows. Still, Rowena had a feeling Lady Preston ruled the house.

She and Nate were also greeted by the Preston's two young daughters, Amethyst and Camrielle, and by Jack Chapman, looking relaxed and at ease in the Preston home. The Prestons' daughters were as lovely as their mother. Though Amethyst had her father's height – at sixteen she was as tall as Rowena – she seemed untroubled by any gawkiness. She moved with an easy grace, and her smile was as warm as her mother's. Rowena was sad that Cecily would have to continue to play the part of a young page and could not get to know the Preston girls.

"Now, my dear," Lady Preston said, "I intend to take you right up to your room. I know you must be exhausted and sick of all the dust." Taking Rowena's arm, she directed her toward a sweeping staircase. "I have told Cook we will have supper late this evening that you may first have a bath. The footmen have just finished filling a tub in your room."

Looking over her shoulder, Lady Preston beckoned to Cecily. "You come, too. I will show you where you will stay, and then you may set out and dust Mister Blucher's clothing while he washes up." As they mounted the stairs, Lady Preston continued, "Knowing from Mister Blucher's other visits how early he rises, I was certain you would not want him disturbing you. So, I have put you and Mister Blucher in adjoining bedchambers with the page in the closet between your rooms. That way the page can be on call for either of you. I hope that meets with your approval."

She knows we are not married, Rowena thought. She knows and has worked out the perfect accommodations for us. She may well know Cecily is not a boy. Well yes, she would know about Cecily. Mister Chapman initially told her Nate was bringing a woman and her daughter. Yet no servants would be privy to what Lady Preston knew.

"You are most kind, Lady Preston," Rowena said. "The accommodations are perfect. Thank you. You are so very thoughtful."

As they reached the top of the staircase that opened into a long gallery, Rowena heard Sir Lionel's booming voice inviting Nate into the parlor for a taste of some fine port before he went upstairs to wash and change. "You, too, Chapman. I know you promised to show my girls a new patterned silk sample, but they can wait." No doubt Sir Lionel was eager to learn how his son fared. She wondered if he knew his son was a highwayman. If not, why did he think his son was on the run? Unable to use his own name or return to his own home?

"Just this way, Mistress Blucher," Lady Preston said.

"How open and bright your gallery is," Rowena said, admiring the outside wall lined with windows. The opposite wall was hung with various portraits and a couple of busts. Stopping before one portrait, she questioned, "Oh, is that Sir Lionel when he was young?"

Lady Preston shook her head. "Nay. 'Tis a portrait of our son, Myles. 'Twas painted two years before he died. The ague took him from us."

"I am so sorry. Must be so hard to lose a child."

Lady Preston gave her a faint smile, and looked back at the portrait. "I am but glad we have this portrait. 'Tis so easy to forget what someone looked like. We have a portrait of my mother, but not one of my father or my brother. Both died of wounds they suffered in the first battle of the war."

"Oh, dear, 'tis most sad. The war has devastated so many people."

Brightening, Lady Preston said, "Let us not dwell on the past that cannot be changed. Come, you must be eager to get to your chamber."

Following Lady Preston down the gallery, Rowena glanced at the paintings as she passed. She saw no portraits of Dev. Could it be he was not their son? Was she imagining Dev's resemblance to Lady Preston and her daughters?

Lady Preston led her into a charming bedchamber where a fire blazed in the hearth despite the warmth of the day, and a large copper tub lined with white linen sat on another large cloth protecting the floor before the hearth. A four-poster bed with a gold canopy and a gold floral patterned quilt was against the opposite wall. An oak hutch stood open and a middle-aged maid in a blue gown with a huge white apron was placing Rowena's toiletries in it. The maid had been unpacking Rowena's panniers the footman had carried upstairs. Rowena was glad she had kept the bottle of stain in her pocket along with her small pistol and her jewelry which she slept with under her pillow every night. At times the pistol and the jewelry seemed to be weighing her down, but she dared not leave them off her person.

The maid had spread her gowns as well as Cecily's out on the bed and had seen to brushing out the wrinkles of each gown. Rowena hoped the maid would not be suspicious of the smaller gowns. She feared she should never have kept them, yet at some point, when Cecily could become a girl again, she would need the gowns. Even more worrisome, her shoes and Cecily's had been placed at the foot of the bed.

Lady Preston pointed to a door beside the hearth. "That leads to the closet between your room and Mister Blucher's. There is a cot in their for your page."

"Peter," Rowena said, "you may unpack and settle your things, then see you wash up before you handle Mister Blucher's clothing."

"Yes, Peter," Lady Preston said. "You will find water for washing in Mister Blucher's room. As well as extra towels."

"Thank you, Lady Preston," Cecily said, giving a little tip to the cap on her head before disappearing into the closet.

"Well, I will leave you to your bath. Mildred will see to your needs, and when you are ready, you will find us in the parlor. Door to the right when you come down the stairs."

"Thank you, Lady Preston. Indeed, I cannot thank you enough."

"Nonsense. As Mister Blucher is always our welcome guest, certainly his wife is also most welcome." With that, Lady Preston exited.

"Might I help you to undress, Mistress Blucher?" the maid asked.

"Thank you, Mildred, but do you please repack the smaller gowns and petticoats and the shoes. They are meant as a gift to a friend's daughter. Poor dear lost her husband in the war and has been on hard times. Her daughter is in need of some suitable wear is she to find a husband."

"Oh, yes, Mistress Blucher," Mildred said, beginning to neatly fold up Cecily's clothing. "How very kind of you to be thinking of your friend."

"Many people have suffered much. Since the war, many people are in want. I cannot help them all, but I can at least help a friend."

Nodding, the maid continued folding the clothing while Rowena slipped out of her boots, hose, and then her gown and stays, but before removing her petticoat which would reveal her laden pockets, she said, "I wonder would you check to see if Peter has been able to pour the water for Mister Blucher. He is yet weak from a fever that killed his parents, and he might not be able to manage a heavy pitcher."

"Aye, Mistress Blucher," the maid said and hurried to do as bid.

Hastily slipping out of her petticoat, she untied the strings to her pockets, and tucked the pockets under the bed. Down to naught but her shift when Mildred returned saying she had poured the water up for Mister Blucher, Rowena let Mildred bind up her hair that it would not get wet, then she slipped out of the shift. Feeling a little self-conscious about being completely bare before a stranger, she quickly stepped into the tub and sank down into the water.

"Oh," she breathed, "this is heavenly."

"You soak for a bit, Mistress Blucher, while I finish repacking those things for your friend's daughter, then I will wash your back for you."

"Thank you, Mildred." Rowena would have liked to close her eyes and immerse herself in the liquid paradise, but she needed to keep an eye on Mildred. Would not do for the maid to discover the hastily hidden pockets containing all that stood between security and desperate poverty for her and Cecily. And besides, supper was being held for her. She hoped Nate would remember to tell Lady Preston that Cecily needed an early supper.

All too soon, she was washed, rinsed, dried with a large linen towel, and had donned a clean shift, yet another gift from Mistress Tavers. With the warmth from the hearth, Rowena never felt a moment's chill. She had heard Nate enter his room. Heard him and Cecily talking, then heard a door close. She guessed Cecily had been dismissed to the closet that Nate might change.

She was wondering how she would get her pockets back on when Mildred asked, "Which gown will you be wearing, Mistress Blucher."

"I suppose I shall wear the blue one with the dark blue petticoat, but I wonder, might you go round and tap on Mister Blucher's door and ask if he will await me before going down."

Mildred nodded. "Yes, Mistress Blucher."

No sooner was Mildred out the door and Rowena had the pockets out from under the bed, tied securely about her waist, and was stepping into the dark blue petticoat and pulling it up when Mildred returned.

"He says he will await you, Mistress."

"Thank you, Mildred. Now do you help me with this gown, and oh, I near forgot my hose. See can you find my other garter. Mayhap it came off when I pulled off the boots."

"Here it is. Shall I help you with your hose?" Mildred was holding up a clean pair of hose, another gift from Mistress Tavers.

"Nay, I shall do it, but I hope you have a way with hair."

"I have been in the Preston's employ since my husband died of the ague in forty-five. My son inherited my husband's tenancy. But when he married, I wanted them to have the house to themselves, and Lady Preston was kind enough to take me on here. However, I do mostly cleaning. I fear I have never dressed a lady's hair, but I shall ask Mistress Amethyst's maid to come do your hair as soon as we have you dressed. And do you wish, I will wash out your hose and shifts. What with the remains of the fire, they should be dry by morning."

"Thank you, Mildred. You are so kind."

"'Tis naught, Mistress. I but hope I have properly served you."

"Indeed, you have," Rowena said, standing to let Mildred slip the gown over her head. The bodice was adjusted and laced and a scarf tucked around the low neckline. Mildred left to get another maid to do Rowena's hair, but while she was gone, Rowena checked on Cecily. She was not in the closet. Had she gone down to eat? Rowena hoped so.

❦ ❦ ❦ ❦

Her gnawing stomach pacified by a cold goose leg, two slices of buttered bread, and a mug of ale, Cecily was enjoying herself. She had always enjoyed spending time in the kitchen at Crossly Oaks, and though the Britteridge kitchen was larger and had more people working, it was just as warm and cheery. The cook, a large burly man with huge arms and a thick neck, had four helpers, two young scullery maids and two older youths, all hopping to do his bidding. The cook was grousing about trying to keep the hens on the spit from being overcooked and not knowing when to start sautéing the fish, what with supper being delayed.

"Normally, 'tis not so fancy a meal," a youth said, stirring a pot simmering over a fire in the hearth. "'Tis your master and mistress what makes this supper near as grand as dinner."

"Humph!" the cook said, taking a whack with a large cleaver at the gutted carcass of a small hog splayed open on his thick table. "Here I am worrying about supper when I have much to do to get this pork a-roasting for the morrow's dinner." Glancing at the youth, he snarled, "Dub, is that mush not thickening yet, build up the fire under it."

The youth placed his spoon on a brick at the edge of the hearth and added more wood to the fire, stirring it up to get a blaze going. "What are you cooking?" Cecily asked.

"'Tis an oats porridge what needs to thicken more is it to fill the bellies of the staff. Cook added eggs and cream and honey, and currants and nuts. Makes for a nice treat. Especially when he fries it up."

"Hmmm, it sounds good."

"'Tis good," the cook said. "Learned it from me Scottish grandmother. Not what I would serve the master's table. I got a strawberry flummery and a baked custard for Sir Lionel's table, but the young misses have been known to slip down here do they learn I have the porridge cut up and fried. After it thickens enough, I dump it into a flat pan to cool overnight. Come morning, I cut it up and fry it. Makes a good nuncheon for the staff."

"Do you think I might try one tomorrow?"

"Aye, young lad. You come down here mid-morning to break your fast and you may have some, be there any left."

"Oh, might you not save me a piece?"

"I will save you a piece do you tell me more about Virginia," the youth, Dub, said.

"Ah, here comes Picard," the cook announced, "must be time to ready the final items for supper."

The tall distinguished gray-haired butler in spotless livery entered the hot but heavenly smelling kitchen. "Lady Preston says their guests have joined them in the parlor," he said. "She asks how long before supper will be served?"

"The oxtail soup is ready now. It can be served immediately. I will sauté the fish, and it will be served with the scalloped oysters. Next will be the roasted hens, are they not burned, finishing with the pigeon pie and dandelion sallet."

"Very good," the butler said. "I will send Hassen and Wood in to get the soup while I pour the wine."

"I best get back to my closet and out your way," Cecily said. "But, Dub, do you save me some of that fried porridge, and I will tell you more of Virginia."

The youth nodded. "Aye, I will save you a piece."

Cecily returned by way of the staircase she had used to go down to the kitchen. She had learned in this new modern house, the servants were to use a back staircase, the family and guests used the one leading off the hall. Her home, Crossly Oak, was so old, it had but one staircase, and everyone used it, family and servants. She found Britteridge beautiful, but wondered if she would ever see her own home again. As she trudged up the staircase, for an instant she felt a little homesick. She missed her brothers and Liverna, her mother's maid, who had also been hers and her brothers' nurse. Sadly, she even missed her father. She could not forgive him for what he had done to her, but she still missed him. And loved him.

Chapter 15

Britteridge Hall had a large dining chamber, but Lady Preston had chosen to have supper served in the smaller family dining room. The room had large glazed windows that had been opened to let the late afternoon breeze drift into the room. Candles on the table and on the mantle occasionally flickered, but the flow of air was not enough to extinguish them.

Relaxing in the genial atmosphere, D'Arcy looked across the table at Rowena. Gads, but she was a beautiful woman. He feared it would take very little for him to fall in love with her. He was pleased she no longer felt the need to distance herself from him. During their day's trek, he had enjoyed having her arm about his waist and her body pressed against his back. And he had liked that she had asked him to await her that he might escort her down the stairs to supper. He had been pleased to tell her that he had sent Cecily to the kitchen that she might have her supper early. The smile she had given him caused his breath to catch in his throat, and he had come near to choking.

He enjoyed watching her talk to Lady Preston. She was animated, yet careful in the subjects she chose to discuss. She never brought up the subject of children, and neither did Lady Preston, except to say, "I hope you will not mind that the girls join us for supper. Normally, when we have guests and dine in the main dining chamber, they are relegated to this room. They being young yet for formal dining. Though Amethyst has recently turned sixteen, and I have started to include her at some of the dinners. Especially if 'tis but the locals."

"Of course, I could not mind. They are both lovely girls. The portrait in the gallery of your three daughters shows them off beautifully."

"Yes, we had that painted shortly before Hestia was to be married. We wanted a picture of the girls together. But tell me, Mistress Blucher," Lady Preston said, directing the subject away from her children, "have you encountered any bad weather on your journey thus far?"

"Nay, it has been most pleasant, fortunately."

"'Tis good, but the thunderstorms that can at times blow in can make travel unpleasant. Still, no doubt you can always take shelter somewhere along the highway does the rain start."

"Indeed," Chapman said, breaking in on the conversation. "'Tis few folks would not offer shelter to travelers in a rain storm. Especially do they have coin to offer in exchange."

"So true," Sir Lionel said, his voice a low rumble. "Adonia, my dear, do you not remember the autumn we went to London?" He glanced at Rowena and then D'Arcy. "'Twas the first year we were married. Adonia had never been to London, and I had been there but once. We decided before we started a family that we should see London. Really see it. Visit every museum and park. Maybe catch a glimpse of the King or Queen. Sail down the Thames and go to the theatre. Sample foods we might never encounter again. We did have us a time."

Lady Preston's smile lit up her face as she looked down the table at her husband. "'Tis a memory I shall always hold close to my heart. But our return journey home was not so pleasant."

Sir Lionel chuckled. "That is an understatement, though it has given us many a laugh over the years. Though leery, Father allowed we could take his coach. You may think the highways today are poor. I tell you, they are works of art compared to what the highways used to be like. And coaches then, compared to coaches now. Well, anyway, even though we had perfect weather on our way to London, I do believe our insides had been jostled so 'twas a wonder we could keep our meals down. And the inns!" His voice boomed out across the table. "The inns! Sheer luck we ne'er caught some devastating disease. We certainly arrived in London with extra baggage clinging to our clothes and our hair."

"Yes, dear, but your father's lawyer had made arrangements for us to stay in the most delightful inn in London. Baths were brought up to our room, and a laundress washed and pressed our clothes, and within two days' time, we were ready to see London. The lawyer had one of his clerks escort us all about London. And indeed, it was grand."

"Have you ever been to London, Mistress Blucher?" Sir Lionel asked.

Shaking her head, Rowena said, "No, I have not."

"'Tis a place to experience, even do you but visit it once. But back to my tale. Our trip home could not have met with more obstacles. Rain, sleet, coach stuck repeatedly in the mud. The inns were just as bad as the ones we stayed in on the way to London. Oft times the food barely edible. Had to wait at one inn for a couple of days while a wheel was repaired. Another wait when one of the horses went lame. Naught we could do but purchase another horse at an exorbitant price. Yet we could not leave Father's good coach horse, so we had to wait until the horse was well enough to follow along behind the coach."

"But we made it safely home," Lady Preston said, "and we have had many a laugh over the mishaps. And fond memories of the people who gave us shelter or helped us get our coach unstuck or gave us directions when we had taken a wrong turn."

"Yes, yes," Sir Lionel boomed. "So that was what I was getting at, Mistress Blucher. Do you encounter bad weather before you reach your destination, I have no doubt people will give you shelter or whatever help you may need, as they did us."

"I am certain you are correct," D'Arcy said, giving Rowena a smile. "We have been lucky with our weather, but I trust we will find those who will help us do we have need."

Rowena returned his smile, and his heart thudded against his chest. "I am certain you and Sir Lionel are right," she said. "Look how Sir Lionel and Lady Preston have welcomed us into their home. Already we are being given the utmost care."

"Deserved, well deserved," Sir Lionel said. "Know I can always depend on Blucher do I need legal advice."

As the various supper courses were served and passed around the table, conversation ebbed and flowed. At times Amethyst, if directly asked a question, cheerfully contributed to the conversation, but D'Arcy guessed both girls had been told to speak only if someone spoke to them first. When supper ended, Sir Lionel suggested they retire to the parlor for a while before going to bed. The two girls said their good nights and headed off to do whatever young girls did before going to bed. D'Arcy had no idea.

"We retire early here in the country," Sir Lionel said.

"Indeed, after this day, I will welcome my bed," Rowena said.

"Do sleep in tomorrow," Lady Preston said. "The girls and I have a commitment tomorrow. We will return before dinner, but please feel free to wander the gallery, or the garden is the day pleasant. Or you might find a book you like in our library. We have not as many books as we would like. Many of the books are ones that were my father's. He did so love to read. He was a gentle, kindly man. 'Twas so wrong that he should have died in a hateful war."

"Now, dear," Sir Lionel said, taking his wife's arm and urging her toward the parlor. "Let us not dwell on the unpleasant past tonight."

"You are so right," she said brightening, and led the way into the parlor.

"Chapman, do you really leave us on the morrow?" Sir Lionel asked when they were all seated, and the butler had served them sherry.

"Aye, Sir Lionel. I have any number of homes to visit ere I return to Chester." His blue-gray eyes twinkling, he added, "And I have a long list of items your daughters have requested."

"Not just your daughters, dear," Lady Preston said. "Your wife has put in an order as well." She turned to Rowena and held up a corner of her skirt. "This lovely silk I ordered from Mister Chapman on his last visit. There is never any telling what all he will have in his pack."

Chuckling Chapman said, "I will always have pins and needles, thread, small cooking pans, fabric samples from silk to brocade, combs, usually a looking glass or two. Items that are lightweight for I must also carry my formal clothing," he indicated the clothes he was wearing, the same dark green coat and waistcoat trimmed in gold and buff-colored breeches he had worn at the Taverses'. "And numerous other items that can be ordered from my store in Chester."

"You have a store?" Rowena asked, and D'Arcy frowned. That was not something Chapman should have mentioned. The less Rowena knew the safer he and his men would be was she recognized and captured.

"Aye," Chapman answered Rowena. "I have a store, but I prefer to roam the country, visiting old friends and making new friends. A young couple runs the store in my absence."

"Well," Rowena said, "It does seem like a most interesting life."

"I began in the trade with my father. And he with his father, and his father with his father. To be honest, I know not how many generations back the men of the family have been chapmen. But 'twas far enough back that we bear the surname."

"How fascinating," Rowena said. "And do you know, has your family always lived in Cheshire?"

Chapman shook his head. "Could not say. But as I said before, I enjoy making my rounds." He smiled at both the Prestons. "I like that I am made welcome here at Britteridge and can enjoy gracious company. At other times, I may find myself in a cottager's dwelling dipping into a bowl of porridge that may have been keeping warm over a fire for several days. But the cottagers' share what they have, and are eager to hear the news of the cities, and maybe buy some pins or mayhap a ribbon for a daughter or new wife."

"You must have had many rare experiences over the years," Lady Preston said, her sweet smile lighting up her eyes.

Nodding, Chapman said, "That I have, that I have."

"Well, we all have our past," Sir Lionel said. "For generations my family was in the salt mining. But in fifteen-ninety-four, my grandfather bought this estate from Lord Huntington. The earl was selling many of his properties and manors. Simply to finance his grand living, so I heard tell. Then in sixteen-eleven, my father purchased our baronetcy title from King James. Father sold our salt mines and salt houses to pay for the title and to build and furnish this house." His eyes and even his voice went soft. "I came of age in this house. Brought my lovely Adonia home as my bride to this house, and she birthed our children in this house. Both my father and my mother lived out the end of their days in this house and are buried in our own consecrated cemetery near a small mere surrounded by a shady glade. Someday my bones will rest there." He snorted, his dreaminess ended. "Now we are into cattle and sheep rearing and trading, along with some well-placed investments."

'Twas a history D'Arcy had heard numerous times. Sir Lionel was proud of his family roots and never tried to shroud his family's past in fake pretensions. During the recitation, D'Arcy had remained on the alert should Sir Lionel chance to mention Deverette. But Sir Lionel had guarded his tongue despite the amount of wine he had consumed.

"I am thinking," Chapman said, rising, "as I plan to leave early on the morrow, I should find my bed."

"Good thought for the lot of us," Sir Lionel said, also rising. He turned to Rowena. "Mistress Blucher, is there aught we can get for you before you retire?"

"I cannot think what it might be," Rowena answered. "My room is lovely and most comfortable."

"Fine, fine," he said, clamping a hand on Chapman's shoulder. "I will see you in the morning before you leave, as no doubt will Blucher. Candles have been left on the stand next to the stairs. I will take one of these candles," he said, removing a candle from atop the mantle, "and will light one for each of you to see your way to your rooms. Picard, our butler, will see the rest of the candles are extinguished before he retires."

At the foot of the stairs Lady Preston put a hand on Rowena's arm. "Do sleep as late as you wish, Mistress Blucher. Mildred has been told not to disturb you, but I left a bell in your room, you may ring for her when you wish. You may break your fast in the room we took our supper in this evening. There will always be something set out on the sideboard, and the butler will see you have ale or cider do you so wish. My daughters and I will return in time to dress for dinner." Patting Rowena's arm, she wished her a good night.

Candles in hand, D'Arcy and Rowena mounted the stairs side by side. "You are satisfied with the sleeping arrangement," he quietly asked her.

"Aye, I would have to think Lady Preston knows the truth."

"She and Sir Lionel know little but that there is a need to keep you and Peter safe. They know naught else, and 'tis best that way."

"I agree," Rowena said as they reached her door.

"I will bid you good night here," he said, and bending he lightly brushed his lips against her cheek, and whispered, "In case we are observed."

Opening the door to her room, she answered, "Most wise. Have a good night's sleep, my husband." With that, she entered her bedchamber, and closing her door, left him standing in the corridor wishing he was not going to a separate room.

❋ ❋ ❋ ❋

Upon entering the room, Rowena found Mildred sitting in a chair staring out the window at the sky's early stars, but she jumped up saying, "Ah, Mistress Blucher, might I help you to bed. I have laid out your night shift, but I found no slippers. However," she nodded toward the hearth. "I laundered your hose, and other shifts, and brushed off your travel gown and those breeches."

"Oh, Mildred, how very good of you. I know you must also be wanting your bed. Just help me out of this gown, and then you may go. I will wash up and see myself to bed."

"Are you certain, Mistress Blucher?"

"Aye, I wish to relax, and slowly comb out my hair. I mean to sleep late on the morrow, so I have no wish to hurry over my ablutions."

After helping Rowena out of her gown, Mildred said, "Well, then, good night, Mistress Blucher. I will be cleaning Mister Chapman's and Mister Blucher's rooms in the morning, so you just ring that bell on the stand by your bed, and I will come right away. Have no fear, I will hear it."

"Thank you, Mildred and good night to you."

After Mildred exited, Rowena waited by the door. She wanted to make certain the maid would not return for any reason. When all remained quiet, she hurried to the closet door, and opening it, found Cecily sitting cross-legged on her cot, a book propped on her lap. A candle burned on a small stand next to the bed and cast a pretty glow over her daughter's walnut stained face and rumpled hair.

Setting the book aside, Cecily jumped up to hug her mother. "Oh, I am so glad you returned before I fell asleep."

"Have you been terribly lonely, dear?"

"Oh, no, Mister Blucher gave me this book earlier when he told me how to find the kitchen to get an early supper. I was very well fed, I promise you."

"I am so glad. Seems we are to spend another day here, mayhap two. Will you manage all right?" Rowena asked, looking at her daughter in some concern.

"Aye, I will be fine. The cook and his apprentices and helpers are all nice. And one of the scullery maids did flirt with me. At least, I think she did."

Chuckling, Rowena said, "Was she pretty?"

"Who could know. Poor thing, her hair was stuffed under a grimy cap, and the rest of her was covered near head to toe in grease and sauces and who knows what else. I cannot think she could be more than fourteen, and the other maid might have been no more than ten. Both the young apprentices are nice, and one has promised to save me a piece of fried porridge, do I tell him more about Virginia."

"Does sound like you are managing well enough. Lady Preston and her daughters will be gone all morning tomorrow. Mayhap you and I can take a walk in the gardens together. I can see no reason I should not have my page accompanying me."

"That would be lovely. After I have broken my fast, I will return here to be on hand when you return. I heard you tell your maid you meant to sleep late."

"I doubt I will sleep too late, but before you leave to break your fast, do you come in and awaken me. I want to have my shift and pockets and petticoat on before I ring for Mildred."

"I will. Mister Blucher said he will be up very early, but he will have poured the water so I might wash when I rise. He is awfully good to us, Mother."

"Yes, he is. But you must remember, I am Mistress Blucher. No mistakes, dear."

"You are right, but then you should not be addressing me as, 'dear'."

Nodding her head, Rowena agreed. "However, I will take a good night hug from my sweet page."

Issuing forth one of her guffaws, Cecily said, "I think 'tis safe."

"Do you need help getting into your night shirt?"

"Nay, Mistress Blucher. I can manage."

"Well then, good night, Peter."

Back in her room, Rowena shed her remaining garments, slipped into her night shift, and secured her jewelry and pistol under her pillow. She sat on the chair Mildred had occupied, and while combing out her hair, she looked out at the dark sky with its twinkling stars. She prayed this lovely summer weather would continue. She had no desire to be drenched in a rain storm. And what the rain might do to Cecily's stain, she could not guess.

Finally crawling into bed, she reveled in its comfort after the previous night's sagging horror that had left her little refreshed. She had not felt particularly sleepy, but soon found herself drifting into sleep. Her last thought was of Nate's light kiss on her cheek.

Chapter 16

Settling back with a glass of brandy, Deverette patted his sister's hand. Seated next to him on the floral printed couch, she seemed to want to stay as close to him as she could. They had to be more circumspect in front of the servants, but in the parlor with the door closed, Hestia chose to ignore caution. "Now, you must tell Errol and me who this woman and her page are and how they come to be with you."

Errol agreed. "Aye, Dev, tell all."

Deverette and Errol had been friends for as long as Deverette could remember. Their fathers' estates bordering each other, and he and Errol not but a year apart in age, they had become fast friends. They had attended the same petty school and local grammar school in Nantwich. Both had been expected to go on to Eton before attending Oxford, but the war had put a stop to those plans. The two had instead shared a tutor housed with the Prestons.

Errol might not be considered truly handsome, his dark brown hair was too curly, his nose a tad too long, his mouth too wide, but that wide mouth was ever smiling, and his brown eyes were ever laughing. Deverette doubted anyone would ever think Errol aught but the most genial gentleman. Hestia adored her husband, and Errol was equally besotted by his wife. They made a charming couple, and Deverette was looking forward to becoming an uncle. He was just sad he had not been able to attend their wedding. It would have been too risky.

After a sip of his brandy, he told his sister and brother-in-law how the Crosslys came to be with them. They were immediately sympathetic, and Hestia said they had done an excellent job of turning Cecily into a young boy. "I never even gave him…," she giggled, "I mean her a glance. She had me fooled."

"But where will you take them?" Errol asked.

"I have no idea what Nate has in mind. Might not now be safe for them in Chester. I will leave it to Nate. He will know what is best. He has served us well thus far."

"Yes, but I never stop worrying," Hestia said, putting her head on her brother's shoulder. "I am with Father, though I would miss you terribly, I do think I would feel less frightened for you were you with the King in Europe like Mister D'Arcy's brother."

"Or, if not that," Errol said, "mayhap you could find a permanent place to hide rather than being ever on the move."

Deverette shook his head. "Nay, being on the move I think is best. I have no wish to end up in prison or forced to serve in Cromwell's army in Ireland or Scotland. Besides, people are growing dissatisfied with Cromwell's rule and with his Major Generals and their commissioners. I will not give up on the hope King Charles may yet return to England. So, in the meantime, I help keep Charles fed and clothed."

"Well, Father, rest his soul, thought highly of your goals," Errol said with a firm nod. "I suppose had I not been laid up with that broken leg when you rode off to fight for Charles in fifty-one, I would have been right there beside you then and now."

"I will ever love that horse that threw you and kept you safe at home," Hestia said. "We would not now be married and have our babe on the way had you gone off with Dev. And who would be here to see to your mother?"

Blowing his wife a kiss, Errol said, "Agreed. Worked out for the best. My leg mended perfectly. I have no limp, thank the Lord. I have you for my wife, sweet Hestia, and our babe on the way, and I am not living on the run like Dev."

"I do look forward to seeing the family on the morrow," Dev said. "Not seeing the family, not sleeping in my own bed in my own room, that is the hard part of the life I now live."

"Speaking of bed," Errol said, "I do think 'tis time we go to bed. I have to finalize the deal with the cattle buyer tomorrow. And I need to check with the tenants on the amount of oats and barley they think they will harvest this season so I have an idea how many cows and sheep I can overwinter."

"Your father would be proud of you, Errol," Deverette said. "With what he had to pay in fines and fees to have this estate returned to him after it was sequestrated, to see how you are making it pay would be a reward in itself."

"Aye, he would be pleased, but I can still hear him muttering nightly about what it cost him to buy back his own land. We were but lucky he had the finances to compound for the estate before it was leased out or the forest destroyed. That they assessed his degree of delinquency at only a tenth of the estate's value was but good fortune. I have heard tales of some estates being assessed at anything from a third to half its value."

"You heard correctly," Deverette said. "Nate's, father, the Earl of Tyneford, was assessed at a fourth of his capitalized value. Had to sell one manor and a lot of timber off a couple of others in order to buy back the rest of his manors. And Nate's brother-in-law, the Earl of Grasmere, was hit even harder. He borrowed from his cousin, who is immensely wealthy, to pay his fines until he could sell off enough timber to repay her. He let a couple of smaller manors go, but he thinks he will get them back. Anyway, as you said, 'tis time we took to our beds."

Deverette rose as did his sister and her husband and with more hugs and good nights, they retreated to their bedchambers. All too soon their days together would be ended, but until then, Deverette meant to enjoy his time with his family.

※ ※ ※ ※

Ethelinda cuddled up close to her husband. They had made delicious love, and Herman now snored peacefully, but her mind was still awhirl. She wondered if she dare send a letter to Nate. But where to send it? To her mother? Might the militia be watching her mother's house? Might they intercept the letter? Too risky. She but hoped Cecily's disguise would keep the child safe until she and her mother found someplace they could hide. She frowned. Possibly she should write to her niece, Gisela Blucher, or mayhap Nate's sister, Lady Grasmere.

Ethelinda had known the militia would discover she and Herman had housed a dark-haired woman and a young fair-haired beauty. Someone was bound to talk. She took unrepentant pleasure knowing her coachman had dismissed without a reference the groomsman who had been the one to report their guests to the militia.

"Pardon, the interruption," the coachman had said when he had been shown into their parlor after the militia left, "but I thought I should let you know I will be needing to hire a new groomsman. I dismissed Gowdy. Gave him no reference. He spluttered and blubbered, but I told him did he ever think to hold on to a good position, he had best learn to put loyalty ahead of dreams of ill-gained rewards."

"Thank you, Wilton. I feel certain you will find a good replacement," she had replied and Herman had applauded the coachman and told him he could expect a bonus.

"Servants need to know loyalty is what will be rewarded," Herman had proclaimed. "Fact is, I should see all the staff gets a reward. Mayhap declare a holiday or some such. I will give it some thought."

"Yes, dear, and maybe a nice gratuity to the seamstress and her assistants. I heard the militia captain complaining to one of the militiamen that he could get nothing from the seamstress or her assistants, despite the offer of the reward. They all proclaimed the girl they made the gowns for might have been a bit on the chubby side, and they would not call her fair-haired. The captain said he could tell they were lying same as were our staff. Indeed, I was right behind the captain when he questioned Charlotte, she being singled out for having been the Crosslys' maid. She said in answer to his question about hair color, 'I do think I would know the difference between blond and brown hair.' She pulled a strand of her hair from under her cap and said, 'See, my hair is blond.' The captain groaned, and moved on to the next servant."

Myron, their house steward, had the staff lined up in the hall for questioning by the captain while the militia searched their house. Ethelinda wondered how many small items would be missing after the militia went unescorted from room to room of her home. She and her maid would have to make a search on the morrow. At least her jewelry case and Herman's strong box had both been securely locked.

As the captain questioned one servant after another, they each had different descriptions of the Crosslys and Nate and Deverette Preston, known to them as Mister Drummer and Mister Mills. The young scullery lads stammered and shrugged and stated they had not seen the guests, being kept ever busy by the cook. When the youthful captain questioned the ruddy-faced cook about the man named Drummer, the cook batted her red-rimmed eyes at the young officer and said, "Some might say he was handsome, but I am more partial to blue eyes like yours, Captain, rather than to brown eyes."

Blushing the captain demanded, "But where did he say he was bound?"

"I have not the least idea. He is not apt to be telling me 'bout his comings and goings. Why would he?"

The captain whipped around to Ethelinda, "I can see I will get no information from the rest of your staff. Seems your groomsman is the only one wanting to see these highwaymen captured, and the stolen bride returned to her husband."

"Captain, as my husband and I have told you repeatedly, Mister Drummer's father and my husband's father were old friends. Mister Drummer is no highwayman. He is a cattle buyer and drover. He occasionally visits when in the area. The two women with him had been beset by thieves, and he was but escorting Mistress Hall and her daughter, Agnes, to her sister's in Chester."

Though she hated to do so, Ethelinda had decided she must stick to the story Nate had devised. At present, with her and her husband near to hand, none of the servants were cooperating with the captain, but the reward being offered might be enticing enough to tempt another of the servants, especially ones new to their employ, to report they had heard the people in question were going to Chester. Then the militia would be back to do more questioning and more threatening.

"Where does this Drummer live?" the captain asked.

"Why, I am not sure he has a home any longer. I think he lost it due to sequestration. I do think it was in Leicestershire." She had turned to her husband. "Is that not right, dear?"

Herman had nodded. "Aye, now he but travels around buying cattle to take to the London market, and come winter, I do think he takes rooms in London. Nothing permanent, though."

Narrowing his eyes, the captain asked, "And the men traveling with him?"

"Drovers. Nice men. Always enjoy their company."

"But what do you know of them!"

"They are gentlemen," Herman said. "They have worked for Drummer for several years, and they tell good yarns after a few drinks."

Rubbing his forehead, the captain said, "Chester? You say they are headed to Chester?"

"Yes," Ethelinda said, "they left early yesterday. Does the weather hold, I should think they might well be there by this evening or some time tomorrow." She knew Nate was stopping to visit Deverette's family near Nantwich. There was a more direct route to Chester. If the militia went racing up the more direct route, they would not encounter Nate and his desperate little party. Dear God, she prayed, let them safely reach their final destination. Where that might be, she had no idea.

※ ※ ※ ※

Liverna finished saying her prayers, and wearily rising from her knees, crawled into her bed. It had been another dreary day. Sir Lindell spent every day locked in his study, coming out only long enough to eat his lonely meals. His two sons offered him no comfort. They would not have lost their mother and sister had he not forced Cecily to marry Haspel. And Haspel had returned again. And again he had threatened Sir Lindell, demanding he be told where Lady Crossly might have gone. Of course, Sir Lindell had no idea. No one had any idea.

Liverna wished the boys' tutor would return early. Milo and Godwin would be so much better off if they had lessons to keep them occupied. As it was, they had nothing to take their minds off how much they missed their mother. Pulling the sheet up around her throat, Liverna wondered if she might convince Sir Lindell to send the boys to Derby for a fortnight. Let them stay with their great uncle, Gaylord Doggett. Doggett was fond of the boys and of their mother. And he was furious with Sir Lindell for marrying Cecily off to Haspel.

In the hopes of saving Crossly Oaks for Milo, Doggett was trying to secure a loan for Sir Lindell by borrowing against Rowena's monthly stipend. "I would not lift a finger to help you after what you did to Cecily," Doggett had angrily stated, "did I not know Rowena would want me to do what I can to save the manor for Milo."

Rowena's brother, Artus, was also furious. He and Rowena, being the only two Plaisance children to survive into adulthood, had bonded. They had grown even closer when their mother had left them that she might care for her own ailing mother. Their father had shown them little affection, he being more interested in fishing, hunting, and horse racing. More often than not, he had been off to some event with various other gentlemen of the hundred.

In speaking privately to Liverna, Artus had told her, did she hear from his sister to let him know. And did Rowena need money or anything else, he and his wife, Dorisande, were ready to help in any way they could. The militia had already searched his house looking for Rowena. He knew they were still keeping his house surveilled as they were Crossly Oaks.

He would like to have Milo and Godwin come stay with him, to give them some diversion, but he was in the midst of fighting his tax assessment and was back and forth to Derby. He believed, as his father was dead, and he personally had never fought against the Parliamentarians, he should not be required to pay the decimation tax. He was hopeful he might win his case. Yes, he was a Royalist at heart, but he kept his views to himself, and he formulated no rebellions. Liverna had wished him well and promised to let him know did she hear anything.

"Where are you my sweet child?" she murmured. "Dear Lord, keep her safe."

Chapter 17

Rowena had not expected to enjoy herself so much. The Prestons and Tourneys were delightful people. Easily as gracious and generous as the Taverses. She was made welcome in both homes, and at no time did anyone question her too carefully. Conversations were kept light, mostly centering around the lovely weather they were enjoying, the blooming gardens, and the fabrics they had ordered from Mister Chapman and that they hoped would soon be delivered. The men talked of looking forward to autumn when they would go hunting, though due to the war, many deer had been killed by soldiers and hungry citizens on both sides, but Sir Lionel swore he believed some herds were rebounding.

Seated at the Tourneys' table with its white linen tablecloth and soft white napkins, Rowena took a sip of wine. Refusing another offering of candied roses, she said, "Oh, indeed, no, I cannot eat another bite. But everything was delicious. You have an outstanding cook."

"We are very happy with Huntly," Mistress Tourney said in her sweet voice. "He is ever trying new recipes, and he is most inventive. We pay him an ungodly wage, but he is worth it."

"All your staff seems so young," Rowena said. "Yet they are all so efficient. So well trained in their jobs."

"That would be due to Errol's mother," Mistress Tourney said, smiling and nodding to the Dowager Tourney at the end of the table with Sir Lionel seated to her right and Lady Preston to her left. "Mother Solange trained every one of them."

"Humph!" Sir Lionel said. "Little choice she had. On his death bed, Cuthbert pensioned off near every servant. Never heard of such a thing."

"Now Sir Lionel," the dowager said, her low voice sounding amused, but she raised her chin and slanted her brows. Despite her weakened condition, Rowena doubted not the dowager had an iron will. "You know Cuthbert had good reason to grant those pensions. Most of the staff had been with his family since he was a youth. They were all old, and they had earned their pensions and their retirement. Though I did keep my personal maid, dear Lucinda. She is still with me."

"My goodness," Rowena said, "What a change."

Chuckling, Errol Tourney said, "As Mother said, the staff was old. I then had no choice but to go to Chester and work with our solicitor to find new servants. The only ones we could find were young ones. More experienced servants had no desire to give up their positions and their future pensions. So, for our house, grounds, stables, garden, everything... the servants are all young. Most have been with us five years now. Thus far, none have wanted to leave. But then, they receive good wages. Fortunately Grandfather made so much money from wise investments after he sold off his tannery, that even with the fines and taxes and compounding, we have managed to survive and are now even prospering."

"And that made a short story long," the dowager said, and everyone chuckled.

Still enjoying the genial mood at the completion of the tale, Rowena glanced at Dev. Seated next to Lady Preston, he was smiling into her eyes. *No wonder he can safely stay here with the Tourneys. None of the servants know he is a Preston.* She looked back at Nate. She could read in his eyes that he knew she had discovered their secret. He, of course, would deny it.

Dowager Tourney asked Rowena if she would like to see the garden. "I know Hestia would be pleased to show it to you."

Rowena smiled. *Did she take a walk in the garden with Hestia, it would give Sir Lionel and Lady Preston more time alone with their son.* "Yes, I would enjoy seeing your lovely garden. Yesterday, while Lady Preston and her daughters were away, I had the pleasure of enjoying the Britteridge garden. The weather has been so perfect. I took my young page with me. He has not yet regained his strength after the fever that near killed him, so I thought a turnabout in the fresh air would be good for him. I do believe it was."

She looked from the dowager to Lady Preston. "I told Peter did he feel up to it, he might wander the gardens again. I hope that was all right."

"Of course," Lady Preston said. "Poor lad. Good thing he is getting a couple of days to rest here before you resume your journey."

"Yes," Rowena agreed, wishing Cecily could be there with her. She hated being so far away from her daughter. She could but pray Cecily would be careful and not give away her disguise, and that the Prestons would not choose to linger overly long at the Tourneys'.

※ ※ ※ ※

D'Arcy decided he would walk with Hestia and Rowena. He could not say why he wanted to walk with them other than he liked seeing Rowena in this relaxed social setting. The previous day he had only seen her at meals. In the morning, he had been closeted with Sir Lionel in his study going over various accounts. He had not been lying to Rowena when he told her he had helped Sir Lionel with legal issues concerning his manor. After dinner, he and Sir Lionel had made the excuse they were to ride about the estate. They had instead gone to Reverie that Sir Lionel might see his son.

D'Arcy learned Rowena had slept late then enjoyed the garden before dinner. After dinner, she had spent a lazy afternoon enjoying the Prestons' rather extensive library. The books were Lady Preston's father's books, some of the few personal items of his that she still had. Lady Preston's father's estate had been sequestrated. Preston, by selling a portion of Lady Preston's late father's estate, including the house, had been able to buy back the timber and grazing acreage along with what animals had not been stolen. Those sections would continue to produce an income. Lady Preston's mother had moved in with the Prestons until her death, two years almost to the day after her gentle, scholarly husband and their son died of wounds suffered at the battle at Edgehill. Those grazing lands now belonged to Lady Preston and would someday augment Deverette's wealth.

Having no love for Charles I and his high-handed ways, Preston had remained neutral as best he could throughout the war. He had paid his taxes, but had given no aid or support to either side. The Royalists when besieging Nantwich had confiscated food and other items from surrounding manors and farms to feed their troops. Once the Parliamentarians won, they had done the same. Soldiers had to be fed. But the Prestons and the Tourneys had survived, and both families now prospered.

D'Arcy wondered if he had been wrong to convince Deverette to become a highwayman instead of surrendering. Dev's father would have paid his fine. With luck, Dev would not have been in prison long, and he could now be living peacefully in his home with his family. Unless he had been impressed into Cromwell's army and forced to fight the rebels in Ireland. D'Arcy knew all the members of his gang put their lives on the line each time they took to the highways to rob their Puritan rulers. At times he wondered if they should disband, but then he would meet with his brother, Ranulf, give him the moneys they stole from the Puritans to give to King Charles II, and his brother would declare how much each and every pound meant to the King, the shortage of funds being ongoing. "Creditors are ever after us, we often cannot afford wood or coal for our fires. And our clothes..." Ranulf ran a hand down his body, and D'Arcy had been surprised how shabby his brother looked. The next time they met, he had given his brother a new set of clothes. "From Kenrick," he said when Ranulf protested the moneys should not have been spent on clothes for him. "Your older brother has no wish for his brother to go about in rags."

Ranulf was suffering much for his King, and D'Arcy decided he could do no less. Besides, his friends knew did they wish to leave his gang, he would never nay say them. Even if at times their efforts seemed hopeless, they were all still loyal to their King. When war had broken out with Spain in fifty-five, Royalists had been hopeful. Some had even joined the Spanish army, but even Spain appeared to be no match for Cromwell. Though the war still raged on, Cromwell and his Protectorate remained in power.

Walking behind Rowena and Hestia, D'Arcy enjoyed their idle chatter. When they stopped to look at flowers or discuss various herbs, he waited patiently. He liked observing Rowena in this setting. He liked the sound of her voice, liked her laughter. He liked her intelligence. She was not an easy one to fool, and she minded her tongue well. And he liked her beauty. The beauty of a mature woman. What he could see of her figure, and admittedly it was not much what with the long full skirts women wore, but he liked what he could see. The fullness of her breasts, her graceful neck, and the occasional glimpse of a slim ankle.

"Mister Blucher," Hestia said, jolting D'Arcy away from his contemplation of Rowena's many merits. "Must you truly leave on the morrow?" Hestia asked, and D'Arcy knew she was wishing her brother could stay longer. But that would not be safe. They needed to keep on the move. Never stay any place too long.

"I fear so, Mistress Tourney. We have a bit of a journey ahead of us yet."

"Mistress Blucher, can you not convince your husband to delay the journey at least another day or two?"

Rowena blushed, but answered calmly, "I fear I cannot. When Mister Blucher says we must renew our journey, then so we must."

The blush gave Rowena's face a pretty glow. No doubt she was embarrassed at being considered his wife, and that Hestia might think she would have some say in when they would resume their journey. She could not know Hestia was aware of her true identity. He also guessed Rowena would be eager to go. She would be wanting to reach a safe destination, and she was dependent upon him to find her that safe locale.

When the afternoon started drifting into evening, Sir Lionel declared they must be returning home. The Tourneys were thanked for their hospitality, and Hestia told Rowena she would hope someday she might see her again. Rowena was then herded out to the couch, that she would not see Lady Preston give her son a good-bye hug. They arrived back at Britteridge to find Cecily engaged in a game of backgammon with ten-year-old Camrielle, and with Amethyst watching.

"I found poor Peter wandering the gardens all alone," Camrielle said, "so I asked if he would like to play hoops with me. We did that for a while, then I asked did he know how to play backgammon. He said he was not good. And so he was not, but we have played a couple of games, and he is getting better, is he not Amethyst?"

"He is," Amethyst agreed. "Poor soul, to think he is now an orphan and must make his way in the world. 'Tis sad." Stricken, she looked at Rowena. "Oh, not that you and Mister Blucher are not being wonderful to take him in. So kind of you."

Rowena smiled. "Peter is near like a son. We are most fond of him."

"Oh, and he told us such grand stories about Virginia," Camrielle said. "What a strange land it must be."

"Aye, 'tis different," D'Arcy said, "but now young Peter, I would have you come with me. We leave on the morrow, and I would have you well rested. You must see to your supper, then 'tis an early bed for you."

"Yes, sir, Mister Blucher," Cecily said, rising. "Thank you, Miss Camrielle, for teaching me more about backgammon. And thank you, Miss Amethyst, for your hints at which moves would assist me."

"You are welcome, Peter," both girls said, and their mother told them they should ready themselves for supper.

"I will see to my ablutions, too," Rowena said.

"Splendid," Sir Lionel said. "Would not do to hold supper up again. Cook can get cranky. Mister and Mistress Blucher, we will meet in the parlor before we go into supper."

D'Arcy nodded to Sir Lionel and held out his arm to Rowena. Taking his arm, she let him escort her up the stairs. Cecily followed after them, and then with an elfish grin to her mother, Cecily followed D'Arcy into his room. The three of them met in the closet between the two bedchambers. "I could not think 'twould hurt for me to play the games with Miss Camrielle," Cecily said. "She was most kind. And I never let on how good I really am at backgammon."

Rowena looked at D'Arcy, and he said, "Nay, I think it could not have been wrong, but 'tis good we leave on the morrow. Now, I will leave the two of you, but I want you both rested and ready to leave when the sun is up on the morrow. I mean to make our next stop by evening."

"We will be ready," both promised, and he returned to his room. With their next stop, they would not have to pretend he and Rowena were married, or that Cecily was a boy. Their hosts, the Haywards, of the yeoman class, had but two trusted live-in servants. Otherwise, they had only day laborers who worked on the grounds or out in the fields, and beyond the woods, a couple of cottagers, but no one lived close enough to tell tales. So guards could be dropped for at least one evening.

Chapter 18

The day had been long, and Rowena hated the tedious time on the pillion, but knowing she and Nate would not have to be the Bluchers, and Cecily would not have to be Peter while staying at their next destination made the wearisome ride worth it. At least they were staying on the main highway and not taking the many back trails like they had taken to Nantwich. Nate felt confident they would not be stopped, but if they were, he believed Cecily had become so adept at playing her role, she would have no trouble convincing any militiamen she was a male youth.

"I have decided I will now tell you more about me and my gang," Nate said. "Dev and I and others of my gang have warrants on our heads for having fought with the King in fifty-one. For that reason, we must ever be cautious and use names other than our own."

"I see," Rowena said. "'Tis not fear you will be recognized as highwaymen, 'tis fear you will be recognized as Royalists who fought for the King and failed to surrender."

"Aye," Nate answered, "Caleb, the Haywards' son, fought with us, but the militia never suspected him of being part of our unit. It being a cavalry unit and Caleb being yeoman, a farmer. He has no price on his head so he is free to live at home with his family. To keep neighbors or laborers from being suspicious when Caleb goes off with us, they believe he is going to deliver speeches to other farmers concerning newer farming methods that have been proven to increase production of crops and the number of animals that can be overwintered. He has done these speeches often enough, should he be questioned, he could offer proof."

"And these methods he speaks about truly do increase crop production?" Rowena asked, wondering if this was but another of their fabrications.

"Oh, aye, they do indeed. Caleb learned much from my brother-in-law, Lord Grasmere. Being confined to his parish and needing to pay off a loan to his cousin, Grasmere began studying every book and treatise he could lay his hands on concerning improving the profitability of his land. My brother brought him a treatise from Flanders expounding on their farming methods and increased production. Berold experimented, followed some of the ideas in the treatise, especially as related to sowing his fields with clover rather than leaving them fallow, and indeed his production has increased as it has for Caleb and his family, and for nearby neighbors, including wealthier neighbors, the Yardleys and the Jaggers. The clover enriches the soil, and it serves as fodder for his sheep and cattle. I have heard my brother-in-law now has plans to sow ryegrass in with the clover, and he means to experiment with a root crop he calls turnips that can be used as feed to overwinter more of his animals. Caleb is most interested in learning more about my brother-in-law's new plans. In the meantime, Caleb tells others what has worked for him, but not everyone will pay heed and profit from the knowledge."

"Why would they not?" Rowena was thinking she would like to learn more and maybe write her brother and share the ideas with him. If Nate's brother-in-law truly was a lord, and that was not just another of Nate's tales, and if Lord Grasmere found the methods profitable, her brother might think more of trying them.

"Some people are afraid to try new things," Nate said. "Some are against anything that their father or grandfather would not have done. Old customs die hard. Then, for those tenants who farm on the champion or open field lands, they must cooperate with all the other tenants. Everyone must agree to any changes. Here in Cheshire, we have less open field farming, but our farmers are often backward and conservative. 'Tis their loss."

Rowena thought 'twas their foolishness. She would hope Artus, was she able to get a letter to him, would be willing to try new crops. She was not so certain her husband would be as ready to experiment with new methods, but did Artus's experiments do well, mayhap her husband would try them. 'Twas for Milo's sake she would like to see the manor prosper as her older son would one day inherit Crossly Oaks. Did her husband have to sell a portion of the manor to pay his taxes, what was left would need to be more productive.

'Twas late afternoon when they arrived at the Haywards' home. It was very much a working farm, but Rowena still found it charming. The square stone house was two stories with a slate tile roof. The downstairs windows were glazed, but the upstairs windows had no glass, only shutters. The house had two chimneys, one at either end of the house. No sweeping lane led up to the grounds. No decorative trees or shrubs graced the grounds, but she could see an orchard with low hanging ripening fruit, a number of outbuildings behind and to the side of the house, and fields and pastures stretching off to a hardy looking stand of oaks to the north and the west. Chickens and a couple of piglets roamed about in the dirt in front of the house, and a yellow dog, its tail a-wag, rose from a spot in the shade to stretch then advance toward them.

The sturdy oak door opened, and Jack Chapman emerged. His hand raised in greeting, he was the first to welcome them. Apparently, Chapman would always be a day ahead of them, his job being to make sure their next destination was safe. He was a likable man, full of good cheer, ever ready with a smile. 'Twas terribly hard to think of him as a highwayman. Well, it was hard to think of any of her saviors as highwaymen. They seemed so honorable.

A woman who looked to be in her early fifties followed Chapman out the door. After wiping her hands on a large apron, she tucked a strand of brown hair back under her cap, shook her skirt at the trespassing hens, and hurried forward to greet Rowena. When Chapman handed Rowena down from the pillion, he introduced the woman as Goody Hayward.

"Welcome, Lady Crossly," Goody Hayward said, and glancing at Cecily who had hopped off her horse, added, "and welcome to you, also, Mistress Crossly. I know you must both be tired and ready for a nice mug of cider. Do come in the house. 'Tis cool inside."

A pretty dark-haired, dark-eyed woman, holding the hand of a little boy who could not be more than two years old stood in the doorway. The boy had red hair, extraordinarily green eyes, and he wore a bright infectious grin. "My daughter-in-law, Mistress Sidonie Hayward," Goody Hayward said, "and her son, my dear grandson, William." She reached down and tousled the child's hair, her pride in the little boy, obvious.

"Pleased to meet you, Lady Crossly," Sidonie Hayward said. "Mister Chapman and Caleb have told us how brave you were in rescuing your daughter. I have been looking forward to meeting you." She stepped aside. "As my dear Mother Yolande said, we have a nice cider and some biscuits awaiting you."

"Thank you," Rowena said, though she could not help being wary that the Haywards should know hers and Cecily's true identities after they had gone to such extremes to conceal their identities for the past few days. But after a glance at Nate, who seemed unconcerned, she slipped an arm around Cecily's waist and followed Goody Hayward inside.

The ground floor of the house appeared to be naught but a large hall. One side of the hall served as a kitchen and dining area, a long heavy oak table with heavy chairs at either end and benches along the sides dominating a good portion of the area. An oak hutch displayed pewter as well as porcelain dishes and mugs. On either side of the huge flagstone hearth were work tables and above the tables were shelves holding mixing bowls, various size pots, platters, and boxes and bags of what Rowena guessed were various food items. In a dark corner, dried herbs hung from the ceiling. The tantalizing smell of a couple of lamb haunches roasting on a spit over a low wood fire wafted out into the air, and the plopping sound of something bubbling in a large black kettle added to the appeal and set Rowena's stomach to rumbling.

The other side of the room could be a parlor in any country gentleman's home. Decorative tapestries graced the stone walls, no doubt adding warmth and brightness to the room in winter months. A floral couch and two burgundy-colored tufted chairs were arranged before a smaller and more decorative hearth. A blue vase with an arrangement of summer flowers and a brass candelabra sat on a chest under the window, and in the far corner, a narrow curving staircase led up to the first floor.

Rowena and Cecily were directed to the couch and Goody Hayward set up a low gate-leg table in front of them. "Now you just lean back and relax. We will serve you the cider and biscuits, then Sidonie will take you up to your chamber while I help Dody, our cook, tend the supper." She nodded to a slender, gray-haired woman with her sleeves rolled up who was mixing something in a large wooden bowl.

Nate took one of the burgundy chairs, and Chapman and Dev pulled up the chairs from the table. While Sidonie went to help Goody Hayward with the light repast, Nate swung William up on his lap. "Well, young fellow," he said, "you are looking handsome today. Would that be a new gown?"

The little boy shook his head, and his mother answered, "Nay, Mister D'Arcy, that would be his Sunday frock. And he did promise he would not dirty it, but he wanted to dress for our guests."

D'Arcy! Rowena's eyes widened. Had she just learned Nate's true surname, or was it another fake name like Drummer and Blucher?

Chuckling, Nate bounced the child on his knee and said, "Well, William, I cannot blame you for wanting to impress the ladies."

"I think he might have been more anxious to impress you," Goody Hayward said, arriving with a tray of mugs and setting it down on the gate-leg table. "William does enjoy when his father's friends visit. Now I must see to supper. Caleb and Ralph will be home shortly, and after a day of marling, they will be starved." She nodded at her daughter-in-law who was placing a platter of biscuits on the table. "When you are refreshed, Sidonie will see you to your room. Even now, her maid is seeing to your gowns, and she just took up some warm water. Sorry we cannot be offering you a bath."

"Oh, no," Rowena said, "I had a lovely bath at our last abode, and today was not a terribly dusty ride. Do we but wash our hands and faces, I know Cecily and I will be much refreshed."

Taking the other burgundy-colored chair, Sidonie said, "Lady Crossly, you and your daughter are so brave. And how well you have disguised your daughter. I have no doubt, however, Mister D'Arcy has had you rambling here, there, and everywhere. He is ever cautious."

Nate frowned. "Now, Mistress Hayward, be not reminding me of the one time I was not cautious enough. I will say that one error taught me to be even more cautious. And so, yes, we do move a bit more deliberately now."

"I meant not to bring up that incident. 'Tis long past and all ended well. Better than well, for I had the pleasure of meeting your sister, and then we had that wonderful trip to the lakes. And if you learned from the mishap, then 'tis for the best. I want my husband to be safe."

Rowena could not help but wonder what incident Sidonie referred to, but she sipped her cider and refrained from asking. Mayhap 'twas better not to know. That the Hayward family knew about Nate and his gang of highwaymen and their robberies she found confusing. Goody Hayward hardly seemed the type of woman who would condone such actions, and yet she seemed to know Nate and his men well. Her son rode off with them.

Her confusion must have shown on her face for Nate started chuckling. "Mistress Hayward, I fear we have told Lady Crossly and Cecily little about ourselves. In every place we have stayed, we could not be certain slips would not be made. The servants, you must know. And as you have said, I am now more cautious than ever. Lady Crossly knows we are highwaymen. She has but recently learned we fought for the King and have warrants on our heads. However, we have not told her what we do with the moneys and other items we take from the Cromwellians." He turned to Dev. "Would you care to tell her, Dev?"

His handsome face alight with a broad grin, his hazel eyes glittering, he said, "Aye, I will tell her." He looked first to Rowena and then to Cecily. "We give near all of it to the King, keeping but a small amount for some of our needs, like a new horse, or more gunpowder, or even sometimes, unexpected lodging costs."

"What?" Staring wide-eyed at Dev, Rowena shook her head. "What do you mean?"

"King Charles has no income," Sidonie said, a slight frown on her face. "So my husband and these other fools ride around the country robbing Cromwell's tax collectors and any other Cromwellian supporters they chance upon. Then every so often, Mister D'Arcy's brother comes over from wherever the King happens to be living at the time, collects what the Cromwellians have unhappily donated, and takes it all back to the King. In other words, they are helping to support the King. And no matter how many times I ask my husband to stop, he will not. He has a prized letter from the King thanking him for his service, so he continues in his dangerous occupation."

Looking slightly cowed, Nate said, "The wives of my fellow highwaymen are none too happy with me, but we all yet serve our King. For us, Cromwell will never be our ruler."

Rowena knew not how she felt. She had trusted Nate and his men with hers and Cecily's safety, yet she had had trouble condoning their nefarious actions. Now, to learn why they had turned to such thievery had her head spinning. But apparently not her daughter's.

"I just knew you could not be bad highwaymen," Cecily said, clapping her hands. "You are all so kind. And the poor King. So kind of you to help him."

Chapman burst out laughing and was joined by Nate and Dev, but Sidonie continued to frown. "You should not encourage them, Mistress Crossly." She looked up. "Ah, but here is Clare. She must have your room readied." Rising, she said, "Do follow me."

"All is ready, Mistress Hayward," the maid said. "Towels are fresh, bed has been aired, coal is in the brazier should it be needed come morning, and I shook out a gown and petticoats for each of them."

"Thank you, Clare," Sidonie said before leading Rowena and Cecily up the stairs.

Rowena was surprised that the maid was undoubtedly a lady's maid. Dressed in a dark blue somber gown with a large white square neckerchief fastened at the throat with a brooch, and just below her elbows, large white cuffs trimmed in lace, she presented a neat appearance and carried herself with the dignity of a maid of her station. Rowena had wondered that the younger Sidonie was addressed as Mistress Hayward while her mother-in-law chose to be addressed as Goody Hayward. She guessed Caleb Hayward, in marrying Sidonie, had married above his station. Yet, Sidonie and her maid, who appeared to be but a few years older than Sidonie, both seemed perfectly at home in their more humble abode.

She also guessed Clare and the cook, Dody, were completely trusted by the Hayward family – and more importantly, by Nate. She could not understand how learning Nate was not robbing people for his own gain but instead to send funds to King Charles II had set her heart to fluttering and her mind to scurrying about in numerous directions – all of them leading back to Nate. Nate when he smiled, Nate when she caught him watching her, Nate when she remembered the feel of his strong muscled legs when he held her in front of him on his horse. And Nate who had offered her and Cecily protection and safe conduct to Chester. Somehow, when she thought him a highwayman, she had been able to push thoughts of him away, but now … But now, what?

"Once you have washed away the dust," Sidonie said, "do stretch out and have a rest. Caleb and his father will not be home until they finish their marling, and then they will be forever out at the well trying to wash away the smell." She giggled, and her dark eyes danced. "Caleb knows is he not scrubbed and shining, he will not be sharing my bed this night. And as Mister D'Arcy, Mister Chapman, and Mister Preston are already sharing our other guest chamber, he would find himself on a cot in the parlor."

Mister Preston – so Sidonie had referred to Dev. Rowena half-smiled remembering how much Dev looked like his sisters and his mother. She had been right. At the same time, she was saddened that Dev could not stay at his own home. Thanking Sidonie, Rowena admitted she and Cecily would be grateful for a rest before supper.

"Do you wish, I could send Clare to help you dress," Sidonie said.

"Thank you, but we can help each other," Rowena said. "Mayhap if she could but do something with my hair."

"Clare can work miracles with hair. She manages to keep my unruly locks safely in place and under my cap." Looking at Cecily, she added "She will be able to do something with your daughter's hair as well. So now, rest. I will let you know when 'tis time to ready yourselves."

Once the door closed behind Sidonie, Rowena and Cecily hastily striped down and began their ablutions. The water was a comfortable temperature, the soap had a lovely lavender scent, and the towels were soft. The bedchamber was small, but not crowded with excess furniture. It had but a bed, one chair, a table beside the bed, one candle on the table and another candle in a holder to the side of the small looking glass hanging above the stand holding the porcelain basin and water pitcher. On a chest at the foot of the bed, Clare had laid out their gowns and petticoats for the evening. Cecily would finally get to wear one of the gowns Ethelinda Tavers had had made for her.

After putting on clean shifts, Rowena and Cecily stretched out on the bed. As tired as she was, Rowena could not keep her thoughts from straying to Nate. Why had Nate finally chosen to make himself known to her. They could have again put on a performance. She and Cecily could have again been Anna and Agnes Hall. What changed? Yes, the Haywards and their two servants could be trusted. But what made Nate decide to trust her and Cecily? Her thoughts tumbling about, she finally drifted into sleep.

※ ※ ※ ※

Knowing they would be leaving early the next day, Preston wondered if he would have a chance to see Arcadia Yardley. He knew he should not be wanting to see her. The last thing he needed was to form any kind of attachment to any woman. Yet, at times, Arcadia haunted his dreams. Her brother Cyril had warned him to be watchful.

"Am I not mistaken, my sister has set her eyes on you. Unless you are thinking to take a wife, you had best be wary."

Well, he was not ready to take a wife. Still, Arcadia had her charms. Needing time to think, he had told D'Arcy he meant to stretch his legs. He had rambled around the Hayward grounds for a bit and was soon bored. But did he set out through the woods to the north of the Hayward property, he could find himself coming out at the Yardley manor, Woodspring Hall. But was that a safe thing to do. Most likely D'Arcy would not approve. As long as they had Lady Crossly and her daughter with them, they would have to be even more cautious than usual – especially now that Lady Crossly knew their true identities. The bounties on their heads would be even larger did the militia learn they were also highwaymen, not just soldiers on the run.

When he had agreed to join D'Arcy in his enterprise, it had seemed the right thing to do, the loyal thing to do. Support the King. But now he often grew tired of always being on the run. Always moving from one place to another. He missed his family. Yet, when he thought of giving it up, turning himself in, taking his chances with the Cromwellian law, he could not bring himself to do it. He was not afraid of prison. Most likely he would only be in prison a week or two before his father paid his fine, and he was paroled to his parish. No, it was giving up on a cause he believed to be right that he could not bring himself to do. He was loyal to his King, and he ever would be. And was he paroled, and then the King decided to fight again and he joined him, was he captured, he would be hanged for breaking his parole. No. He sighed. Better to go back inside. Better to forget about Arcadia.

Chapter 19

Rowena enjoyed supper at the Haywards' table. A white linen cloth had been spread over the table, spoons and linen napkins had been placed at each setting. Ale or cider were the drinks offered, and all the food was placed on the table by the cook, Dody, and by Goody Hayward. Goody Hayward then took her place at one end of the table. Her husband was at the opposite end. They sat in the only two chairs. Goody Hayward had offered her chair to Rowena, but Rowena had refused, declaring she would be perfectly comfortable on the bench. She had been a bit surprised when Dody and the maid, Clare, joined them at the table. She had never known such informality, but she rather liked it.

Goodman Hayward, though in his late fifties, was still a robust man, and though he was slightly balding and had a ruddy complexion from years of working outdoors in all kinds of weather, his bright smiles and jovial disposition made him seem younger. Needing little encouragement from Nate, he was happy to expound on the merits of the new farming methods Caleb had introduced to their farm. That Caleb would, in little more than a week, be off on another lecture tour could only be for the best. The more farmers Caleb could help, the better.

"Where will you lecture this time, Mister Hayward?" Rowena asked Caleb.

"I have one lecture in Chester, another in Whitby. I go 'round to farmers and talk to them individually. Most are at least willing to listen."

Rowena wondered if this was all for her benefit, yet another tale, or did Caleb really spend time talking to farmers. Nate had said he did enough that he could prove he had good reason to be absent from his home. Talk to farmers – rob Cromwellians. Would make for a busy schedule.

She could understand how Sidonie had fallen in love with Caleb. His hair was a dark auburn, his sea green eyes had a beguiling, sleepy, or come-hither look to them, and he had the same robust build as his father, broad shoulders, strong legs, but his stomach was flatter, his waist, trimmer. Yes, with his slim nose and shapely mouth, he would turn most women's heads. She would have to say, he was near as handsome as Dev Preston. And Preston bordered on perfection.

From what she had seen of the baby, William, he had definitely been marked by his father in his coloring. He was yet too young to determine if he would be as good-looking as his father, but with two attractive parents, all boded well for his future. Assuming his father did not get caught or killed while robbing people on the highways.

When supper ended, Nate invited Rowena to take a stroll around the grounds. "See what a good working farm is like. All the day laborers have long gone home. 'Tis safe to be about."

She was curious why he wanted to be alone with her. She looked at Cecily. Lovely in the silky pink fustian gown she was finally allowed to wear, her daughter said, "Go ahead, Mother. I have learned Mistress Hayward has been reading the same book I was reading, Don Quixote, and I wish to discuss it with her."

"Very well, dear," she said, and after again thanking Goody Hayward for the tasty meal, she followed Nate outside. She noted that Dody and Goody Hayward were the only ones involved in the cooking and the cleanup. The maid, Clare, disappeared upstairs, most likely to ready beds and bed gowns and to put out clean towels in all the rooms. Rowena doubted Clare would empty chamber pots, but she might toss out old water and refill the pitchers with warmed water. And, as Sidonie had promised, Clare had dressed Rowena's and Cecily's hair in becoming fashions so they both felt presentable when they went down to supper.

"Take my arm and mind your step, Lady Crossly," Nate said. "The hens and pigs have been locked up for the night, but some have left reminders of their daytime presence."

"So they have," Rowena said with a laugh. "As I now have on shoes rather than my boots, I will be doubly careful. But tell me more about the Haywards, please, Mister D'Arcy. The house is humble, but the furnishings, at least those in the area opposite the kitchen, are as rich as any that might be found in a country gentleman's parlor."

"And so they are. Mistress Hayward is the daughter of a local and well-heeled baronet. When Sidonie Hayward determined she would marry Caleb despite his being below her station, her mother insisted she must have suitable furnishings for when she called upon her. Or should any of the other neighbors call. So, Sir Bertran, Mistress Hayward's father, not only gave her a substantial dowry of a prime grazing field abutting the Hayward property as well as ten cows, he also paid for the parlor furniture and the finest furniture for her bedchamber. Caleb once told me it took him a month before he could adjust to the finery."

Rowena chuckled. "I also noticed Mistress Hayward did nothing to help with the meal or the cleanup."

Nate harrumphed. "That would be Goody Hayward's doing. She respects the fact Mistress Hayward is a lady, and Sidonie is treated as such in the Hayward home. No way would Goody Hayward ever let her daughter-in-law do menial tasks, especially not in the kitchen. Goody Hayward and Dody do the house cleaning, the laundering, and the cooking. The maid, Clare, helps with some things, but she, too, knows what duties are acceptable for her position. A day laborer sees to the egg gathering, pig slopping, and milking, and helps with the kitchen herb and vegetable garden. But Goody Hayward and Dody do their own baking, and they make their own cider. The ale, they get from one of their cottagers.

"Mistress Hayward takes care of her son. She has no nurse for him. She does some sewing and mending, mostly anything that needs delicate stitching. She reads aloud to the family, takes walks with her sister, and putters in the flower garden that is next to the herb garden. Before William was born, she went riding or visiting her family or friends. Basically, she occupies her time doing all the things any lady would normally do."

Thinking her life had not been much different from Sidonie's, Rowena said, "You know a lot about the Haywards it would seem."

Nate harrumphed. "I should. Caleb has been riding with me since we first formulated our plan. Often times the Haywards have hosted some or all of our gang. Do we put the Haywards' lives in jeopardy? Possibly, but they have been willing to risk our presence as have other Royalist families who offer us succor and a place to hide. Many people are loyal to King Charles, and we yet carry hope in our hearts that Charles will one day return to the throne. Charles is young. And Cromwell grows old. Without Cromwell's strong hand, I doubt the Puritans can hold onto the rule. In the meantime, we do what we can to give aid to our King."

"So you are particular about whom you rob?"

He snorted. "Aye. As you witnessed with Haspel, we lay our plans well. Now, tomorrow when we leave, we must resume our disguises. We are again the Bluchers."

"Why the Bluchers?"

"I am John Blucher because John was the brother of Ailred Blucher. John went to the colonies, Virginia to be exact, and promptly died there of a fever. However, no one but the Bluchers know John died. So, am I ever stopped and questioned, though thankfully it has yet to happen, I am a real person, not fictitious. So, back to tomorrow. We dare not take you to Chester. When we were at the Taverses, too many of the servants could have overheard us talking about Chester. They could be watching Ethelinda's mother's house. That being a possibility, we will bypass Chester and go directly to the Bluchers in Whitby. We will need make but one overnight stop on the way, and that because we must need ride sedately down the highway. We want not to draw any attention to ourselves by traveling too fast."

"I understand." Rowena also noted Nate had referred to Mistress Tavers as Ethelinda. That use of her given name had to indicate a closer relationship than just friends. Bringing her thoughts back to Nate's plans, she asked, "Will Cecily be my page again?"

"Well, that brings us to what I wish to discuss with you."

"Oh?" She had wondered why he had needed to take a stroll with her. He had not been showing her anything about the farm. Fact was, they had walked directly to the orchard and were presently standing under a tree burdened with ripening apples.

"I cannot but feel you and Cecily will both be much safer if you separate."

"What!"

He held up a hand. "Hear me out. Together you and Cecily are too identifiable. You must know Cecily cannot endlessly continue on as a boy. And you have been accused of being in league with highwaymen. Untrue, yes, but if caught, you risk being hanged, at best transported, did Haspel testify against you. You were aided by us in recovering your daughter. He could make a good case."

Her heart pounding in her chest, Rowena knew what he was saying was true. She could only stare up at him as his words coiled around her heart.

He reached out and took her hand. "Lady Crossly, Rowena, I mean not to frighten you. I have a solution that I think you will find amenable."

His eyes bored into hers, willing her to trust him. His hands holding hers felt warm and comforting. But to be parted from Cecily – how could she?

"My sister, Lady Grasmere, would be a suitable foster mother to Cecily. 'Tis common to foster children with relatives or friends. I and my brothers and my sister were all fostered out. Cecily could be the daughter of a friend of my sister. No one would be the wiser. And she would be safe. She would receive the best of care and guidance. And we could arrange upon occasion for you to visit her. But you would not be visiting her as her mother."

As she continued to stare at him, he asked, "Were you never fostered?"

"No. Fact is, at the age of ten, I was often in charge of running the house. My mother's mother, my dear grandmother, was very sick for near five years before she died. Mother took care of her, so she was seldom home."

He nodded and she was certain his eyes filled with sympathy. "Why would your sister want to take on raising a foster child?" she asked. "She knows us not."

"My sister is not only a Royalist, but she has a caring heart. She has a little daughter of her own, and wishes she could have more children. She will understand a mother's love for her child. And Cecily is a lovely girl. I know Phillida will love her."

"And what becomes of me?"

He shook his head. "That I have yet to determine. Once we are at the

Bluchers, we can think more on it. I have little doubt a plan will come to mind. Mayhap, you could even stay on with the Bluchers for a while. They are not far from Harp's Ridge, my sister's husband's primary residence. Though, it being summer, they are presently at Grasmere."

Pulling her hand free, Rowena said, "I will think on all you have said, Mister D'Arcy. Sadly, much of what you say is true. But to be parted from all my children …" She sighed. "I so wish I could know how my sons are doing."

"Could be that could be arranged," Nate said. He cocked his head. "Could be."

She looked up at him. "Truly?"

"We will talk more on it once we have Cecily safely hidden from Haspel."

She nodded. "Yes, we have much to think on. I suppose we should return to the house. Am I to be parted from my daughter, I want to spend as much time with her as I can. Not that I have agreed to be parted from her. I must think on it."

Giving her an understanding smile, he offered her his arm, and they made their way back to the house.

※ ※ ※ ※

D'Arcy could understand Rowena's feelings. She had risked all to rescue her daughter, then to have her daughter taken from her. It would be heart-wrenching. While at the Prestons, he and Jack Chapman had discussed how best to keep Cecily and Rowena safe. Chapman had come up with the idea of fostering Cecily with Lady Grasmere. But what to do with Rowena.

"It may not be our fault," Chapman said, "but we did help Lady Crossly rescue her daughter from Haspel. Does Lady Crossly now have a bounty on her head, 'tis partly our doing. Our consciences would play havoc with us was the lady caught and hanged."

D'Arcy had nodded. "Aye. We must see naught happens to that pretty neck. I do think, though, are we to convince Lady Crossly that she must part with Cecily, we will have to give her reason to trust us. I am thinking she should learn our true identities and learn why we are highwaymen. Otherwise, she will never leave Cecily in my sister's care."

"True enough. I suppose when we stay with the Haywards would be as good a time as any to tell her the truth about us and to introduce her to the idea of being separated from Cecily."

And so they had done so – revealed their names and their schemes. D'Arcy believed Rowena could see the merit of leaving Cecily with his sister. Eventually, she would accept the idea. She would recognize that it would be the best way to keep Cecily safe. But where might they leave Rowena and keep her from going mad with worry for her daughter? Foolishly, he wished he could keep her with him. He knew he was much too attracted to her, all the same, he would feel a loss when at last he had to leave her.

Then, when she had looked so wistful when speaking of her sons, he had thought, why not. Why not take her to Derby? No doubt some arrangement could be made to allow her to see her sons. She had mentioned a nurse, her maid. Could he but get word to the maid, more than likely she could arrange for Rowena to see her sons.

And in the process of taking Rowena to see her sons, he would get to spend more time with her, risky though that might be.

Chapter 20

Rowena and Cecily were up early. Neither had slept well. They had talked long into the night about Nate's plan to foster Cecily with his sister, Lady Grasmere. Neither liked the idea of being separated, at the same time, they could each see the wisdom of it.

When they rose, sleepy-eyed, Cecily again expressed her concern for her mother. "Am I not with you, no one would question who you are. You could be anyone. That Haspel should claim you are part of the highwayman's gang is wicked. But then, he is evil so we should not be surprised. I wonder how Father is doing? I would guess Haspel is ever on his doorstep."

"I care not how your father is doing." Rowena heard the harshness in her voice but had no wish to restrain it. "Never will we return to him. What he is putting us through is unforgivable. What he did to you is unforgivable. No, Cecily, was I not concerned about Milo's inheritance, I could wish your father to the devil."

"Mother!"

Rowena hugged Cecily. "I am sorry, sweetheart. I know he is your father, and you must still bear him some love, but I cannot. Now, let us go down and break our fast. Nate said he wanted to leave early this morning." D'Arcy had been Nate to her for so many days before learning his true surname, she still referred to him as Nate rather than Mister D'Arcy.

She and Cecily descended the stairs at the same moment that a dark-haired, wild-eyed girl burst into the Hayward home. She instantly ran to Nate and grasped his coat sleeves. "Oh, Mister D'Arcy, you must do something. They have taken Cyril."

"What!" Sidonie cried, and chaos soon reigned. Everyone was talking at once, but the girl's voice rang out above the rest.

"The militia with Moreland at their lead arrived before the sun was up. They were tipped off that Cyril was home. Cyril hid in the attic, but despite Father's boisterous complaints, they searched the house and found him."

"Moreland has ever been after Cyril," Sidonie snapped, her eyes narrowed. "He wanted to marry Tamar and never forgave Cyril for winning her hand. Since then, he has been doing his best to catch Cyril."

"You remember, this is not the first time Moreland has tried," the girl said, looking up at Nate, "but sadly, this time he succeeded. At least this time we know who tipped him off."

"Who, Arcadia!" Sidonie demanded. "Who tipped off Moreland?"

Rowena guessed the girl, Arcadia, must be Sidonie's sister. Same dark hair and eyes, same heart-shaped face, though Arcadia's chin was a bit more pronounced than Sidonie's. She was a pretty girl, might be beautiful was her face not distorted with worry.

Releasing Nate and turning to Sidonie, Arcadia said, "'Twas Ada. One of the maids. She snuck out during the night and went over to the Jaggers' and told their stableman, Rupert. He then went to Malpas and told Moreland. Ada was caught by Cook when she was trying to sneak back into the house. After threats from Father, she admitted what she had done. She said 'twas Rupert's idea. He told her did they get the reward money, they could afford to get married. She admitted 'twas Rupert who told Moreland the last time Cyril was near caught. He had been spying on our house for Moreland. My guess is he started courting Ada so he could get her to help him. I doubt he ever intended to marry her."

"Did they take Cyril to Malpas?" Nate asked, interrupting Arcadia's deluge.

The girl turned back to Nate. "Aye, that was their intent, I do think."

"All right. We will get Cyril out of jail, but we need do it tonight before they can move him to another location for his trial. Or worse, ship him off to an island prison without a trial."

"How, how will you get him out?" Arcadia's eyes were glued on Nate's face.

"Well, we must formulate a plan, so give us time to think."

Nate nodded to Jack Chapman, Caleb, and Dev, and they and Goodman Hayward went outside. Goody Hayward gathered both Sidonie and her sister into her arms. "Never fear, girls. You know well Mister D'Arcy will let no harm come to your brother. Come now, Sidonie, look at William, how big his eyes are. You frighten him are you fearful. And Arcadia, never in your life have you ever been frightened of anything. Now is not the time to change."

Sidonie gave Goody Hayward a hug then dropped to her knees to give her young son a hug. "Here, William. Mother was making a fool of herself. We have nothing to be afraid of. Like your grandmother says, Mister D'Arcy will free your Uncle Cyril."

Rowena doubted the child had any idea what his mother was talking about, but her tone was sweet and pleasant, so William was soon smiling. Arcadia, also hugged Goody Hayward and though she stopped wringing her hands, she continued pacing the room until Goody Hayward called her over to the foot of the stairs where Rowena and Cecily still stood and introduced them.

"Now," Goody Hayward said, "Lady Crossly, you and Mistress Crossly come break your fast. Arcadia, I doubt you have eaten. You sit down and join them. Sidonie, you and William, too. You have not eaten, and William will soon start fussing do you not feed him. I made a little custard for him." She looked slightly wistful. "Used to be my Adler's favorite dish."

Rowena had learned that Goody Hayward's elder son had fled to the Dutch colony in the new world after King Charles II's defeat in fifty-one. Goody Hayward missed her son terribly, but he was happy in his new home, so she was happy for him.

Rowena could not help but wonder what this turn of events would mean for her and Cecily. Did it put them more at risk? Should she and Cecily leave? But how could they leave? They had no horses, no money, only her jewels, and who could she sell them to. She tried to eat, but the porridge stuck in her throat. At first she had not known who Arcadia's brother might be, and why Nate should be concerned about him, but she soon figured out he was one of Nate's highwaymen. One thing she had learned about Nate, he was loyal to his men. Did he say he would find a way to free Cyril Yardley, he would find a way.

※ ※ ※ ※

Rowena could only hope she had done the right thing in allowing Cecily to leave without her. But surely, they were both safer were they not together. So Cecily, again dressed as a boy, was being escorted to the Bluchers' by Dev Preston and Arcadia Yardley. Like Cecily, Arcadia was dressed as a boy. Her thick dark hair cut short, a pair of her brother's breeches cinched tight about her waist, one of his coats hastily shortened and the sleeve cuffs turned back and tacked in place by Goody Hayward, and Arcadia was set to pose as Cecily's brother. Dev would be their older brother, and he was escorting them home after a visit to an aunt. They would stay one night at a safe location that had often given Nate and his men shelter. Dressed as males and riding astride, they would have no need to travel sedately, so they should reach the Bluchers by mid-morning the following day.

Arcadia had promised repeatedly that Rowena had no reason to worry about Cecily. "Dev and I will take good care of her. She is Peter, I am Bob, and we are Will Jamieson's brothers." And so after multiple hugs, the three brothers departed.

Rowena had no idea what Arcadia's mother thought of letting her daughter ride off in a male disguise with an unmarried man and with only Cecily as a chaperone, but her father, who had arrived at the Haywards' shortly after his daughter, only said, "Take care with that pistol, Cadia. Keep it tucked in your pocket. Let it not be stolen. 'Tis a true shot should it be needed."

"I am certain the pistol will not be needed," Dev said after a glance at Rowena. She knew her face showed her concern. "We are less than a day and a half from our destination. Simple."

And so Rowena let Cecily ride away, and she spent the remainder of the day waiting for Nate and Chapman to return from setting up their plan to free Cyril Yardley.

When the sky began to darken and a few stars blinked overhead, the rescue party set out for Malpas. Per Nate's instructions, Sir Bertran Yardley, Cyril's father, paid ten pounds to the jailor to remove the irons Cyril had been carted away in. Still secured behind bars in the brick jail with its heavy oak door, Cyril could at least rest easy on his cot until rescued. Moreland had ridden off to Nantwich to get men to help him escort Cyril to London. The local Malpas militiamen, having grown up with Cyril and gone to school with him, had no wish to be part of Moreland's revenge. They had done Moreland's bidding in helping to arrest Cyril, but they had thought Sir Bertran would pay a large fine and see his son freed. Moreland had other plans.

That they could not be suspected of being involved in Cyril's escape from jail, Caleb, Sir Bertran, and Goodman Hayward went to visit the village elder to discuss the possibility of freeing Cyril by paying a fine. Nate, Rowena, Chapman, and Sidonie, dressed as a male youth, were heading for the jail. Rowena was wearing a blond wig Chapman had plucked from his pack, her bodice was pulled low to reveal the rounded mounds of her breasts, and a dark beauty mark had been drawn on her left breast. Her job was to entice the jailor out of the jail. Get him as far from the door as possible so Nate could slip inside the jail.

She was frightened, but at the same time she felt an exhilaration. There was something thrilling about besting the Cromwellians who were responsible for turning her life upside down. And she was determined she would do her part well. A shiver of excitement shimmied down her spine as they rode into the dark streets of Malpas.

※ ※ ※ ※

D'Arcy had no doubt Rowena would entice the jailor out. A beautiful woman with a heavenly figure overly displayed – too well displayed – she stirred things in him he knew should not be stirred. When she had come downstairs after changing into her costume, he had had trouble keeping his thoughts on their plan and not on wishing he could see even more of Rowena. She had already proven herself a competent actress with first his cousin, Ethelinda, and her family, then at the inn where they had had to overnight, and yet again with the Prestons and the Tourneys. She would not fail them.

Neither would Sidonie. When they needed another male to stage a fight with Chapman, and none were available as Dev was escorting Cecily to safety, and Caleb needed to be in the presence of the Malpas elder so he could not be blamed for his brother-in-law's escape, Sidonie had quickly volunteered to play the role. Nor was this the first time Sidonie had come to their aid. When her husband had been shot during one of their robberies, Sidonie, though heavy with child and near her due date, had traveled with the escaping highwaymen to care for her husband. She had saved Caleb's life. D'Arcy trusted both women to play their parts well

Chapter 21

Stars were glinting in the sky, but the quarter slice of the moon offered little light as D'Arcy led Chapman, Rowena, and Sidonie down the dark Malpas streets to Marvin Bussard's stable. Bussard was a Royalist eager to help King Charles. Earlier in the day, when D'Arcy had asked for his aid, Bussard had been more than willing to lend assistance. His modest home was not far from the jail so it was the perfect place to start and end their scheme.

Bussard, with the help of his wife, had been able to send their servants out on various errands, so Bussard was the only one waiting for D'Arcy and his cohorts when they arrived at his stables. "You had no trouble sending your servants off?" D'Arcy asked Bussard.

Bussard chuckled. "Nay. 'Twas almost too easy. I sent the stableman on an errand out to Ascelina's parents. Ascelina had the coachman and footman take her to visit a friend, and she took her maid, our son, Boniface, and his nurse with her. I gave the rest of the staff the night off as I said I would be going out so no one was needed. They were all quite happy with the unexpected treat."

"You will tell your wife we appreciate her help?" D'Arcy said.

"Aye, she was pleased to be able to help."

With their horses securely hidden in Bussard's stable, D'Arcy was ready to set his plan in motion. Chapman and Sidonie took up their positions beneath an open window a little way down the street from the jail. D'Arcy had paid a widow having fallen on hard times after her husband had been killed fighting for the King to keep a bright light shining from her window. Another Royalist, she was eager to oblige.

Rowena and D'Arcy made their way to the jail, and the play began. Hidden in the shadows but able to see the door to the jail, D'Arcy watched Rowena hammer on the heavy door with a rock. "Help! Oh, help! You must help me!" she cried. She repeated her cries until at last the door creaked open a crack and a burly man peered out at her. Reaching inside, Rowena grabbed the man's coat sleeve.

"Come quickly. You must help me before that man kills my brother!" Her voice broke with a sob. D'Arcy was impressed.

The jailor held a lantern out and its glow illuminated Rowena's low-cut bodice. That the jailor was ogling her was apparent as he lowered the lantern to cast more light on her breasts. She continued to tug on his sleeve with one hand and point down the street with her other hand. Under the muted gleam of light cast from the open window, Chapman and Sidonie were staging a fight.

"My brother, you must help my brother," Rowena continued to cry. "That man! He swore he would kill Billy. Oh, please, help me."

The jailor tore his gaze away from the alluring display before him and glanced up the street. He stumbled a little as Rowena tugged him out the door. "You must stop them!"

Still holding the lantern, he raised it and shouted at the two combatants. "Hey you two clodpolls! Desist and be gone with you!" Ignoring him Chapman and Sidonie continued to fight, and Rowena half dragged the jailor further from the door.

Deciding he needed to act, D'Arcy slipped from the shadows and slid inside the jail. Hidden behind the half open door, he waited in the dark for the jailor to return. Peering through the crack of the open door, he could see but a tiny glimmer of the lantern, but he heard the jailor call out again to stop and desist or the two louts would find themselves in jail. He then heard Rowena cry, "Oh, Billy, Billy, wait for me. Wait for me!", and he knew Rowena, Sidonie, and Chapman were running away from the jailor.

"Hey, you! You woman!" the jailor hollered. "Come back here. Come back! Damn!" he cursed, and lowering the lantern, made his way back to the jail.

Staying in the shadows, D'Arcy waited until the jailor closed the door, threw the bolt, and hug the lantern back on its hook near the door before stepping forward. "Just rest easy now and there will be no call for this popper to go off," he said.

The jailor jerked around to find D'Arcy pointing a large double-shot pistol at him. "Gads! What would ye be wanting? I have no money."

"I want not your money. I want your prisoner." Waving his pistol a little, D'Arcy indicated the keys attached to the jailor's belt. "I need you to unlock Yardley's cell. He will be leaving with me."

The man shook his head. "Oh, nay. Moreland will have me head."

"Better your head than your life." D'Arcy waved the gun again. "I have not much time. Open the cell. Now!"

An angry scowl on his face, the jailor unfastened the keys from his belt, and inserted a big heavy key into a rusty lock. The jail had but two tiny cells, one with naught but straw on the floor and a slop bucket. The other cell, meant for the more well-heeled prisoners, had a cot, a washstand and bowl, and a chamber pot. The jailor's own meager accommodations were little better.

Emerging from the dark cell, Yardley said with a chuckle, "You took your time getting here."

"Did the best I could," D'Arcy answered with a slap on Yardley's shoulder. He waved the gun at the jailor. "Sorry, but I am going to need to lock you in this cell. As you have no other prisoners, there will be no one to disturb you, so hopefully you will get a good night's sleep and will be well rested and ready to break your fast when the morning guard arrives."

Still scowling, the jailor said, "You will regret this. You and Yardley will be caught and brought back here in irons. I will wager on that."

Locking the lock and then tossing the keys onto the table near the door, D'Arcy said, "Did I think you could afford it, I would take that wager, but I fear you are not paid enough to make a wager worth my time."

As D'Arcy and Yardley started to exit, the jailor called, "And that woman. I will have that woman in my jail, too. And I will enjoy myself with her."

D'Arcy looked back over his shoulder and frowned. "What woman? I know of no woman." Before the jailor could answer him, he closed the door and removed the kerchief from his face. He was not worried about the jailor being able to recognize Rowena. The jailor would describe a woman with blond hair. Besides, the man had barely glanced at her face. She could walk right past him and never be recognized.

Hurrying down the dark street, D'Arcy led Yardley at a fast but silent pace. In a matter of moments, they reached their destination.

When D'Arcy and Yardley arrived, they found Sidonie had already changed back into a gown, and after a hug for her brother, D'Arcy boosted her up onto a pillion behind Chapman. Chapman would see Sidonie safely home, and come morning, he would set off for the Bluchers. Yardley had to quickly change into the servant's clothing his sister had worn. Bussard would dispose of Yardley's richer clothes. Yardley would be playing the role of a servant.

After again thanking Bussard for his generous aid, D'Arcy, Rowena, and Yardley set off for their night's abode. Yardley was riding the horse Sidonie had ridden into Malpas, and Rowena, seated on a sidesaddle, now rode her own horse. She admitted to being pleased she would not again have to ride on a pillion.

Rowena, too, had changed clothes, and her blond wig had been tucked away in Chapman's pack. She now wore a crisp white lappet cap, a modest gown showing no cleavage, and a light-weight brown cloak to protect her from the evening chill. All paint had been removed from her face, and her creamy skin glowed with health. D'Arcy had found her alluring when dressed as a strumpet, but he found her even more attractive as her natural self. She was indeed a captivating woman, and he was pleased he would be spending more time in her company, though he knew he should instead be looking forward to distancing himself from her.

※ ※ ※ ※

Rowena felt an exhilaration she had not felt in years. From the moment the jailor opened the door to the jail, all fear had flown, and she had immersed herself in the role she was playing. She wondered if actors on stage felt that same moment of thrill when the curtain rose, and they saw their audience, and their performance began.

Now she was playing a repeat role. She was again the sedate wife of John Blucher. They would be staying with Marvin Bussard's in-laws, Basil and Rose Guildford. Basil Guildford was the heir of a wealthy wool and cloth merchant. When the Basil's only surviving child, Ascelina, married Bussard, the well-educated younger son of a prosperous yeoman, Guildford had trained Bussard to take over his mercantile business. Basil and Rose had then retired to a country home a little way outside Malpas, not far from his sister's and her husband's manor. According to Nate, the Guildfords, to their neighbors, seemed an elderly couple leading a quiet, dignified life, but they had on several occasions offered Nate and his men a safe haven, and they loved every moment of deception.

Upon arriving late at night at the Guildfords' home, Rowena saw little of the house and grounds. She was escorted upstairs by Mistress Guildford to a room she would be sharing with Nate. There was nothing showy about Mistress Guildford or her home. The woman wore a dark, rouge-colored gown tucked up on the sides to reveal a beige petticoat, and her grey hair peeked out from under a creamy white lappet cap. Her voice was sweet, pleasant, but uncultured. She was obviously country-born and put on no airs.

"I hope you will be comfortable in this bedchamber," Mistress Guildford said, opening a door off a central corridor. She whispered, "There is a cot in the closet where Mister Blucher can sleep. The servants believe you are married, so I fear you must share a room."

Rowena nodded. "I understand. But do you know where Nate, or rather John, and your husband disappeared to?" When they had arrived at the Guildford home, Mistress Guildford had taken charge of Rowena, and Nate, Yardley, and Mister Guildford had headed off to the stables. Nate appeared to be half holding Yardley up while a groom followed behind leading the horses.

Mistress Guildford looked over her shoulder then closed the door. In a low voice she said, "They will be transforming Mister Yardley's appearance. He will be put to bed in our head groom's room and will be terribly sick. We are suspected of being Royalists, and the militia will search the homes of all Royalists in their search for Mister Yardley. They must not be able to recognize Mister Yardley. Our head groom has been with us since my husband and I were newly married. Him we trust, but we must be cautious around the other servants. Rewards can be tempting even though we pay our servants well."

"Must be quite the transformation if the militia will not recognize Mister Yardley," Rowena said.

Mistress Guildford chuckled. "Oh, it will be. By the time they are finished with Mister Yardley, his own parents would not recognize him." She patted Rowena's arm. "I have assigned my personal maid to see to your needs. She, too, can be trusted, but I would still advise caution. My husband and I may know your true identity, but I think it best none of the servants know."

"Yes, 'twould be best. And thank you. I will be cautious. Truth be, I am now used to guarding my tongue."

"Well, I know you must be exhausted. You will wish to ready yourself for bed. I have ordered warm water to be brought up. I also ordered a small glass of sherry. Should help you sleep. You might as well sleep as late as you wish tomorrow. You will not be leaving here until Nate decides 'tis safe for Mister Yardley to travel. That could be a couple of days."

"Yes, so he has told me."

A tap at the door had Mistress Guildford turning to open it. "Ah, Hilda," she said, "you have brought the water. Do go ahead and pour some into the bowl." She glanced back at Rowena. "This is my maid, Hilda. She will ready your bed, help you unpack, and she will ready Mister Blucher's cot in the closet. I have already informed her you need a good night's rest without your husband's snoring keeping you awake. Now, I will see your sherry is brought up and will bid you a good-night."

"Thank you, Mistress Guildford. You are kind to have waited up so late for us."

"Nonsense. Basil and I are always pleased to see Mister Blucher. And now to meet his wife. I but hope your servant will soon recover from whatever might be his illness."

"As do I," Rowena said, wondering if she would get to see the transformed Cyril Yardley.

After Mistress Guildford left, Rowena turned to her ablutions while Hilda readied the bed, laid out Rowena's nightshift, and unpacked her panniers.

After setting Rowena's few toiletries on a small table by the bed, Hilda said, "I believe I should take your gowns with me and press them, Mistress Blucher. They have become crumpled stuffed into the panniers."

"Yes, thank you Hilda. That would be good. I fear there is scarce room for my gowns and sundry items in the panniers." Rowena was glad she no longer had Cecily's gowns in her panniers. They were now in the pack Chapman would be taking with him as he rode to his meet up with Cecily, Arcadia, and Dev Preston at the Bluchers'.

Again a little shiver of misgiving shot up Rowena's spine. Had she done right letting her fourteen-year-old daughter ride off with two people she barely knew? She had seen the way Arcadia looked at Preston. Would Arcadia make a mistake and look at Preston that way in front of other people? Might she give them all away? She was glad Chapman would be joining them at the Bluchers. He had promised her he would watch over Cecily until she and Nate arrived. Pray God they would not need to stay at the Guildford's more than a day. She wanted to join her daughter and be certain she was safe and well.

While Hilda went into the closet to ready Nate's cot, Rowena slipped her pistol and jewels under her pillow. She hoped she would be able to sleep and would not spend the entire night worrying about Cecily.

Hilda helped Rowena ready herself for bed then answered a light tap at the door and accepted the glass of sherry for Rowena. "Do you not be needing me for aught else," Hilda said, "I will take these gowns with me and bid you goodnight."

"Goodnight to you, Hilda, and thank you."

The maid exited after snuffing out all the candles but the one on the table beside the bed. Sitting up in the bed, Rowena sipped the sherry and looked about at the bedchamber. The stucco walls were painted a creamy white. The furnishings, from chair, to washstand, to bed, to chest at the foot of the bed, to the nightstand were of maple. Even the mantle shelf above the hearth was of maple. Curtains at the windows were a bright yellow, and the patterned quilt on the bed was mixture of yellow, orange, and a pale green. A most attractive room.

The house was obviously new as it had a central corridor with doors opening off both sides of the corridor. It was a fairly large house. She had counted four doors on each side of the corridor. That would mean eight bedchambers and possibly each one with a servants' closet off them. Nate would be sleeping in the closet off her bedchamber. She forcibly pushed that thought away, sipped the last of the sherry, and squiggled down into the bed.

Fluffing her pillow, Rowena pulled a quilt up closer to her chin. The night had cooled and a single window was open just enough to let the fresh night air into the room. Excitement still dancing about in her head, Rowena feared she would not be able to go to sleep immediately. She wondered what was to become of her. Cecily would be safe with Nate's sister. But what would she do? Where would she stay? She was already accused of being in league with Nate's highwaymen. She was already wanted, so what had she to lose? She had been of assistance to Nate and Chapman in freeing Yardley. Might she again assist them? Nate said she was a good actress. She played her part well. Did she help them gain information, she could earn her keep with them. She could leave her jewelry with Lady Grasmere to be used on anything Cecily needed. Then she would not be constantly worrying about it. She was a good horsewoman. She would not slow them down. She had good reason to hate the Puritans. Look what they had done to her and Cecily with their unfair taxes. She would feel no guilt robbing them. Yes, she could see no reason she could not aid Nate and his highwaymen.

What would it be like to travel all over England? She thought she might like it. Until Nate rescued her and Cecily and provided them a safe escape from Haspel, she had never been anywhere more distant than Derby. She rather thought she would like seeing more of England. With such thoughts darting about in her head, she drifted into sleep. She never heard Nate tiptoe into the room and peer down at her before blowing out the candle on the stand beside her bed and treading softly across the room to the closet and his bed.

Chapter 22

Cecily missed her mother. At the same time, she felt safe and comfortable with Arcadia, or rather Bob. Arcadia played the part of a boy perfectly. And she seemed fearless. Not long after they set off from the Haywards', they were met by two militiamen who recognized Dev from the inn they had stayed at on their way to the Prestons'.

"I know you," the larger of the two said. "You were on your way to Wrexham. To buy cheese you said."

"Indeed I did. Placed my order and am on my way to Chester to arrange shipping for it."

"And who might these two lads be?" questioned the other militiaman, peering intently at first Arcadia and then Cecily.

Cecily's heart was in her throat, but Arcadia piped up, "I am Bob Jamieson and this is my brother, Peter, and Will is our older brother. He is taking us back home to Chester. We have been visiting our aunt and cousins in Malpas." She pursed her lips and stared intently at the man questioning her. "By the by, might you be unmarried. My aunt is intent on finding a husband for my cousin, Anna. She is now four and twenty and her mother fears she will end up a spinster does she not soon get married." Giving the man no chance to speak, Arcadia blathered on, "Anna is a good cook, and she has a good hope chest. She is fair enough to look upon if a bit on the skinny side. Now would you be needing a wife, and are you headed to Malpas, I could be telling you more about Anna. My aunt's home is not hard to find."

"I am not needing a wife!" the militiaman shouted, breaking in on Arcadia's discourse.

The larger militiaman was laughing. "I have me a wife. But, Hill, this Anna that young Jamieson is describing might be the perfect woman for you."

Glowering, Hill snarled, "Let us tend to business. Have any of you seen a dark-haired woman traveling with a young fair-haired woman? Mayhap in company of several men."

"Nay. I cannot say I have seen such women as you describe," Dev said. "I recollect you said there was a reward being offered for them."

"That is right," Hill said.

"Oh!" Arcadia said, taking off again and giving neither militiaman a chance to speak. "A reward! I saw a dark-haired woman near a week ago passing through Malpas with her husband and two children. One of the children had light colored hair if I recall correctly. Had a wagon full of furniture. Saw them stop at an ale house for a respite. Might they be the ones you look for. I could use a reward. I could buy me that new saddle I have been wanting and…"

"Hold there!" Hill shouted. "You beat all. Does he prattle on like that all the time?"

"Pretty near," Dev said. "He can be a trial. 'Tis why Mother was eager to let him spend the summer with our aunt."

"Well, I have had enough of him. Just keep in mind a large reward is being offered for the capture of those two women. Word is, they may be headed to Chester." Glaring at Arcadia, he glanced at his comrade and growled, "Let us be on our way."

The hammering in her chest slowing and her heart resuming a more regular beat as the militiamen rode away, Cecily said, "You were wonderful. Once you started chattering, they never again looked at me."

"'Twas as I intended. I meant to draw their attention away from you. You make a convincing enough lad, but did they look closely, they might have seen the fear in your eyes."

"Oh, and I was frightened."

"No need to be afraid. Dev and I will see you reach the Bluchers' safely. Then before you know it, your mother will again be with you."

Dev said, "Yes, Arcadia, you did well, but use caution. Watch your mannerisms. You must not forget you are a lad. Keep your voice low, it rose a bit as you hurried your speech."

"Did it? I will be more careful does the need again arise. I would say, though, 'twas a good thing I am the one here with Cecily and not her mother. Those militiamen are eager to claim that reward. They might have been more suspicious of Lady Crossly."

"'Tis true," Dev said. "'Tis why we decided 'twas safer did Cecily and her mother travel separately. Now, let us continue. With luck, we will reach our destination in time for supper."

And they had reached their destination in ample time to sit down to supper, but Cecily had been surprised by the humble abode offering them shelter and sustenance. The Nadlers' home was naught but a two-room house consisting of the hall and the Nadlers' bedchamber. They were served a home-brewed ale, rye bread, and a porridge rich with rabbit, carrots, and beans for their supper, and after Dev told them what news he had of what the Nadlers termed the outside world while they sat around the dying fire in the hearth and sipped cider, the Nadlers announced 'twas time for bed.

Bed for the three Jamiesons was naught but a cornhusk mattress placed on the floor in the corner of the room, out of the way of Goody Nadler who would be up early to stir up the fire and warm up the porridge which would be their breakfast. The two Nadler children that were still living at home, the oldest son and the youngest, went out to the barn for the night. The cornhusk mattress serving Cecily, Arcadia, and Dev was the sons' bed when the family had no guests. There being no chamber pots, Cecily again experienced the outhouse aromas. She and Arcadia giggled together over them until Dev reminded them that boys would not be giggling.

When they settled down on the mattress for the night, Cecily was placed in the middle. She understood why. She was considered too young to tempt Dev, but was Arcadia next to him, that could be too inviting. Dev turned his back to her, but Cecily still had a tingly feeling throughout her body knowing she was sleeping right next to such an extraordinarily handsome man. She knew he had no romantic interest in her, but she wondered if he might have feelings for Arcadia. She was pretty certain Arcadia had placed her interest in Dev. Well, mayhap a romance would bloom between the two. Did it, they would make a handsome couple.

※ ※ ※ ※

Arcadia listened to the rhythmic breathing of her two companions.

She was pleased Dev did not snore. Not that, did he snore, she would refrain from marrying him. No, she had determined the first time she laid eyes on Deverette Preston that he was the man she meant to marry. But that was five years ago. She was now two and twenty and had turned down several suitors, much to her mother's annoyance. Her father seemed not to care. "Does she fail to marry, that is one less dowry I have to come up with," he declared when her mother wrung her hands.

She knew getting Dev to consider marriage was a problem in itself, even did she win his love, and she was determined she would do so. First problem, like her brother and D'Arcy, Dev was a wanted man. He was a Royalist who had not surrendered. And he was a highwayman, ever on the run. But that had not stopped her brother from marrying. And he now had two daughters, three-year-old Beatrice and new born Juliet.

The thought of her brother made her wonder if D'Arcy had yet freed Cyril. Cyril had taken a chance spending several nights in their home, but he wanted time with his wife and children. He could not be blamed for that. Her father believed his servants were loyal so had acquiesced and agreed to let Cyril stay. Cyril's capture had put them all at risk. Her father could have been arrested or at least fined for housing an unrepentant Royalist.

Arcadia guessed her mother was worried sick, and not just about Cyril. She would be furious with Arcadia's father for letting Arcadia dress as a boy and ride off unchaperoned with one of the highwaymen. But did her mother know her daughter was set on winning the love of that highwayman and of marrying him, she would be less upset. Someday when the King returned to the throne, and Arcadia's father was always saying 'twas but a matter of time before even the Puritans were sick to death of their leaders and would welcome King Charles II to the throne, Arcadia's mother would be pleased to have Deverette Preston for her son-in-law.

How to go about winning Dev's love was the hurdle Arcadia had yet to figure out how to surmount. If she had more time with him, she knew she could win his love. She had seen the way he looked at her covertly when he thought she was unaware of his gaze. She believed he found her attractive. She but needed to build on that. She had to take advantage of every day she could have with him. Sadly, being dressed as a boy precluded any flirting. Mayhap once they reached their destination, and while they awaited D'Arcy, she could find ways to be alone with him.

Twisting from her back to her side, Arcadia heard the mattress crunch under her. What an adventure. She wondered what bugs she and Cecily were picking up. Two gently reared girls, they were experiencing things they could never have imagined. Sighing, she knew she needed to sleep. Dev would have them up and on the road at first light. She listened to the soft breathing sounds from her two companions and let them lull her into a drowsy state, and at last she slept.

Chapter 23

The militia arrived earlier that D'Arcy expected them, but he, the Guildfords, their head groomsman, Wally, and Cyril were ready for them. When the militiamen pounded on the door, the Guildfords' head footman, still half asleep, answered it. D'Arcy, watching from the top of the stairs, saw the footman shoved aside, and four militiamen pushed their way into the house.

"Where is your master!" one militiaman snapped as Guildford brushed past D'Arcy and headed down the staircase.

"What is the meaning of this! Why do you break into my home?" Guildford demanded.

"We are searching for Cyril Yardley. He was aided in an escape from jail last evening. We are searching the homes of known and suspected Royalists. You could well be hiding him."

"We are hiding no one here, but as you can see, you have awakened my entire household." Servants in various degree of dress and undress were coming into the hall. Some still had their bed jackets and nightcaps on.

"Mister Guildford, what is happening?" asked a middle-age woman, waddling up, her hair mussed, her robe askew.

"Look how you have frightened my housekeeper," Guildford said.

His chin jutting forward, his eyes narrowed, the militiaman who appeared to be in charge, said, "We care not about your servants or you. We intend to search this house."

"Well, then," Guildford said, "get on with it, but I will have one of my servants accompanying each one of you. Bear in mind, too, that my wife is still abed as is Mister Blucher's wife. 'Tis shameful that you will be bursting into their bedchambers."

The militiaman blushed, but with a wave of his hand, he directed his three men to set about their search. One would search the servants' quarters, one the ground floor rooms, and he and the other man would search the bedchambers on the first floor.

D'Arcy returned to the door of the bedchamber he shared with Rowena. He would put up a small protest, but not one that would cause him to get into trouble with the militiamen. He had no doubt Rowena would play her part well. She would blush and be outraged and would have the bed quilts pulled up to her chin. Mistress Guildford would do the same. Once the house was searched, the militiamen would start on the outbuildings. How the head groomsman and Cyril carried off their parts of the charade was what truly mattered.

Guildford assigned a servant to each militiaman. They would watch that the militiamen were respectful and stole nothing. Not all militiamen were honest Christians. Some simply joined the Puritan militia because they hoped to confiscate or steal Royalists' possessions. The leader of the militiamen was the one to search Rowena's bedchamber. She gave him a tongue lashing, first for being so brazen as to enter her bedchamber while she was still abed, and second for coming so early and awakening her from a needed rest. After searching under the bed, and in D'Arcy's closet, the militiaman apologized and scurried from the room. At the same time, the other militiaman was just leaving Mistress Guildford's chamber with a tick in his ear. Rose Guildford was the daughter of an estate steward, and though she had married into the gentry class, she knew how to forcefully address the labor class.

Soon the house had been searched, and the militiamen were ready to start on the outbuildings.

※ ※ ※ ※

No sooner had the militiaman exited her room, and Rowena was up and getting dressed. She had every intention of being ready to flee should the need arise. She also hoped to get to see Cyril Yardley. Nate seemed not in the least bit worried that Yardley would be recognized, but he could just be trying to calm any fears she might have.

As soon as she was dressed, she slipped her jewels and her small pistol into her pockets and hurried out the door. A couple of servants were ambling about still in partial undress, but as Rowena started down the stairs, the housekeeper appeared, dressed and ready for work, and she set the servants to scurrying. She greeted Rowena and told her she would soon be able to break her fast, but Rowena was more eager to follow after Nate, Mister Guildford, and the militiamen. Hurrying out the door the footman opened for her, Rowena spotted Nate, Guildford, and one of the militiamen headed to the stables. She followed after them.

"You say he may have the plague?" the militiaman was saying as Rowena neared the three men.

"Aye," Nate said. "He was feeling ill two days ago and kept getting worse. By the time we arrived here last night, he could barely walk. I near had to drag him to his cot. We put him in with the head groomsman that the groomsman might alert us did he die during the night."

A worried look flashed across the militiaman's face, but he squared his shoulders, and throwing out his chest, said, "All the same. I need to see him."

"And see him you shall," Mister Guildford said. Turning to the stable doorway, he hollered, "Holloway, we have come to see Mister Blucher's man servant. Open your door."

The head groomsman had his own room on the ground floor. The other groomsmen and laborers slept in a dormitory above the stable. Some, rubbing sleepy eyes were coming down the outside staircase as the head groomsman opened the door to his private chamber.

"Is my man still alive?" Nate asked.

"Aye," the groomsman said. An aged man with gray, wiry hair peered out from under bushy eyebrows at the three men outside his door. "Might even be a bit better. He stopped groaning once the rash broke out all over him. Scratched himself raw in a couple of places, but come in and see for yourself how he does."

Rowena slipped into the stable and absently petted one of the horses while watching the men enter the groomsman's chamber. She could hear voices but could not make out what they were saying. Then the men exited. All were shaking their heads.

"I know Cyril Yardley," the militiaman said. "Have known him near all my life, and that man in there is not Cyril Yardley. Damned if I am not feeling sorry for the poor bloke. Does he live, he is apt to be bad scarred." He scratched his arms through his coat sleeves. "Hope he has nothing contagious. You say it all started after he ate his supper the night before?"

"Aye. Was not long afterwards he started feeling poorly."

"Poison, you think?"

"Might have been, but cannot think why him. Unless it was meant for someone else," Nate said. "'Twas a crowded inn."

The militiaman nodded his head as his three companions joined him and declared they had searched everywhere but upstairs above the stables. The head militiaman told them to search there, but he doubted they would find Yardley. "My guess is he and whoever broke him out rode away from Malpas as hard and fast as they could go. They could be in Derby by now to my way of thinking. But will Moreland be angry when he returns. He will have that jailor's head."

Once the militiamen trod down from the dormitory above the stables, they headed to their horses and were soon riding away. Rowena decided it was her chance to see Yardley. The other laborers and groomsmen were not privy to the deception, so she had to play her part in the drama. "Poor Jed," she said, Jed being the name they had given Yardley. "I must take a peek at him. Does he die, I must be the one to write his poor mother."

Nate chuckled. "Aye, come ahead, my dear. You shall have a peek at our poor servant."

Rowena stared at the man on the cot. Could he really be Yardley? His dark hair, cut in a bob, was dirty and straggly, his dark eyes were bloodshot, and his nose was no longer trim, but was blotchy and bulbous. His face and hands were covered in a red rash, his cheeks were puffy, and his neat mustache was gone, replaced by the rash. One section of his face below one eye was raw and weepy looking. His nails were ragged and dark with grime. She would never have recognized him as the handsome gentleman D'Arcy had brought back to Bussard's stable. His appearance came close to making her gag.

"Well, Mistress Blucher, are you satisfied your servant is yet alive. Mayhap now, you might wish to return to the house to break your fast," Mister Guildford said. "Looks as though you will be spending a day or two with us until your servant is well enough to travel. My wife thought a trip over to my sister's home might be diverting for you today."

Rowena had turned from Yardley to Guildford when her host started speaking. Slowly nodding her head, she looked back at Yardley and said, "Yes, I suppose I should return to the house, but I think mayhap my appetite is not what it was. Poor Jed."

D'Arcy took her arm. "Come my dear, I will walk you back. I promise you, Jed will soon recover. In the meantime, let us enjoy the Guildfords' hospitality."

※ ※ ※ ※

Liverna pretended to be busying herself folding linen napkins, but she was listening to every word passing between Sir Lindell and Gaylord Doggett, Rowena's uncle. The two men were in a room just off the main hall where Sir Lindell saw his tenants and conducted other business. She could not see Sir Lindell or Doggett, but she could hear them. No doubt other servants could also hear them. Doggett was not known for his quiet voice and at present, Doggett was furious with Sir Lindell.

"A fool! I call you a damned fool!" Doggett bellowed. "To marry your wee daughter off to a man like Haspel is repugnant. And now to have my niece accused of being in league with highwaymen – to have a bounty on her head. Man, were it not for your two sons, I would be calling you out."

Sir Lindell's voice was pleading. "You have to understand, I was desperate. I feared I would lose half the manor. What would that leave me for my sons or for Cecily. And you told me you could not help me."

"I told you to be patient. I could not immediately help. I needed time to study the situation. To work on finding a solution. Now I have the solution, and my niece and my little grandniece are missing. Lord only knows what will become of them."

Liverna heard Doggett pound his hand on Sir Lindell's table. "Was it not for Milo and Godwin, I would wash my hands of you. For them, I have arranged for a loan for you. Rowena's stipend will make payments on that loan until the loan is paid off. The interest is high, and it will take her entire stipend to make the tri-monthly payments. I do this only because I think it is what Rowena would want. She would want it for

Milo."

"Thank you, Gaylord, thank you. Since Cecily ran away with her mother, and Haspel raised my taxes, I have been at a loss as to what to do. For Milo, I thank you."

"Ehhh, I want not your thanks. Now what are your plans for the boys' education? You cannot think to continue with a tutor forever."

"I cannot afford to send them to Eton at present. I have a good tutor for them. I will keep them here at home at least one more year."

"Mayhap 'tis for the best." Doggett's voice had softened, and Liverna had to strain to hear him. She knew he had a deep love for his sister's children and grandchildren. His own two sons were yet childless as was Rowena's brother, consequently, Milo and Godwin were looked upon as the future heirs to the Plaisance and the Doggett family legacies.

At present the boys were packing to go stay with their Great Uncle Gaylord in Derby. Liverna would not be going with them. She wanted to stay at Crossly Oaks Manor in case Rowena should try to contact her. The boys would be well cared for by Gaylord's wife. With her own two sons married and living in their own homes, Rosamond missed having children about her home. Liverna knew the kindly woman was hoping her sons would eventually have children that she might again hear the patter of little feet in her home.

Hearing the boys clattering down the stairs to the hall, Liverna picked up the napkins and carried them over to the sideboard to tuck them into a drawer. A manservant assigned to go with the boys followed behind them carrying their panniers.

"I wish you were going with us," Godwin said, his blue eyes, so like his father's, a little damp with unshed tears.

Stooping to hug the child, she quietly whispered, "I know, Godwin, but you know I must stay here should your mother try to contact me to learn how you boys are doing. I know she is missing you as much as you are missing her. And you know your Aunt Rosamond will spoil you rotten with all kind of sweets and toys. You will have a grand time. But you remember to brush your teeth every night." She drew back to look the boy in the eyes. "You promise me?"

"I promise, Liverna."

"Good boy. Now, look," she said, rising. "Your Uncle Gaylord is done with his business and is ready to take you home with him. Have a good time and before you know it, you will be back here to begin your lessons with Mister Hail. He has said he will return from his visit to his family by September."

"That is good," Godwin said. "I miss his lessons."

"You may," Milo said, coming over to give Liverna a good-bye hug, "but I cannot say I do. I much prefer to be out of doors."

"And so you shall be," his Uncle Gaylord said. "I have arranged for both of you to attend a riding school while you are with me. Are you to ride to the hunt, you must learn how to jump your horses." He looked at Godwin. "Well, maybe you are a bit young for that yet. But Milo here," he clamped a hand on Milo's shoulder, "you are not too young to start on the low bars. I care not for the sport myself, but I know it will be a part of your life, and you must do it well and safely. Now, let us be on our way. Your aunt is eagerly awaiting you."

The boys again gave Liverna a quick hug, but they refused to even say good-bye to their father despite the fact he followed them outside to their horses. Liverna could almost feel sorry for the man. Then she pictured the forlorn little Cecily being forced to marry Haspel, and she again saw her darling Rowena climbing down the ivy outside her window, and all sympathy for the man faded.

Godwin was boosted up onto his pony by the servant, but Milo managed to mount his larger horse by himself. His uncle praised him, and they were soon trotting off. They would be in Derby within the hour. Liverna hoped the change of scenery would help heal the pain in the boys' hearts. She feared the only thing that would heal the pain in her heart was to hear from Rowena. Where was the dear child?

Chapter 24

Rowena was vastly relieved they had safely arrived at the Bluchers' home in the tiny village of Whitby. She would get to see her daughter. Hold her in her arms. Rejoice in their reunion. Oh, but what adventures she would have to tell Cecily – everything from helping in Yardley's escape from jail, to fooling the militiamen who came searching for Yardley, to her delightful visit with the Guildfords and Mister Guildford's sister and brother-in-law, the Drapers. Then the trek from the Guildfords' to the Nadlers', and what a night that had been on a cornhusk mattress with Nate sleeping at her side. Nate had had no choice but to pass her off as his wife. Nate trusted the Nadlers, but the fewer people who knew her true identity, the safer they all would be. Yardley, still in disguise, slept in the barn with the Nadlers' two sons.

Upon being helped to dismount by Nate, Rowena noted the Bluchers' home was substantial if old. Nate had belatedly informed Rowena that the Bluchers were his cousins. At least, Ailred Blucher's wife, Gisla, was his cousin. When pressed, he admitted Ethelinda Tavers was his cousin, too. Gisla was the daughter of Ethelinda's older sister. Ethelinda also had a younger sister and two brothers, and they all had children. Rowena wondered how Nate could keep up with so many cousins. She had but two cousins, her Uncle Gaylord's two sons.

Nate, masquerading as Ailred Blucher's brother, John, again had no choice but to introduce Rowena as his wife. As Gisla and Ailred had not married until sixteen fifty-two, a year after Nate changed his identity and became a highwayman, none of the Blucher servants had previously met Nathaniel D'Arcy so they had no knowledge of Nate's and Gisla's relationship. Nor had the servants known Ailred's brother, John, or that John had gone to Virginia and promptly died there, so they readily accepted Nate as Ailred's brother.

Rowena had expected to embrace Cecily, but Chapman was again the first to greet them. He quietly informed Rowena that her daughter and Arcadia were still young boys. In fact they were Will Jamieson's young brothers. Consequently Rowena had to wait until Gisla Blucher escorted them into the parlor and sent the servants on various errands before Rowena and Cecily could at last rejoice in their reunion.

"My sweet child," Rowena said. "We have so much to speak of, but when we may have the chance, I can only guess."

"Not here," Chapman said. "We dare not chance the servants becoming suspicious."

"I fear, too," the pretty blond-haired, blue-eyed Gisla said, "that as you are posing as Nate's wife, we will have to put you and Nate in the same bedchamber." Unlike Ethelinda, Gisla bore no resemblance to Nate.

Giving her hostess a wry smile, Rowena said, "Considering we spent last night together on a cornhusk mattress on the floor in the Nadlers' main living quarters, they being but small landholders of the yeoman class, I think we will manage here."

"Oh, Mother," Cecily said with a giggle, "we stayed at the Nadlers' and Dev and Arcadia and I slept on that same cornhusk mattress, and the husks stuck through the ticking and crunched every time one of us moved even the least little bit."

"That will need be enough exchanges for now," Chapman said. "Walls can have ears. Remember, Arcadia is Bob and Cecily is Peter, and speak no more in a familiar fashion."

"Jack is right," Nate said. "Mind your tongues. Much depends on how well we play our parts in this drama."

"We had an early dinner," Gisla said, sweeping her arm around to indicate Chapman, Dev, Arcadia, and Cecily. "With Ailred in Chester everyday but the Sabbath, we have our larger meal in the evening when he returns home. But, on the chance you might be arriving today, I had Cook keep the porridge warm, and he has tarts he can bake that will be ready once you have seen to your ablutions. So, let me escort you up to your room." She looked at Chapman. "You will see Mister Yardley receives a meal?"

Chapman smiled. "Aye. I will also see he is settled in the dormitory, and that the groomsmen are seeing to the horses."

"Thank you, Jack," Nate said and chuckled. "No doubt Cyril will enjoy the jocularity of the groomsmen. He is so relieved to have that paint washed from his face, he will be ready to swig a little ale and tell a tall tale or two. But all of you remember, he is but Jed." 'Twas a role he had played more than once when at the Bluchers.

With Chapman headed for the stables, Nate and Rowena followed Gisla up to the room they would be sharing. "This is the room we reserve for my mother when she visits," Gisla said, opening the door to the bedchamber. "Ailred's mother never visits. She says she hates this house. True, it is dark and can be drafty, but Ailred and I are slowly making changes, making it brighter. Anyway, this room has a day bed. Mother likes to come up for a nap after the noon meal. I think it should provide an adequate sleeping couch for you, Nate."

"It will be perfect," Nate said.

Gisla looked over her shoulder to make certain none of the servants were hovering near-by, then she looked at Rowena. "I know under other circumstances this would be unacceptable, you sharing a room like this, but all caution must be preserved."

"I am way past worrying about my reputation, Mistress Blucher. All that matters is keeping my daughter and everyone else safe."

Gisla smiled. "Yes, you are right. Well, fresh water is in the pitcher, and I will have a maid come up to help you change once Nate, I mean John, is done with his ablutions, and comes back down to the parlor."

"Thank you," Rowena said, thinking how kind the Bluchers were to help her and Cecily, knowing if they were discovered they could be hit with a large fine if not imprisonment. She marveled that so many people were so ready to help them – the Tavers, the Prestons and Tourneys, the Haywards, the Bussards and Guildfords, even the simple Nadlers, and now the Bluchers. Generous and good-hearted were all these people.

※ ※ ※ ※

D'Arcy hurried his ablutions so to give Rowena her privacy. He had never been so drawn to any woman. The more time he spent with her, the more time he wanted to spend with her. Their sojourn at the Guildfords' had been relaxing for both of them. The militia had been fooled. Yardley was safe, though he would have to spend the day in the head groomsman's room. With that worry dissolved, D'Arcy had determined he would get to know Rowena better. Since he no longer had to keep secrets from her, when alone with her, he could answer her questions and amuse her with tales of some of the robberies. And he had learned more about her. He had learned she had been a good and faithful wife, but that she now despised the husband who had sold her daughter to Haspel. He could not blame her. The thought of Haspel taking Cecily to his bed turned his stomach.

Their excursion with the Guildfords to Rowell and Amata Drapers' Pine Knoll manor had been a delightful way to keep Rowena from worrying about Cecily. Amata, Guildford's sister, was the perfect hostess, and enjoyed showing Rowena around the ancient manor house. The house dated back to Henry IV, and Amata Draper, once she married Rowell, had insisted the house be kept as it had originally been designed. The only things she allowed to be added to the ancient dwelling were more and better drawing chimneys. She took great pride in showing her guests around her home, and D'Arcy had enjoyed watching Rowena take in all the details of the intriguing establishment. Portions of Rowena's home, Crossly Oaks, dated back to the rule of Stephen, and Rowena and Amata had exchanged several tales of their homes' heritages.

The Drapers' older son and his wife had joined them for dinner. The couple had their own modern home past a stand of pine trees and across the stream that ran the length of Pine Knoll manor. The younger Drapers not only preferred having their own abode, they liked the lightness and brightness provided by the many windows, the decorative stucco ceilings and walls, and the comfortable, elegant furnishings and lighting in their home. D'Arcy admitted the sparse, heavy wood furniture of Pine Knoll offered little comfort, but it seemed to suit Amata and Rowell Draper. D'Arcy knew, too, the house concealed a number of secret rooms and passages, though their existence was not mentioned to Rowena.

Bringing his thoughts back to the present, D'Arcy dried his face and hands, brushed his coat and breeches, and with a nod to Rowena, he vacated the bedchamber that Rowena might have her turn at cleaning up. Later they would dress for supper when Ailred Blucher returned home, but for the present, they were being treated to a light repast.

The Bluchers' home was also old, but it had no grand history. It dated from Elizabeth's time on the throne and had been Ailred's mother's dowry. His mother had never wanted to live in or even visit the house. She liked Chester, so Ailred and Gisla had eagerly accepted it for their home. Ailred rode the six miles into Chester daily to work with his father in his counting house and warehouses.

Blucher's father, grandfather, and other ancestors had ever been in trade, but over the years, his family had shrunk. Blucher had but a widowed sister who lived with her parents in Chester. The Bluchers were prosperous merchants, and Ailred and Gisla had every reason to believe their one-year old son, Merrill, would one day continue in the trade.

D'Arcy regretted that Rowena's reunion with Cecily would be all too short. They would be leaving the following day. He wanted to get Cecily to his sister. Lady Grasmere, her husband, and young daughter were currently, as was their usual in summers, at Lord Grasmere's manor in Westmoreland. For his part in fighting for and supporting Charles I, Lord Grasmere had spent time in prison, but after paying his large fine, he had been released but was restricted to his two manors, Harp's Ridge in Cheshire and Knightswood Castle in Westmoreland.

D'Arcy also wanted to get Yardley far away from the Cheshire militia. Not until they neared Whitby had Yardley been allowed to remove his disguise. They stopped by a stream, and Yardley set about scrubbing away the alabaster powder and red ochre from his face. He peeled away the beeswax that had been used to make his bulbous nose. After four days of enduring the disguise, his skin was red and raw, but at least he was no longer painful to look upon. He would continue as their servant until nearing Grasmere, but he no longer had to look so hideous, though his hair still needed washing. That would be accomplished before they set out in the morning.

They would be traveling in two separate groups. D'Arcy and Rowena and Yardley would travel together, and Chapman would join Dev and Arcadia and Cecily. Still best to keep Cecily and Rowena separated.

They would stay at different dwellings at night, though they might occasionally encounter each other when they stopped in inns or taverns for meals. Such encounters would give Rowena the opportunity to see that her daughter was safe. At night, Chapman and his group would stay, when possible, with known royalist supporters. D'Arcy had no choice but for him and Rowena to stay in inns as man and wife. He wondered how long he would be able to keep his distance from Rowena. If she gave the least little hint she would encourage his advances, he would be lost.

Yardley, as their servant, would stay in a dormitory with other men. D'Arcy wished he could keep Yardley in the room with him and Rowena as they had been able to do when traveling with Cecily. Well, they would ride as hard and fast as they could without drawing undue attention. He wanted to get to Knightswood as quickly as he could. What then? What would he do to keep Rowena safe? He had no idea, but at least when at his sister's, he would not have to be sharing a bedchamber with Rowena.

The night they spent on the cornhusk mattress at the Nadler's had been a sore test for him. Though they were both near fully clothed, he had ached to touch Rowena, to taste her lips. He had forced himself to breathe slowly until he heard her steady breathing and knew she slept. He had his back to her, and she had turned from him, but sometime during the night, she had rolled over, and he had awakened to her breasts pressing against his back. Gads! How much temptation was he to be forced to endure?

At least at the Prestons' he had had his own room, and at the Guildfords' he had been safely ensconced on his cot in the closet. Here at the Blucher's he would have the daybed. He would sit up late with Ailred so hopefully Rowena would be asleep as she had been the nights they spent at the Guildfords'. But what he would do at an inn, how he would control his urges to hold Rowena, he simply had no idea.

Chapter 25

Rowena was stunned by the beauty of the lake country they were traveling through before reaching Knightswood Castle, Lord Grasmere's manor. The land was breathtakingly beautiful. Chapman, as was his usual, had forged ahead to prepare Lord and Lady Grasmere for their guests' arrival. The last night of their trek, both groups joined up and stopped at a secret enclave, a partial cave halfway up a mountainside and hidden by a dense stand of trees, that had more than once be a refuge for Nate and his highwaymen.

Rowena wondered how Nate had ever found it. He had chuckled. "'Twas but chance. We need know every place we can find that will offer us a place to hide are we being chased, so we are ever alert to what nature may offer us. I was heading back to Knightswood after turning over our gains for the King to my brother when the rain poured down in sheets. I needed out of the storm. I saw a deer and her fawn disappear into these woods. I decided that mother deer might know something, so I made my way up here, and following the deer path, I found this cave."

The cave was large enough to shelter all of them. Stashed under what appeared to be a pile of fallen rocks were several blankets bound in canvas. After the horses had been watered at a stream trickling out of the mountainside, and hobbled, Nate declared they had best settle down for the night before darkness was upon them. He would allow no fire for fear the light would be seen and give away their hideaway. They shared a supper of bread and cheese washed down by water from the trickling stream. The blankets were spread as bedding for the three women. Situated to the back of the cave, Rowena at last had time to sit and talk with her daughter, to hold her close and pray she was doing the right thing in deciding to leave Cecily with Lady Grasmere.

In the morning, Cecily and Arcadia would be turned back into young women, and Yardley would no longer be a servant. He was known to the Grasmere servants as a gentleman. This was not the first time he had masqueraded as a servant, and he played his part well, but he was ready to resume his own identity. Cecily would have to keep her hair tucked up under a lappet cap until the darker color faded and her own hair grew back out. Or mayhap 'twas best did they keep her hair covered even when it grew out. Cecily's pale hair was so distinguishable.

Rowena heard Nate discussing with Dev and Yardley how they were to get Arcadia back to her home. Would not be safe for some time for Yardley to go home so he could not escort her. She could not travel alone with Dev or Nate. No plan being formulated, Nate suggested they all get some sleep. Surely his sister would help solve the dilemma.

Arcadia whispered to Cecily, "Do I have my way, they will not quickly be finding a way to send me home. I have a mind to spend more time with Dev."

Cecily giggled, and Rowena smiled. She could not blame Arcadia for wanting more time with the handsome, Dev. Was she not hoping to find a way that she could spend more time with Nate? She knew she should not be thinking about Nate. She was a married woman, even if she never wanted to set eyes on her husband again. But her reputation had already been so compromised, she could not see that she could do it much more harm. So why not enjoy Nate's company?

Stretching out on her blanket, she wished her daughter and Arcadia a good-night. The cave was near pitch black, but soon she could make out the shadows of the three men as they settled down for the night. They were resting against their saddles, and having given all the blankets to the women, they had naught but their horse saddle blankets to throw over their shoulders. At least the night chill was not great.

Soon she heard her daughter's soft even breathing followed by Arcadia's. The men's heavier breathing was punctuated by an occasional snort. The sounds of nature floated about in the air; an owl hooting then the flutter of wings, frogs croaking, the horses stomping about and munching on what grass they could find, the call of some bird not yet settled in its nest. All seemed peaceful, and Rowena expected to be lulled into sleep, but instead her mind went racing back over the past week. Days and nights she had spent alone or near alone with Nate.

The better she got to know Nate, the more she wanted to know about him. That he was the second born son of the Earl of Tyneford had been a surprise. She had not realized he was a member of the D'Arcy family that dated back to the Norman invasion. It was an old, aristocratic family with manors scattered about England and Wales. Nate's older brother, Kenrick, the Earl of Tyneford, was confined to his parish for his support of Charles I. Ill from his months in confinement after Charles I's defeat, Kenrick had not broken his parole to fight for Charles II, but Nate had. That could be a hanging offense, and it made Nate a wanted man who dare not return to his home, or at least not for extended visits.

Nate traveled openly about the country and seemed not to fear recognition, but Rowena had learned he was ever alert. He heard things and saw things and even seemed to feel things that she was not at all aware of. Even at the Bluchers' he had not let down his guard. He had checked the door, the windows, and had his weapons always handy. His concern for her safety and for Cecily's was ever apparent, especially now they were again together.

If she had not known before, she now knew with certainty that she and Cecily must be separated. 'Twas too dangerous, not just for them, but for all the people who had helped them. She hoped she would like Nate's sister. He had assured her she would. All the same, she would be leaving her daughter in the care of a woman she would spend no more than a couple of days getting to know. She had told Nate about her jewelry. If she could not trust him with that knowledge, she could not trust him with hers and Cecily's lives. He had agreed would be best to leave the jewelry with his sister, though he doubted his sister would have any need of it.

A hot flush crept up Rowena's neck to her face as her mind drifted back to that night on the cornhusk mattress with Nate. They had each turned their backs to each other, but she had not been able to go to sleep until she heard his rhythmic breathing. 'Twas her action during the night that caused her embarrassment. In her sleep, she had rolled over and cuddled up next to Nate. She awoke when Goody Nadler came from her bedchamber and started stirring up the fire in the hearth. She had near gasped out loud when she found herself pressed against Nate. She had hastily rolled away from him, but the mattress had crunched under her, and she had little doubt but what Nate had been aware of her nearness and her hasty move away from him.

She had tried to joke about sleeping on the mattress with Nate and make light of the situation to her daughter, but all the same she wondered about Nate's thoughts. Was that why he decided when they left the Bluchers' they would pose as brother and sister rather than husband and wife at the inns they stopped at on the way to Grasmere. That way she had a room to herself, and he slept in the inns' dormitory rooms with Yardley. She had missed having him near after so many nights of having him within calling distance if not closer. He had made her lock her door and told her not to open it to anyone but him or Yardley. She liked that he was protective of her. At the same time, she worried his fear for her safety would make it harder for her to convince him to let her join his gang.

Well, she hoped in the couple of days they would be spending with Nate's sister that she would be able to convince him she would be an asset to his highwaymen and their schemes.

※ ※ ※ ※

Preston shifted enough that he could see out of the mouth of the cave and up to the stars. D'Arcy had not been concerned that they would be discovered in their hideout, yet he felt they needed to keep a lookout. Did any animal or human advance on their sanctuary, the horses would sense them and would alert them, but the guard on duty would need be aware of all sounds. Preston had volunteered to take the first watch.

His thoughts turning to Arcadia, as they had been doing all too often, he wondered if he dared consider taking a wife. That Arcadia favored him, he had no doubt, but would she continue to wait year after year for him? Might she grow tired of waiting and decide to wed another? Other members of their gang, Madigan and LaBree, had married, yet they still took to the road when D'Arcy beckoned. Yardley was married. But how seldom was he able to be with his wife and children. And look what had happened on his last visit.

Preston frowned. If he were to marry Arcadia, where would she live? Would she continue to live with her parents, and he, like Yardley, would have to grab what few chances he had to be with her? He could hardly leave her with his parents. No, how could he marry Arcadia? Yet, how could he not? His desire for her had grown even greater since being in her presence the past fortnight. He had needs, physical needs, and he had no mind to relieve them with a doxy that might give him the plague.

D'Arcy and Chapman had to have the same needs. He wondered what they did. He knew D'Arcy had to be struggling with his attraction to Lady Crossly. That Lady Crossly was attracted D'Arcy was just as apparent. He could not help but feel sorry for them. Unless Lady Crossly allowed her reputation to be besmirched, they could have no chance of finding love together. Well, on the morrow they would arrive at Knightswood. He would have to wait to see what the future might offer him and his friends.

※ ※ ※ ※

D'Arcy was pleased he had the last watch. He liked seeing the day break, watching the stars disappear and the sky turn pink then orange as the sun slowly rose. He would have everyone up early. Arcadia and Cecily had to be turned back into young ladies, Yardley into a gentleman. He expected his sister, Phillida, to have all ready for her guests when they arrived. Cecily would be introduced to the staff as the daughter of a dear friend, and all would be told Phillida would be fostering Cecily. Rowena would be the chaperone who had been hired to escort Cecily to Knightswood. She would next be escorting Arcadia home after her visit to a friend. Did all go as planned, they, minus Cecily, would be back on the road in a couple of days.

Where they would go, he had yet to determine. He had near promised Rowena he would take her to Derby to see her sons. But was that a safe thing to do – for her, or for him and his highwaymen? Yet, the thought of being separated from Rowena was not to his liking. Besides, he had yet to come up with any place he thought would be safe to leave her. And how would she support herself? Then there was still Arcadia, and they had not decided how to get her home.

Two of his other henchmen, Madigan and LaBree, were expecting to meet him at the Bluchers' to head out on their next expedition, but he would have to send Chapman to tell them the plans were changed. They would meet in Manchester instead. Repeatedly, Madigan's wealthy wife, Delphine, Grasmere's cousin, had offered to send funds to the King so they could stop their robberies, but he had not believed that safe. Did anyone discover she was supporting the King, her wealth could be confiscated or at best greatly taxed. She proclaimed she would rather have her wealth confiscated than her husband shot during one of their robberies, but her husband agreed with D'Arcy. 'Twas too risky. The Major-Generals and their assistants were poking into everything and were suspicious of anyone who might be a Royalist and owe a decimation tax. They would love to get their hands on Delphine's vast wealth.

So the highway robberies would continue. But for how long, D'Arcy was beginning to wonder?

Chapter 26

Within moments of meeting Phillida Lotterby, Lady Grasmere, Rowena no longer feared leaving Cecily in her care. The lady was regal, yet gracious, and laughter danced in her blue-green eyes that were so like Nate's. She was a handsome woman with dark hair, a high forehead, a straight jaw line, high cheek bones, and a curvaceous mouth often spread in a winning smile. Her daughter, Timandra, was an adorable five-year-old with her mother's eyes and her father's slim aquiline nose, jutting chin, and firm mouth. Lord Grasmere was equally welcoming, and despite his often austere visage, he showed naught but gentleness and bright smiles to Cecily.

Knightswood Castle was a square, dark-stone, two-story keep with a high wall circling it. Nate told Rowena that Lady Grasmere had insisted Berold, Lord Grasmere, make some major improvements to the keep was she going to spend her summers there. A decorative screen was added to cut the great hall in half. The front portion of the hall was still used for greeting guests and for Berold to meet with his tenants or to hold court to settle disputes. The back half, with its new chimney, was now a dining chamber. Lady Grasmere had the chapel remade into two bedchambers. One was a dormitory for their female servants, the other was for the couple, Tomas and Claudia Burch, who maintained the keep and were its only inhabitants nine months of the year.

Lady Grasmere retained the solar for her and Lord Grasmere. It served as their bedchamber and private parlor. The rest of the first floor was turned into four small bedchambers to house Timandra and her nurse and any guests, which they had more often than not.

Within the surrounding courtyard, the separate kitchen had been rebuilt in stone, and the stables were moved further from the keep. Lodging for the male servants who came with them from Harp's Ridge were housed in a dormitory close to the keep. All the other various out buildings from pig sty to hen coop to dovecot to laundry shed were located beyond the gardens next to the back wall. The keep had a bowling green on one side and a small formal garden on the other side where the ladies could sit beneath beech trees and talk or read or sew. And to please his wife, Lord Grasmere built a small pavilion just outside the wall where Lady Grasmere could enjoy a view of the lake and the hills and the village of Grasmere.

The village of Grasmere was not part of Knightswood Castle manor, but its residents had long been on good terms with the Lotterbys. Rowena had not been surprised by the immense swath of denuded land beyond the keep that was naught but stumps and grassland filled with grazing sheep. So many Royalists had had to sell off their woods to pay their fines for having supported their King. At least with the denuded land, Lord Grasmere could graze more sheep, and wool was profitable.

Rowena wondered if the lack of woodland created a hardship for the Lotterby tenants who would depend on the wood for fires and the acorns for feed for their pigs. "What of his tenants? How do they fare?" she asked Nate.

"Most still farm," Nate said, "but some work the fulling mill, others raise cows and make cheese, some are growing hemp, and others are grazing more sheep. These tenants have tenure that allows them more freedom than in many sections of England. Many have prospered and are yeoman farmers or close to it. The fells still supply many of their needs, not just for fuel, but for thatching, and peat is available if wood is hard come by. I think 'tis the beauty that is missed as much as the woods and the acorns."

"I have thought to put the three women in the chamber Venetia and Delphine use when here," Lady Grasmere said, interrupting Nate. "Lana," for such was the name they had given Cecily, "will sleep on a cot for a couple of nights. I have made up the other two guest chambers for you and Mister Chapman and for Mister Preston and Mister Yardley."

"'Tis perfect, Phillida," Nate said.

Rowena was pleased Lady Grasmere had put the women in one bedchamber so she and Cecily could have at least a couple more nights together. But to think that from the present into the unknown future,

Cecily would be Lana Marcroft, Rowena found sad. Cecily would have to tell everyone she met that she was from a village outside York. Nate told her much about York and the surrounding area, and Cecily, being a quick study, promised she would have no trouble remembering her York home, though she said she found being from Virginia more fun.

Briefly joining Lady Grasmere in her brightly decorated solar, Rowena handed over her jewelry to her hostess. Lady Grasmere readily accepted the jewelry, promised to keep it safe, but said she doubted she would have need to sell any of it. "I will take great pleasure in having new gowns made for Lana, though we will be able to do little until we return to Harp's Ridge, there being few choices of fabrics here. But I know a seamstress in the village who can alter a couple of my gowns so Lana will have more choices of things to wear."

"We could hardly ask you to give up your gowns, Lady Grasmere," Rowena said.

Fluttering her hand, Lady Grasmere said, "'Twill give me good reason to have new gowns made for me. My blue bombazine silk and wool blend gown is showing its wear, but it can be cut down to make a good travel gown for Lana. Now, you are not to worry about her. We will also see she has a warm cloak by the time the weather cools and we head back to Harp's Ridge. And Timandra already adores her. Lana will be like a big sister to my daughter.

"Tomorrow morning," Lady Grasmere added in a lowered voice, "after everyone is rested, we will go out to my pavilion where we may be certain of our privacy, and we will discuss what is to be your fate, Mistress Holloway."

Rowena sighed. Her new name was to be Bess Holloway. She wondered how many more names she would adopt before she would ever be able to resume her own name, if ever. With a little smile, she thanked Lady Grasmere for all she was doing for her and her daughter. She knew she was leaving Cecily in the safest possible position.

※ ※ ※ ※

Though she loved dressing as a boy and riding astride, Arcadia was pleased to again be in a gown. Now she could flirt with Dev Preston and no one would think aught of it. She had decided did she have to seduce Dev she would. She meant to marry him. That he was attracted to her she had no doubt. And with Cecily's helpful questioning, she had learned he was not promised to any secret lover. Cecily, upon learning of Arcadia's love for Dev, had fallen in with Arcadia's plans to win Dev's heart. Arcadia found Cecily to be a bright and spirited girl, and she had developed a true fondness for her.

Upon learning of Cecily's forced marriage to Haspel, Arcadia had said, "Should anything happen that you should again fall into Haspel's hands, take a knife with you to bed and stab him in the groin. That is what I would do was I forced to wed someone like that. For certain, he would quickly be seeking an annulment."

"Mother thinks within the year he will seek an annulment," Cecily said. "But I will not feel free and safe until I am turned twenty-one and cannot be forced into a marriage."

"Well, you will be safe with Lady Grasmere. She and my sister, Sidonie, became good friends, and they correspond on a regular basis. Sidonie even says does she ever have a daughter, she intends to name her Phillida after Lady Grasmere. Anyway, I have no doubt you will have a grand time being fostered with Lady Grasmere."

Her thoughts turning back to Dev, Arcadia looked at herself in the mirror hanging over the washstand. She hated having to tuck her dark hair under a lappet cap, but it was too short to let it hang lose or to braid it. Cecily had the same problem, but she was not trying to seduce Dev. Pinching her cheeks and biting her lips, Arcadia brought some color to her face, but she wished she had some kohl for her eyes. Not that her mother would approve of that, but then, her mother had seldom approved of anything she had ever done.

She had to admit, she had always been in trouble for one thing or another. Some things were her own fault, but not everything. Her brother William should be blamed for the time she climbed into the meadow with the bull. Had he not dared her, she would never have been so foolish. Well, mayhap it was not exactly a dare, but 'twas close enough. William and his dearest friend, Adler Hayward, had been standing at the fence admiring the bull when William said, "Father has warned us all that bull is a mean one. Not even Arcadia will get in the pasture with him." Was that not a dare? At least she was swift and had outrun the bull. William and Adler had grabbed her and pulled her up and over the fence before the bull could jab her with his horns.

And then the time she and Sidonie had been admiring the new piglets, and Sidonie's kitten had squiggled out of her arms and fallen into the pig sty could not be blamed on her. Sidonie had screamed and Arcadia had naturally jumped into the pig sty to save the kitten from the mother pig. It was not her fault the kitten had been hard to catch, and she had slipped more than once into the mud. How William and Cyril had laughed, and of course they had told Adler and Caleb Hayward about the escapade. Arcadia could not do a thing that her brothers failed to share with the Haywards. Not the time she fell from the tree when again rescuing Sidonie's kitten. Or the time she hid in the cook's outdoor bread oven and nearly got closed inside. She could not now remember why she had been trying to hide, but she must have had a good reason. The list went on. So why should she now worry about whether her mother would approve of her plan to make Dev marry her? Of course, she would not.

Chuckling to herself, she turned from the mirror and smiled at Cecily who looked oh so pretty in the pink fustian gown that had been made for her when she had stayed with D'Arcy's cousin. 'Twas a true shame to have to keep Cecily's beautiful pale blond hair tucked under a cap, but it would be a necessity for many a year to come.

"Shall we go down to supper?" Arcadia asked.

"Aye, I am ready," Cecily said. "Are you ready, Mother? I mean Mistress Holloway."

Arcadia caught the wane smile Lady Crossly gave her daughter. Poor woman, having to leave her daughter and having no place she could call home. She could not help but feel sorry for the older woman. Brightening at Lady Crossly's nod, Arcadia slipped her arm in Cecily's and the two left the room together with Lady Crossly following more slowly.

Chapter 27

After placing wine, cheese, pasties, and nuts on the trestle table in Lady Grasmere's pavilion, the servants departed, and Lady Grasmere asked for attention. "Berold, dear," she addressed her husband, "will you please pass out the cups of wine. Everyone else, are you at any point hungry, help yourself to the pasties and cheese."

Everyone thanked Lady Grasmere and Lord Grasmere when he handed them their wine. They were all settled on the benches on either side of the table, but Rowena's nerves were frayed. Her future would be determined on this day, in this pavilion. Could she convince Nate to let her join him? Or would he find her some position in some home, and she would not know if she would ever see him again or when she would see her daughter?

Seated around the table were Lord and Lady Grasmere, Nate, Dev, Yardley, Arcadia, Cecily, and herself. Chapman had left that morning to take a message about the change of plans to Nate's other highwaymen. Drawing in a deep breath, Rowena tried to calm her racing heart.

"Nate has told me, Lady Crossly, rather, Mistress Holloway," Lady Grasmere said, "that you are wishful of seeing your two sons."

Surprised that Nate had told his sister of her wish, Rowena nodded. "Yes, I had to leave them without so much as a hug. I know not how they feel that I would so desert them."

"Oh, Mother," Cecily said, taking Rowena's hand. "They will understand. Liverna will see to that."

"Liverna?" questioned Lady Grasmere.

"She was my nurse, my maid, and my children's nurse," Rowena said. "She has ever been right hand."

Lady Grasmere nodded. "Good to have such a devoted servant. My maid, Adah, is devoted, but she serves only me. Never would I trust her with any children. She is not the cheeriest of souls, but she can do wonders with my hair and gowns."

"I have told Rowena, uh, I mean Lady Crossly or Mistress Holloway… Gads!" Nate growled. "Can we be a tad informal here. I offered to take Rowena to see her sons. Mayhap I should not have done so, but I did."

"Might I say something here," Rowena said, looking first to Lady Grasmere and then to Nate. "I do believe I have proved myself to be good at assuming whatever role I am given. And I was an asset in helping free Mister Yardley." She looked at Yardley, and with his nod, she heaved a deep breath and continued. "I believe, as I am already considered a member of this gang of highwaymen by the Cromwellians, that I can see no reason not to continue on as a member. I can ride well. I sleep wherever I must lay my head, witness the Nadlers' cornhusk mattress, the barbarous inns, and the cave just two nights ago.

"I am healthy, and I am attractive enough to draw men into conversation." She looked at Nate. "Since we were traveling as brother and sister, when we sat down to eat, men, once they found out Nate and I were not married, were only too eager to converse with me. I have no doubt I can as easily gain information from Cromwellians as Nate or Dev or anyone else. I can wear wigs, wear face paint, ride astride if necessary. So. I wish to join your gang, Nate."

Cecily sat open-mouthed staring at her mother, but Arcadia applauded her. "What a grand idea! I think I would also make a good member of the gang. I can be a boy or I can dress as a woman and flirt with the merchants or tax collectors."

"Indeed you shall not!" Yardley exploded. "Good lord, Mother would have my hide."

Lady Grasmere held up her hands. "Wait, wait. Please, let us talk this out." When everyone looked at her, she continued, "I can understand Lady Crossly's desire to ride with you, Nate, rather than assume a role as a nursemaid or a companion to an elderly woman, or who knows what occupation you might be able to find for her. Certainly, she would not impose year after year on any family you might think to settle her with unless she could support herself.

"As she has informed me, her reputation is already in tatters, and she already has a bounty on her head. Wherever she might stay, she will be at risk. She might possibly be safe acting as housekeeper at Wynn Alawn, Kenrick's manor in Wales." Rowena remembered that Kenrick was Nate's older brother and was the Earl of Tyneford. "But that manor is so far away," Lady Grasmere continued, "and she would never get to see her daughter. I cannot like the idea of Lady Crossly putting herself at risk, but as I said, she will be at risk or unhappy almost anywhere she may be."

She looked at Arcadia. "You, though, young woman, are not to even think of riding with Nate's gang. Did anything befall you, I could never again face your dear sister. However, we do have the problem of how to get you safely home. I would think the best thing would be for you to go with Nate and Dev and your brother to Derbyshire with Lady Crossly as your chaperone. After Lady Crossly has seen her sons, Nate and Lady Crossly must then see you safely home."

Arcadia's lip was in a pout, but as she learned she would not have to immediately start home, she brightened a little. Yardley seemed relieved Lady Grasmere had been firm with his sister. But what did Nate think of his sister's conclusion? Rowena looked at Nate and found him looking at her. She smiled. "What say you, Nate?"

"I say you may ride with us until I can come up with a better plan. But I cannot like it. I cannot think 'tis safe for you."

"Thank you," she said. "You will see, you will not regret it."

Yardley was shaking his head. "I am with Nate. I cannot think it wise. At times, we must ride long and hard. Other times we hide out in most disreputable places. Far more disreputable than the Nadlers' or that cave. Places where the men are coarse and use vulgar language. Places no lady should experience."

"I agree with Yardley," Lord Grasmere said. "'Tis not something a lady should be exposed to. At the same time, I remember Mistress Hayward was of great value in providing her husband and others of your gang with cover. No one expected a woman heavy with child to be traveling with highwaymen. A woman," he glanced at Arcadia, "even two women could make men eye you less suspiciously when you stay at an inn."

"Berold does have a point there," Lady Grasmere said. "Though I would think when you get closer to her home, 'twould be best to disguise Lady Crossly. Perhaps with a blond wig. The description of her is that of a dark-haired woman." She glanced at Arcadia. "The militia will be less apt to suspect a fair-haired woman with a young dark-haired companion."

Arcadia beamed. She was to be allowed to take part in the expedition.

"So be it," Nate said, a scowl darkening his face. "Rowena, take a stroll with me. We will have much to discuss are you to be traveling with our gang, even if for a short time."

"Go ahead," Lady Grasmere said. "I will take Cecily, I mean Lana, upstairs with me, and we will become better acquainted."

"Yardley," Lord Grasmere said, "I have a treatise I wise to give you to give to Hayward. 'Tis on potatoes. 'Tis written by the Royal Horticultural Society. They think potatoes should not just be for swine and cattle, but 'twould be good for people with limited acreage in the place of a wheat or rye crop. 'Tis interesting."

"I will be happy to take the treatise to him. Caleb has two lectures planned. One in Chester, one in Whitby where he was to meet us. When he arrives in Whitby, the Bluchers will tell him to meet us in Manchester instead."

Rising, both men headed off together, and Rowena, after giving Cecily a kiss on her cheek, rose and joined Nate outside the pavilion. As they set off in the direction of the lake, she heard Lady Grasmere say, "Mister Preston, you have been here before. You are familiar with the grounds. Do you show Mistress Yardley about. The garden is quite lovely right now. I wish to have time to talk with my new foster daughter, Lana."

Rowena guessed Arcadia would be delighted to be sent off to view the grounds with Dev. And she hoped Cecily and Lady Grasmere would enjoy getting know each other. Sighing, Rowena could but pray she was doing what was right for Cecily and for herself.

※ ※ ※ ※

Arcadia was near skipping. This was the first time she had ever been alone with Dev. If she could but get him to kiss her, she knew she could get him to proclaim his attraction to her. Mayhap even love. Her insides tingling, she forced herself to keep from laughing joyously. When Dev proffered his arm, she took it and smiled up at him. She had taken special care with her dress. Of the gowns Lady Grasmere had offered her, she had chosen a scarlet-colored gown with a gold petticoat. The petticoat and gown were a little large, but Adah, Lady Grasmere's personal maid, had taken them in at the waist, then she and another maid had hurriedly shortened the hems. Arcadia needed to be careful not to catch a heel in the hems for they were loosely stitched. Adah had also curled Arcadia's short thick dark hair and pinned it atop her head in a most becoming fashion so Arcadia had not needed to don her lappet cap.

Dev lead Arcadia back inside the courtyard and toward Lady Grasmere's garden. It was a lovely garden with the scent of roses in the air. Arcadia and Dev had not spoken on the way to the garden other than when Dev said, "Mind your step here," when they had to skirt around a sunken area in the path leading to the garden. Benches under shade trees dotted the garden and pebbled paths meandered around flowers and shrubs.

"'Tis a lovely garden," Dev said. "My brother-in-law's mother created such a garden at Reverie Manor. Reverie is my brother-in-law and sister's home. It borders on my parents' home, Britteridge."

"You must miss your home very much," Arcadia said. "I know Cyril misses Woodspring terribly. And of course he misses Tamar and his children."

"I do miss my home and family," Dev said. "I was pleased to get to see my family before we headed for the Haywards', but I have to stay with my sister. I cannot stay at Britteridge. Always a chance a servant might report me to the militia as one of your servants reported Cyril."

"Indeed, 'tis worrisome. I doubt not but Father will dismiss the maid who told the Jaggers' groomsman about Cyril being home. And most likely, the Jaggers will dismiss the groomsman who reported on Cyril to the militia. I cannot wager when it might again be safe for Cyril to return home. Tamar will be so woebegone."

"'Tis hard on the wives when their husbands ride off to an uncertain fate," Dev said, turning their steps toward the back wall of the garden where a small fish pond was shaded by a large oak tree. "I cannot think 'tis fair for the wives," he added. "I know Mistress Madigan and Lady Tuftwick are always frightened when their husbands ride off with us."

"Yes, my sister, Sidonie, feels the same when Caleb rides off. I know she has tried to convince him that he has done enough for King Charles."

"My mother and father have said the same to me," Dev admitted, pulling out his kerchief and dusting off a bench next to the pond. He urged Arcadia to sit then sat down beside her, but he was not looking at her. His eyes seemed to be looking at something Arcadia could not see. When he brought his gaze back to her, he said, "I worry my parents grow old, my two youngest sisters turn into young women, my sister, Hestia, will birth her child, and I am not there to see any of it. I could not even be present for Hestia's wedding."

Arcadia was not prepared for Dev to take her hands in his and to raise them to his chest. "I cannot even court you, Arcadia. How many years have we known each other, yet what do we know of each other? I know you are brave and willful and you can ride as well as any man, but I know naught else about you. And was I not in this gang, I would like to pay you court and learn more about you."

Near breathless, Arcadia whispered, "Would you, Dev? I hoped you found me attractive. I prayed I was not mistaken, but to hear you say you would like to court me makes my greatest wish come true."

His grasp on her hands tightened. "Do you mean that, Arcadia? Cyril did tell me he thought you might have a tender for me, but I dared not believe it. Well, even did I believe it, I dared not act on it. I have no right to court you. No right to take a wife. 'Twould not be fair to you. I see how hard it is for Caleb and your brother and Maddy and Tuftwick to leave their wives. Having spent these days with you, I could not go on without telling you of my feelings."

Her heart turning flips, Arcadia slowly shook her head. "My dear Dev, could you only know how long I have been waiting for you to tell me you care for me. I have loved you from the first moment I met you. I have refused every offer for my hand because I kept hoping I could win your love." She looked down then back up. "Have I won your love, Dev?"

To answer her, he released her hands and crushed her to his chest. "Oh, yes, my sweet Arcadia. You have my love. And to know that for all these years you have been loving me. It astounds me. Yet how can I take you to wife and then leave you? In fact where would I leave you?" He pulled a little away from her and looked down at her upturned face. "I should not have used you like this. I cannot ask you to marry me. And yet…and yet…, oh, God!" Again he pulled her to him and claimed her lips in a ravenous kiss.

Arcadia responded with a fervor that matched his. So many years she had waited for this moment. Her arms went around his neck, and she gave herself up to the emotions rampaging through her. He loved her. He loved her and nothing else mattered. They would find a way to make their marriage work. If Cyril and Tamar could do it. If Sidonie and Caleb could do it, then she and Dev could do it. Even if they had to endure long separations, how sweet would be the reunions.

But then, heady thought – was she married to Dev, no one could tell her she could not go with Dev. Like he said, she could ride as well as any man. If Rowena could ride with them, then why could she not. What mattered now was to convince Dev they must be married despite all that might stand in their way.

Chapter 28

Knightswood having no parlor, after dinner Phillida and her guests gathered in her solar. It was an airy, comfortable room with warm mats and large cushions on the floor, and small tables next to padded chairs. A sideboard displayed two candle sets and two crystal decanters, one holding brandy, the other sherry. After accepting a small cup of sherry from her husband, Phillida smiled at her brother lounging on a cushion next to the chair Rowena had seated herself on after carefully arranging the folds of her gown. The poor woman, having but three gowns to her name, was being careful of them.

That Nate had finally fallen in love was obvious, and it pleased Phillida. He was past an age when he should have taken a wife. That he had fallen in love with a married woman was unfortunate, but if the love he bore Rowena Crossly might convince him to give up his precarious game of hide and seek and flee to Europe, she would voice no disapproval.

That Lady Crossly was in love with Nate was just as apparent. Of course, the lady would feel guilty that she had such feelings for Nate, but Phillida was guessing love would eventually win out. Even were they not married, Nate and Lady Crossly could live together as man and wife. Did they go to Europe, and did King Charles accept them as a couple, as no doubt he would, they would not be socially estranged.

For five years, near six, Nate and his gang had been helping to support King Charles. They sought out wealthy Cromwellians, robbed them, and were then forced to live in hiding. 'Twas too dangerous. Yes, Nate was a superb organizer. He was ever cautious, but it would take but one slip for him to wind up with a bullet in his chest or a rope around his neck. She could not forget that two years earlier Caleb Hayward had been shot in the chest and would have died if not for his wife, Sidonie. And now, Cyril had been captured and imprisoned, and Nate had had to put himself, Lady Crossly, Sidonie, and others at risk to free Cyril. No, was there any chance Lady Crossly might be the agent to make Nate give up being a highwayman, then she would support the lady in her desire to stay with Nate and join his gang.

Turning her attention to Arcadia and Dev Preston, Phillida judged the two had finally confided the love they shared. Sidonie had written that her sister, Arcadia, refused all suitors and near had her mother in hysterics. But Sidonie knew Arcadia was in love with Preston. Noting the way Preston cast sly glances at Arcadia when the girl was not looking, Phillida believed Preston was enamored of the pretty lass. What better way to let the young lovers discover their love than to send them off to the garden together? By the way the two were looking at each other, lightly touching each other, whispering together, 'twas obvious their love was no longer a secret.

She chuckled. Berold was attempting to engage Yardley in conversation, but Yardley's attention kept being drawn away to his sister. Soon Arcadia and Preston would have to announce their wish to wed. As Preston, like Yardley and Nate, had a price on his head, finding a way to have their banns posted could prove troublesome. Still, it could be managed.

Her gaze shifting to Cecily, Phillida watched the pretty girl cling to her mother. One more day at most, then mother and daughter would be separated for only the Lord knew how long. Cecily was all any mother could wish for in a daughter, pretty, bright, cheerful, and loving. She would make a wonderful companion for Timandra. Phillida's five-year-old daughter was enthralled by Cecily and was currently having her nap with her head pillowed in Cecily's lap. The chatter of the adults seemed not to disturb the child, and Cecily, sitting on a cushion at her mother's feet, was being careful not to wake Timandra.

Yes, Phillida believed a true bond would be formed between Cecily and Timandra. Torn from her mother, her family, her home, with no idea what lay ahead in her future, Cecily would need someone to fill the void in her life. And Timandra, for a couple of years now, had been longing for a friend. Phillida kept hoping she would have another child to be company for Timandra, but despite a vigorous love life with Berold, she had not gotten with child.

Her musing was brought to a halt when Preston, after being poked by Arcadia, rose from his cushion, and clearing his throat, he looked at Yardley, and said, "Cyril." He swept the room with his arm. "Well, everyone. I wish to tell you that Arcadia and I have decided, or rather, I have asked Arcadia for her hand. She has given her consent. Of course, normally, I would first have asked her father if I might court her, but circumstances being what they are... And both of us being more than of age...Well." He shrugged.

Yardley rose from his chair beside Berold and slapped Preston on the shoulder. "I did warn you she had her eye on you. Are you certain you know what you are doing? You will have your hands full with Arcadia."

Nate was laughing. He had also risen and stretched out his hand to congratulate Preston. "I wish the best to the both of you. I know not how soon you plan to wed. Finding you a safe place to post the banns may prove a problem. You dare not post them at Malpas or Nantwich. Dev's name is too well known." He looked to his sister. "What say you, Phillida?"

"I say congratulations to both. Did we not need take every precaution now that Lana is with us, I would offer the two to stay at Harp's Ridge while their banns were posted at Frodsham. But did anyone question the banns, we dare not expose Lana to any Cromwellian."

"Ahhh, you are right," Nate said.

"The Puritans' new law that banns must be posted and that the ceremony must be done by a Justice of the Peace have made getting married difficult," Phillida said, looking at Arcadia and Preston. "'Twould have been so simple to pay for a special license, and you could be married at your own time and place."

"Well, the wedding will not be taking place any time soon," Nate said. "We have a visit to Derby for Rowena to see her sons, and we might well have a couple of robberies to pursue before Dev and Mistress Yardley can even tell their parents of their plans."

"True," Preston agreed, looking at Arcadia, "but the sooner we can inform our parents and make the arrangements for our marriage, the sooner I will like it."

Nate chuckled. "I understand your feelings, Dev. We will endeavor to get you back to your brother-in-law's manor as soon as may be possible. But until then, Arcadia, like Rowena, must play her role."

"And so I shall," Arcadia said, her eyes bright with enthusiasm.

Phillida hoped Arcadia and Lady Crossly would be safe with Nate and his gang of highwaymen. She admired both women. She would not be willing to put herself at risk for King Charles, as much as she wished him back on the throne. She but wanted her brother safe. And she hoped Lady Crossly would be the one to lead him to a more sedate lifestyle.

Chapter 29

Rowena was thrilled Nate was taking her to see her sons, at the same time, parting from Cecily had been the most difficult thing she had ever done in her life. She trusted Lady Grasmere would take great care of Cecily, but until Haspel requested and received an annulment, she could not help but worry about her first-born child.

Having arrived at an inn in Manchester after two and a half days of hard riding, Rowena was not surprised to find Chapman already there. Caleb Hayward was also there as were two other highwaymen she recognized, but she could not remember their names. As the other two acted as though they were complete strangers, she doubted she would meet them until some future date. She liked that she and Arcadia were riding astride instead of on side saddles. Nate had decided they would not be able to ride hard enough if they rode on side saddles. Nor could they be transformed into men if the need arose. Wearing breeches under their skirts, she and Arcadia had their modesty preserved, and they had much more freedom of movement.

Arcadia, an accomplished horsewoman, was reveling in her role. She and Rowena were acting as sisters, and Nate was their brother. Dev was but a friend who was traveling with them for safety's sake. Having Arcadia along meant Rowena and Nate no longer had to pose as husband and wife. Relieved she would not be sharing a room with Nate, Rowena, at the same time, missed having him near. She knew she was drawn to him. Maybe she was even falling in love with him. But what good would that do her. She was married. She should not be entertaining any thoughts concerning Nate, yet she could not seem to keep her thoughts off him.

That she was now to be a party to a highway robbery was both exhilarating and frightening. Fact was, she was responsible for Nate's decision to relieve their prey of his ill-gotten gains. At the inn in Manchester, she had not deliberately lured the pompous robust man to her side. But once he learned she was a widow, and Nate was her brother not her husband, he had become verbose in his eagerness to impress the pretty widow.

"I am bound for Chester." He patted two hefty panniers stretched across his lap. "I have enough in these pouches to buy whatever I might wish when I reach Chester. The finest house, the finest coach, the finest clothing, all can be mine. And how did I come by such largess you might ask?"

Rowena had not asked, but the man barreled on as though she had. "By being astute," he bragged. "I bought a Royalist's manor for a pittance. The government needs funds to pay its militia, and they are eager to find buyers for confiscated manors. Once the manor was mine, I sold off the timber and raised the rents the tenants pay. Lord knows they were paying too little. And I rented out the manor house." He chuckled, and again patted the panniers. "A wealthy man I now am, that I tell you."

Shrewdly eyeing Rowena and running his fingers over his thin moustache, he said, "And I might well be looking to take a wife."

Rowena smiled. "'Tis sorry I am that we head to York." She nodded at Arcadia who was talking quietly with Dev. "My sister formed an attachment that was not suitable, so our brother decided he would take her to our aunt's. Sadly, I must also go, being a widow as I am."

The man frowned. "York. Quite a distance."

Rowena nodded and grimaced. "Yes, quite a distance. But do tell me, Mister Barr, surely you are not traveling these roads without protection."

"Nay. I am no fool." He pointed across the room. "See those two belswaggers swilling down the ale but keeping their eyes on me?"

Rowena saw two large, shabbily-dressed, unshaven men with lank, dirty hair and narrowed eyes watching her and Mister Barr. She nodded and said, "Yes, I see them."

"They are armed and know how to use their poppers. They will see me safely to Chester. Bonded they are. Anything happens to me, their families could lose all their possessions."

"Oh, indeed, you are a wise man," Rowena praised him, and he beamed at her.

"Yes, yes," he said. "York is quite a distance. All the same…" He tilted his head and licked his lips. "It might be worth my while to visit York."

Before Rowena could form an answer to Barr's lascivious look, Nate put a hand on her shoulder and said, "Anna, 'tis time you got your sister to your chamber. To my thinking, she has spent too much time talking with Mister Jamieson."

Relieved to be rescued from Barr, Rowena rose immediately. "Of course, John. I should have been paying more attention to her."

Barr rose as Rowena did and grasped her hand. "I hope I will see you come morning, Widow March. You have made this evening a more pleasurable experience than I had been expecting." He again licked his lips. "And who knows, mayhap we will meet again."

Forcing a smile, Rowena said, "How nice that would be. Now, I bid you good evening."

Nate, seated at the end of the table, had to all who might have been observing him, appeared to be in deep conversation with Chapman, but Rowena knew he heard every word Barr uttered. When he had heard enough, he ended the play and sent Rowena and Arcadia up to the safety of their bedchamber.

The next day, while she and Arcadia waited restlessly in the woods bordering the highway, Nate and his gang awaited Barr and his henchmen.

Chapter 30

Arcadia wished she and Rowena could join in the robberies, but D'Arcy was adamant – no, they would not participate in the robberies. Fact was, he would not even allow them to witness the robberies. "Do you not see us commit any robberies, you cannot swear on oath that we robbed anyone," D'Arcy said.

And so between Manchester and Derby, three Cromwellians had been relieved of their treasures, but neither Arcadia nor Rowena could offer testimony against D'Arcy or any of his men. Though not allowed to help with the robberies, Arcadia could not think when she had ever had a livelier or more exciting time. She had envied her sister, Sidonie, when Sidonie had been Lady Grasmere's guest and had traveled with her to Knightswood Castle, but now, not only had she, too, visited Knightswood, she was also seeing numerous other parts of England. And, she got to spend her days riding at Dev's side.

Chapman had left with his panniers bulging. He would cache them, and then rejoin them in Nottingham, their next venture after Derby. They would then circle around through Leicestershire, Staffordshire, and Shropshire before finally returning to Cheshire. Now, the objective was to find a way for Rowena to see her two sons. Arcadia was elated when D'Arcy decided she and Dev would be the ones to visit Crossly Oaks and talk to Rowena's maid, Liverna. That D'Arcy would trust her with the assignment was an honor.

Through Liverna, they would arrange some way, some place Rowena and her sons could meet. As the plan fell into place, Arcadia and Dev, pretending to be brother and sister, rode up to Crossly Oaks. Though a small portion of the keep dated from the days of King Stephen, it no longer had a wall surrounding it, just a circular drive that appeared to be lacking in care. After helping Arcadia down from her horse, and with her leaning on his arm, they could not know who might be observing them, Dev rapped on the heavy wooden door.

The door was opened almost immediately by a youth dressed rather sloppily in Sir Lindell's livery. He looked surprised by the couple at the door, but hastily allowed them entrance when Dev explained his sister had taken ill, and he thought to bring her to the nearest house.

An old man, much more neatly dressed, advanced on them. Round eyes under bushy eyebrows looked them over carefully, gauging their status. "I am Sir Lindell's steward. How may I help you?"

Dev introduced himself as Will Jamieson and Arcadia was his sister, Mistress Jamieson. "We have been visiting friends north of here and are headed home, but my sister complained she was feeling faint and feared she might fall from her horse. I saw your house and hoped we might find aid here. Might there be a lady's maid or nurse to see to my sister. She ate little this morning. I hope she is but faint from lack of refreshment."

The steward was immediately solicitous. He sent the footman who had answered the door to fetch Liverna. "She is the children's nurse," he said, then escorted them to the parlor. While Arcadia sank gratefully onto a plush damask covered couch and Dev took a straight-back chair near the hearth, the steward rang for a maid. He ordered the maid to pour some port for the Jamiesons then to ask cook to put together a small tray of refreshments while he informed Sir Lindell of his guests.

Trusting she could maneuver a private meeting with Liverna, Arcadia accepted the port. They had not long to wait before Liverna hurried into the parlor. Arcadia smiled feebly at the woman and placed her hand to her cheek. "Oh, I think the port has helped, but I still feel so weak. I cannot think what has come over me?"

After introducing himself and Arcadia, Dev said, "Mayhap I should leave you in the nurse's care, my dear. I will wish to thank Sir Lindell for his hospitality. No doubt soon the maid will return with a small repast for you." With a bow to Liverna, he exited, quietly closing the door behind him.

"Now, child," Liverna said, taking a seat beside Arcadia. "I understand you feel faint. Does aught else pain you?"

Straightening, Arcadia smiled brightly and grasped Liverna's hand. "I am fine and I come with glad tidings for you and Milo and Godwin."

Liverna's pale eyes grew large, and she drew back from Arcadia. "What do you mean?"

"I mean I bring you tidings from Lady Crossly."

Liverna's hands tightened on Arcadia's hands. Her thin lips quivering, she asked, "She is alive? She is well?"

Arcadia chuckled. "She is indeed, and she is most desirous of seeing her sons."

Releasing Arcadia's hands, Liverna clutched her chest. "She is here?"

"She is nearby, but is well hidden."

Letting out a deep sigh, Liverna said, "My prayers have been answered."

A tap on the door had Arcadia slumping back against the cushions on the couch. The footman, his livery now smoothed and neatly buttoned, opened the door for the maid who carried a tray with thin slices of bread and cheese and two small tarts on a platter.

"Set the tray on the leaf table, Agnes, and be so kind to pour me a port."

"Yes, Liverna," the maid said.

Once the maid left, Liverna took a long sip of her port before saying, "I believe I had need of this. So, please, tell me more. What of Cecily? Is she safe and well?"

Again sitting up, Arcadia took a tart, nibbled on it, then smiled at Liverna. "Cecily is safe and well. She is in a good home where she may remain until she is of age. Her mother hated to part from her, but 'tis safer for both are they not together. They are too recognizable when paired. Besides, Lady Crossly desperately wants to see her sons and be assured they forgive her for leaving them."

"Of course, they forgive her. In fact, they have naught to forgive. They know their mother did what she had to do. But how is it Lady Crossly comes to be with you? Haspel has been spreading terrible rumors that she is in league with highwaymen."

"How silly," Arcadia said with a giggle. "She is with friends, though, and we have brought her here. What we need from you is a way that she may see her sons. Tonight would be a blessing could you arrange it. 'Tis dangerous for her to stay around here too long."

Slowly nodding, Liverna looked thoughtful, the wrinkles around her mouth and eyes more apparent. She cocked her head. "Yes, once the house is asleep, I will awake the boys. Tell Lady Crossly we will meet her behind the dairy barn when the moon is straight up in the sky. I will say naught to the boys until I awake them, otherwise they may be too excited."

Arcadia nodded. "That would be wise. Guess I had best finish this and my port so all will think I was but faint from lack of nourishment."

"You and your brother are most kind to be doing this. To be taking this risk."

"We are happy to thwart any Cromwellian," Arcadia said before finishing off the tart.

"I will tell your brother you are much improved," Liverna said as Arcadia reached for the second tart. She had not realized she was hungry until she started eating.

Playing his part with gusto, Dev returned to the parlor. "Ah, my dear, the nurse says you are feeling fit again. Fit enough to resume our journey."

Gulping down the remainder of the tart, Arcadia nodded, drained her glass of port and smiled at Dev. "Yes, I do believe 'twas naught but hunger. I hope you have thanked Sir Lindell."

"I have. But you must meet him and thank him yourself."

Arcadia was shocked by the man Dev introduced. He had obviously lost a lot of weight for his clothing drooped on him. His disheveled hair was dirty and lank. He was stoop-shouldered, and his face appeared etched with pain. Proclaiming he was pleased he could have been of service to her, he wished her a safe journey to her home, but no joy reached his bloodshot eyes, and naught but a weak smile touched his lips. He seemed eager for his unexpected guests to be on their way. Arcadia could almost feel sorry for the man did she not know what he had done to his daughter and his wife.

Chapter 31

Keeping to the shadows, D'Arcy watched Rowena's reunion with her sons. After the boys had repeatedly hugged Rowena, her faithful maid, Liverna, had her turn. "Oh, my lady, my lady, my prayers have been answered. I have been so worried about you and Cecily, but I understand from your friend that Cecily is well and safe."

"She is," Rowena said, releasing Liverna and again drawing her sons into an embrace.

"Did you really join with highwaymen to free Cecily?" the younger boy, Godwin, questioned, his bright eyes reflecting the moonlight when he looked up at his mother.

Rowena chuckled. "I was blessed that highwaymen had stopped Haspel's coach, and they were kind enough to help me free Cecily from Haspel's clutches, but that is all I can tell you of those highwaymen. Nor must you ask me who befriended us. I will tell you nothing that could give away Cecily's safe home."

"Ah, we would not tell anyone, Mother," the older boy, Milo said.

"I know you would not deliberately do so, my dear son," Rowena answered and planted a kiss on her older son's head. "All the same, do you not know anything, you cannot tell should you be pressed – say should anyone threaten your father."

"Humph! We care not what happens to Father. What he did was rotten. Rotten to the core!" Milo said, his lower lip thrust forward. "We are not speaking to him. We spent the remainder of the summer with Uncle Gaylord, but had to return home just two days ago to take up our studies with Mister Hail. Father says he cannot afford to send me to Eton."

"Things are not good here," Liverna said. "Money is tight. Haspel placed a high tax on Sir Lindell. He said he was in league with would be rebels and highwaymen, which of course he is not. Your Uncle Gaylord arranged a loan and is using your stipend to make the payments, but the interest is high, and it takes your entire stipend to keep the interest rates from going higher. Your uncle said he knew that is what you would want for Milo."

"He is right. Crossly Oaks must be preserved," Rowena said, rubbing Milo's shoulder.

Wagging her head from side to side, Liverna said, "Sir Lindell sold off all his cows. That is why this spot behind the dairy barn was a safe place to meet. He has only sheep now, and he buys our dairy needs from your brother. He let the gardener go so Crossly Oaks is looking rather shabby. For servants, there is but me, the cook, the house steward, a footman, the laundress, one downstairs maid, and one groomsman."

"And Mister Hail," Godwin said.

"Yes, the boys' tutor. He dines with Sir Lindell, but Sir Lindell eats little and drinks much. He has lost a tremendous amount of weight. He is a lonely and sick man to my thinking."

"I fear in my heart I can feel no sympathy for him," Rowena said, her voice cold. "Cecily is in hiding. I have a warrant on my head. It is all his doing."

"We still have the coach horses, but he sold most of the riding horses, Mother," Milo said "We have a pony for Godwin, and we still have your horse, Flyaway. I ride her now. I hope that is all right with you."

"Of course, Milo. I am proud of you that you can ride her."

"Uncle Gaylord had us take riding lessons while we were with him. He says as a baronet, I will have certain standards I must adhere to. And riding to the hunt is one such."

Rowena laughed softly. "Well, 'tis possible you may someday ride to the hunt. However, 'tis more important you learn how to make Crossly Oaks stay solvent. I trust your Uncle Artus, and Uncle Gaylord will see you get the proper education for that." She looked up at Liverna. "Speaking of Artus, he is well? Was he heavily taxed, also?"

"He is well, and he was able to convince a judge he was no Royalist and had not supported any insurrections, but he still was hit with some taxes. Your father having fought for Charles I. He is using a portion of his stipend to pay off the loan your Uncle Gaylord arranged for him so he would not have to sell any of his woodland."

D'Arcy hid a chuckle. 'Twas Rowena's brother's very woodland that had sheltered them until the moon rose, and they could meet Rowena's sons and maid behind the dairy barn. Waiting alone with Rowena beside a trickling stream that Rowena said her father had loved to fish had not been easy. He no longer had any question in his mind, he was in love with Lady Rowena Crossly. Wrongly so, maybe, but her husband's actions had driven her from her home. To him, Sir Lindell Crossly had forfeited any claim to his wife, marriage vows or no.

His thoughts returned to Rowena when she handed Liverna a letter. "This is for Artus. In the future, are we to meet, he must arrange the time and place. I would hope to have more time with my sons. In the letter, I name two men who will contact him, Mister Chapman or Mister Hayward. Mister Hayward knows much about new farming methods that are proving profitable, and I think Artus should pay him heed. Mister Hayward or Mister Chapman will be our connection through Artus with you and the boys. Should the letter fall into the wrong hands, it is not signed by me, nor did I write it, though I did dictate it. You must assure Artus it is from me."

Liverna took the letter and tucked into her bodice. "So will I do, my lady."

"Lady Crossly," D'Arcy said. "We must leave. We dare not linger here too long."

Looking in his direction, Rowena nodded. "Of course, we must not take chances." She hugged her boys again and for a moment, they clung to her. She kissed each of them, gave another hug to Liverna, and with tears glistening on her cheeks, she turned to D'Arcy.

"I am ready," she said.

He brought their horses out from the side of the barn, and after allowing Rowena and her sons one more hug, he hoisted Rowena up onto her saddle and mounted his horse. Rowena waved, her sons waved, and Liverna waved, then he and Rowena trotted silently back across the field and up to the road that would lead them to their night's abode.

※ ※ ※ ※

The hour being late, Rowena appreciated their hosts welcoming her and Nate so graciously into their neat yeoman home. The couple housing them were Royalist friends. D'Arcy seemed to know near everyone, she thought. Two small children slept on a fold down bed in the hall, and Dev was stretched out on a cot. Another cot awaited Nate. Rowena was escorted up to the loft to share a thick mattress with Arcadia. They would rise early in the morning, and with Rowena sporting a blond wig, they would meet up with the other highwaymen and learn whether they had any prospective prey, before they moved on to Nottingham.

Rowena had learned the highwaymen seldom stayed in the same inns or homes. Better they not be seen together. Yardley, Hayward, and Chapman, when not off on one of D'Arcy's errands, would stay at one location. The other two highwaymen, Torrance Madigan and Henry LaBree, Lord Tuftwick, were at a different inn or home. Rowena was amazed that, Lord Tuftwick, a Baron, was a member of Nate's gang. Of course, no one knew he was a baron. Like the others, he had a fake name. They all had fake names.

They seldom stayed in the same inns with any consistency. They preferred their faces not become too familiar to any innkeeper or his help. They also preferred inns in larger cities and towns. More choices of inns, and more choices of travelers meant more opportunities to discover who might be a Cromwellian or better yet, a tax collector.

Hugging herself, Rowena let her tears slide down her cheeks. To be separated from the children she loved so dearly was terribly hard. At least the boys had Liverna. And they had her brother, Artus, and her Uncle Gaylord. And Cecily had the kind and gracious Lady Grasmere. Her children were safe, but she was now riding with a gang of highwaymen. She could at any time tell Nate he needed to help her find a place to stay. Help her find work, but she knew she would not do that. She was in love with Nathaniel D'Arcy. He was everything Lindell was not. Strong, courageous, and honorable. She would not be parted from him.

Her thoughts drifted back to the evening spent with Nate in the wooded area Lindell had surrendered to her father when she had agreed to marry Lindell. 'Twas a marriage settlement. Her father got the woodland and fish stream he wanted, and Lindell got a young wife and her stipend left to her by her mother's father. Some might think her father had sold her, but she had married Lindell of her own free will. She had been happy enough in her marriage, but she had been so young when she got married. She had not known what she was missing. She knew now.

She might not be able to marry Nathaniel D'Arcy, but she had already decided she meant to be more than just friends with him. She wanted to experience what other lucky women were experiencing. She saw the love between Sidonie and Caleb Hayward, between Ethelinda and Herman Tavers, between Lady and Lord Grasmere. She wanted her chance at that love. She had no doubt Nate was in love with her. Had he not put his gang at risk by taking her to see her sons. Had he not insured Cecily was safe with his sister.

And this afternoon, had he not come close to taking her in his arms. She had watched him struggle with his desire versus his honor. To take another man's wife was wrong. He knew it. She knew it. So instead, they had talked of his large family, his multiple cousins, and of her family, her father before he went off to war and after he returned home but a shadow of his former rugged self. She and Nate both knew they would be unable to fight their desire, their love forever. Something had to give. Wrong or right, Rowena meant to claim her love.

※ ※ ※ ※

Preston sighed. He had been sleeping peacefully until Nate and Lady Crossly arrived. He hoped the meeting with Lady Crossly's sons had gone well. He could understand Lady Crossly's feelings. His parents felt the same about him. They hated that he was always on the run. Now that he was committed to marry Arcadia, he found he could not even consider being parted from her. How Caleb or Cyril left their wives was beyond him. With his desire for Arcadia growing more intense each day, he wondered how much longer he could wait until they were married.

They had to find someplace they could safely have the banns read for three weeks. Someplace no one would be suspicious of strangers. And it would not be too soon for him. How he was again to get to sleep with thoughts of Arcadia, her kisses, her soft body pressed against his rampaging through his head was the question? Damn! He needed some solution and soon.

Chapter 32

D'Arcy hated that he would no longer be able to leave his takings with Winnlock Measure. To his thinking, there was hardly a more secure place anywhere in England than Measure's safe. And Measure was a true and devoted Royalist. Yet, the mere act of returning to Burslem to collect what he had already left with Measure was risky. He almost decided not to stay with the Taverses. He would not want to cause more trouble for his cousin, but Chapman had given them an all clear. No militia hovering about. And Ethelinda was now confident her servants were loyal. None would report he and Rowena had again stayed at the Taverses' home.

Rowena had been pleased to learn her husband's horse, Dalton, that she had ridden to rescue Cecily, had been sold to a good home in Leicestershire. "According to Druce Howell, the youth who spirited the horse away," Ethelinda's husband, Herman, said, "he sold the horse and the saddle to a true gentleman. Druce made a good profit and came home by stage. No one questioned his story that he had traded his horse to a dark-haired woman making her way to London. And, he had a nice visit with his sister who lives in Leicester."

"Druce is a good lad," D'Arcy said, settling back in his chair in the Taverses' comfortable parlor. "Now, let me again thank you for housing all of us this evening." Rowena and Arcadia were sharing the chamber Rowena had shared with Cecily. He had his usual chamber, but Chapman was sharing his chamber with Caleb, and Dev was sharing his with Cyril.

Having lucked out on learning about a tax collector on his way to London with his pouch near to bursting, they had robbed the man just outside Leicester. They had left the tax collector and his two armed guards bound up along the highway so the men could not dash back into Leicester and alert the militia. All the same, they had needed to ride hard and long to distance themselves from the robbery.

D'Arcy had decided with the tax haul, when added to their other recent robberies, as well as what he had in Measure's safe, they had enough to send to the King. After Dev and Arcadia's wedding, other than the newly married couple, his gang would need take to the road again before winter set in, but for the present, their pouches were bulging. Knowing that after the last robbery they were no longer needed, Tuftwick and Madigan had headed for their homes rather than continue on to the Taverses'.

Henry, Lord Tuftwick, had volunteered his home, Tuftwick Hall, as a safe place for Dev and Arcadia to abide while their wedding banns were read and posted. Nate had no doubt Tuftwick's and Madigan's wives would see Dev and Arcadia had a lovely wedding celebration. He planned to be there for their wedding as he had been at Grasmere for Tuftwick's and Madigan's weddings two years earlier. And it would be a nice respite for Rowena. She would enjoy meeting the two highwaymen's wives. And D'Arcy hoped his sister, Phillida, would arrange to come to the wedding and bring Cecily. That would be the perfect place for Rowena to get to see her daughter.

D'Arcy had enjoyed seeing his cousin, and he knew Rowena had also enjoyed seeing Ethelinda, especially now she knew Ethelinda was D'Arcy's cousin. To everyone's regret, D'Arcy and his gang could stay but the one night. Bright and early in the morning, they had headed into Burslem. They split into groups, but they were all bound for Nantwich. Dev would get to introduce his future bride to his family, then a quick visit with Arcadia's parents, and Dev, Arcadia, and Cyril would head to the Tuftwick manor in Lancashire.

After a sad farewell to Measure – both men knew D'Arcy would no longer be able to leave his plunder with the old goldsmith, the risk now being too great with the militia on the lookout for the man known as Drummer – D'Arcy, hefting his heavy packs filled with six months' worth of stolen coins and jewelry, exited Measure's shop. He had sent Cyril, Arcadia, and Dev on ahead. Caleb and Rowena awaited him at the edge of town, and Chapman had left at first dawn for Nantwich to prepare the Tourneys and Prestons for their visitors.

While securing the packs onto his horse, D'Arcy saw a pretty woman cocking her head and staring at him. He knew the woman – David Pettigrew's widow. David had been a dear friend, but he dare not acknowledge his friend's widow. Ducking his head, he hoped his hat would hide his face, but his maneuver failed.

"Mister D'Arcy? It is Mister D'Arcy, is it not?" Mistress Pettigrew said, advancing on him, a bright smile on her face.

"Nay, Mistress, the name is Drummer," he said, gruffly. "You have mistaken me."

The woman blushed. "Oh, I do beg your pardon, sir. Just, you look so much like…" She shrugged and shook her head. "Well. Sorry."

A man striding past swung abruptly about. "Drummer? Did you say, Drummer? I know that name. Not three months ago, you stayed at Herman Tavers' with a dark-haired woman and her daughter. I need speak with you."

The man had the look of a militiaman, brown jerkin over a plain linen shirt, loose breeches and floppy boots, and a cape slung over one shoulder. And he was well armed. The mustache over his upper lip twitching, he narrowed his eyes in a menacing fashion.

D'Arcy knew he could not afford to be questioned. Not with what he had in his packs. He had no choice but to ignore the militiaman, swing up on his horse, and ride out of Burslem as fast as possible. He knew the militia would soon be after him, but he also knew he could lead them on a merry chase before he chose to lose them.

"You! Come back here! Come back here, I command you!" the militiaman hollered, running a few steps after D'Arcy.

Glancing over his shoulder, D'Arcy saw the militiaman turn back to Mistress Pettigrew. He was obviously questioning her as he pointed at D'Arcy's fleeing figure. What Maura Pettigrew would tell the militiaman he could but guess, but it would not benefit him. Soon the man would round up other militiamen and the chase would be on.

Galloping past a second man who hollered at him to stop, he spotted Caleb and Rowena. Seeing him on the run, they spurred their horses and joined him. He could wish they had not. The second man who hollered at him would connect them to him. They now had no choice but to flee with him. At least Rowena was again wearing her blond wig. At some point he might be able to risk letting her and Caleb make their way back to Caleb's on their own. But was he willing to take that chance? Caleb on his own would have no trouble, but did he need at any point to explain Rowena's presence, he might run into problems.

His thoughts whirling about in his head, he raced ahead with Rowena and Caleb trailing after him.

※ ※ ※ ※

Rowena had no idea what had happened in Burslem, but she gripped her horse's reins, dug her heels into his flanks, and raced after Nate. She knew Nate had been fearful of returning to Burslem. He had considered bypassing the town, but he had left too many prizes there. Between what he accumulated before she entered his life, and what he and his highwaymen had appropriated since they set out from Manchester, he had a bountiful haul to hand over to his brother to take to King Charles II.

Chapman had some of their more recent prizes buried at the bottom of his pack. He would stop by to inform the Prestons and Tourneys of their visitors and would then go on to the Bluchers where he would wait for Nate and Rowena to join him. Rowena was to stay at the Bluchers' while Nate and Chapman rendezvoused with Nate's brother. Nate would then return for her, and they would go to Lancashire to be on hand for Dev's and Arcadia's wedding.

Rowena was happy for the young couple. She envied them. She had hoped she and Nate might reach some sort of understanding, but though they had traveled through six different counties and had relieved a tax collector and several Cromwellians of their monies and treasures over the past month and a half, Nate kept his distance. To her thinking, the man was a bit too honorable. She loved the way he looked at her, the way his hands lingered on her hips when he helped her down from her horse, and sometimes she heard the deep sigh he heaved when he turned from her after making certain she and Arcadia were secure in their room at night.

Everything had gone so smoothly since she and Arcadia had joined the highwaymen. Chapman had even joked the two women were like good luck charms. Not only had their victims been well-heeled, relieving them of their valuables had been simple, swift, and without mishap. And they had taken great pleasure in relieving the excise tax collector of his funds. The excise taxes not only hurt the poor, they helped fund Cromwell's militia. But now something had gone wrong, and she could but wait, wonder, and ride.

※ ※ ※ ※

The horses needing a breather, and believing he and his companions had put a good distance between them and their pursuers, D'Arcy slowed his horse. Rowena and Caleb rode up next to him.

"What happened," Caleb asked, a worried frown creasing his brow.

D'Arcy explained how the widow of a friend had recognized him. With a wry twist to his mouth, he admitted 'twas the name Drummer that caused the problem. "'Twas unfortunate an alert militiaman was passing at the time I used my fake name. I should have said Blucher. I should have known the name Drummer was now connected with Rowena and Cecily."

"Oh, then this is my fault," Rowena said. Before he could disabuse her of that idea, she added, "And the Taverses. Will they again be questioned?"

D'Arcy shook his head. "Could be. But both Ethelinda and Herman will play innocent. I wish I had paid heed to my instincts and not again involved them, but 'tis always so comfortable with them. I overruled my own doubts."

"We all do that from time to time, Nate," Caleb said. "But what are your plans now? Do we take to the fields and bypaths?"

D'Arcy pursed his lips before answering. "Nay. The militia are apt to spread out and cover the bypaths as well as the highway. I think we will ride hard as far as Nantwich. We will ride through the town heading to Chester, making certain we are seen. Once we have left the town behind, then we will take to the bypaths and make our way to Malpas and the Drapers."

"Ah, the Drapers. Good choice," Caleb said. "What of Dev and Cyril and Arcadia?"

"We will catch them soon and will tell them what has happened. Are they questioned by the militia, they will say they saw us and will tell them we appeared to be headed to Nantwich."

"Think you they might be mistaken for us? Two men and a woman."

"Nay. The militiaman got a good look at me. And with Rowena's blond wig, they will be looking for a blond-haired woman. The good thing is, Dev and Cyril carry none of our bounty. Were they to be searched, they have naught but their clothing, and my clothes, in their packs. My packs being completely filled with our treasure trove."

"Aye, we will trust all will go well with them. I do think the horses are some rested, should we not put them to the run again."

"We will keep them to a slow canter, but do we see the militia approaching at a fast clip, we will take to the fields. These horses can jump anything. I am betting militia horses are not so able." He looked at Rowena. "Now hear me good, Rowena. Does it look as though we might be caught, I will stand and fight. But you must, and I repeat, you must ride on with Caleb. Do you understand me?"

Her dark eyes round, she slowly nodded. "You are thinking of Cecily. She must be our first thought. As must be Caleb and his family." She looked at Caleb. "Yes, I will ride on if need be. But let us get going so we will not need make such a sacrifice."

Nate chuckled. "Agreed." And putting his heels to his horse, off they went.

Chapter 33

Preston played his part well. It being the third time two of the militiamen had encountered him, they now felt they knew him and could vouch for him. One of the two did stare at Arcadia overly long, but she batted her eyes at him and spoke in a shy whispery voice that she felt so much safer knowing the militia were on the highway. "My brother and I are so grateful we fell in with Mister Jamieson, but now we can feel even safer," she added breathlessly.

They gave the militia a good description of the blond woman and the two men, but they were no help with the horses. "What were their horses like?" Preston said when questioned. "I cannot say I paid them any heed." He looked at his soon to be brother-in-law. "What of you, Mister Blake?"

Cyril shook his head. "I was swatting the dust from my face. They left us in a cloud."

And so the militiamen had ridden on, and Preston had breathed a sigh of relief. His only real concern was how quickly they had come up on them after Nate, Caleb, and Lady Crossly had passed. He could do naught now but pray the three would reach Nantwich and take to the country bypaths before the militia could catch up to them.

※ ※ ※ ※

Not but a couple of miles outside Nantwich, Chapman was more than a little surprised when D'Arcy, Lady Crossly, and Hayward came racing up the road behind him. Something had to be wrong. They should be considerably behind Yardley, Arcadia, and Preston. Waiting for them to reach him, he patted his horse. He was as comfortable on foot as on horseback, but when carrying some of their prizes in his pack as he now was, he preferred to be riding. He had never had any highwayman attempt to rob him, but he could never be too careful. He never traveled late in the evenings, and he often took to byways did he feel a highway to be unsafe.

Upon learning the situation, Chapman agreed with D'Arcy's plan. His own plans would change little. He would stay an extra day with the Tourneys before heading for the Bluchers'. Once there, he would await D'Arcy and Rowena, knowing they would be delayed by several days as they would have to wait in hiding until the militia gave up the hunt.

Having ridden with D'Arcy for six years, he had no concern that D'Arcy might lose his way on the back bypaths of Cheshire. D'Arcy now knew them as well as he did. And they could find no better place to hide than with the Drapers. Brilliant.

※ ※ ※ ※

Near dropping from exhaustion, Rowena sighed when D'Arcy turned off the trail they had been following since the moon had come up, and they headed into the woods. Caleb had left them a little ways back with Nate's admonition he should head for his home on the morrow once he was rested. The trail she and Nate now followed was little more than a deer path. Had she not tied a lappet cap tight about her head, the tree branches would have snatched the blond wig from her head. She had no idea how many miles they had traveled since morning. If she had to guess, she would think well over thirty. She guessed the poor horses had to be as weary as she was.

They had stopped for a long respite while they waited for the moon to rise. A sheltered glen with a trickling stream running through it provided grass and water for the horses. Water from the stream also quenched their parched throats. The only food they had to eat was some bread Chapman had given them from his pack when they stopped to inform him about the militia chasing them. Chapman always seemed to have something in his pack to eat, even if naught but bread. Rowena appreciated that Nate had thrown his cape down for her to rest on, but she had been unable to nap. Fear tugged at her heart. She knew they were headed to the Drapers', Basil Guildford's in-laws. Nate assured her no better hiding place existed in all of Cheshire. And he was right about so many things. But until they reached their shelter, she could not feel safe.

That Caleb was headed to the front entrance to the Drapers' house, she understood. He was ostensibly calling on them to talk to them about new farming methods. Traveling on his own, no one would suspect him to be fleeing the militia. But where were she and Nate headed? He told her they would be going in a back entrance, but she could not understand how they were to get there. The Drapers' Pine Knoll Manor was on a knoll, yet they were not climbing upward. They splashed into a stream and to her surprise, Nate indicated they would be continuing in the stream rather than crossing it.

The moonlight shone down on the stream and the water kicked up by the horses danced and sparkled in the lunar glow. Onward the horses trudged until she could hear a loud splattering, and peering past Nate, she saw a waterfall tumbling over a rocky ledge and splashing into a mid-sized pool. She gasped as Nate urged his horse into the pool, crossed it, and disappeared into the waterfall. For a moment, she could do naught but stare before urging her horse forward and sloshing into the pool surrounded by trees and vine-draped stones. Blinking her eyes and drawing in a deep breath, she followed Nate into the waterfall. Wet, but not soaked, she emerged into a low cave and heard Nate chuckling.

"I should have told you about this," Nate said, "but I could not resist saving it as a surprise. 'Twas certainly a surprise for me the first time Rowell Draper showed it to me."

Wiping drops of water from her eyes, Rowena said, "Indeed, who would ever guess this cave would be here. But how long are we to stay here?" She looked around. The cave was not large. Hardly room to house them and the horses. And it was cold. She was already shivering.

Nate swung down from his horse and helped her down. She needed the help, she was so tired. Looking up at Nate, she could barely see him in the dim moonlight filtering in through the waterfall. She could make out his smile, but that was about all.

"Lead the horses over to the side," he said. "I have a few rocks to remove."

She followed his instructions though wondering what he meant. Rocks to remove? She could see little more than his dark form at the opposite side of the small cave, but she could see him moving and hear him grunting. Whatever rocks he was moving must be heavy. She next heard scraping noises, and then Nate disappeared. What now?

In a moment he reappeared and was carrying something. He knelt, but she could not make out what he was doing – not until a couple of sparks flew into the air, and then a flame appeared. He had lit a candle in a lantern. When he rose, she saw him smiling at her.

"Now we can make our way to our evening's abode," he said, his voice light and merry. Holding the lantern up high, he showed her the entrance to a tunnel. He had removed a number of stones, some of them quite sizable. The opening he created was just large enough that the horses could be led through it into the dark passageway.

"How did you come by the lantern?" she asked, looking warily at the tunnel. What might be hiding in its dark interior?

"A lantern, candle, flint, steel, and a box of char cloth are kept just inside on a ledge," he said. "Handy should it be needed, as is the case this evening."

Joining her, he took the reins to his horse. "Let us go. I have much to do before we can settle for the night."

Sighing, she followed after him. The tunnel was not very high or wide. Nate could stand up straight, but his hat sometimes brushed against the top of the tunnel. The horses kept their heads lowered, and their hooves made a soft clopping sound on the hard-packed dirt, or mayhap it was stone they traversed. She kept her eyes on the dim lantern light ahead, and tried not to think what snakes, rats, or spiders might be lurking in the dark. She saw Nate brush away the occasional cobweb and was glad he was in the lead. The tunnel made several turns, but then all of a sudden, it opened into a large cave.

And what a cave. Against one wall it had four open-end horse stalls with feed troughs, buckets, and hay on the ground. On the opposite side was a small pen that could be used to corral smaller animals. In the center of the cave was a table and benches and a couple more lanterns and a metal box she learned was full of candles. Opposite the passageway where they had entered the cave was another passageway that appeared to have steps carved into the stone.

Following Nate's example, Rowena led her horse over to one of the stalls. "We will put long leads on the horses so they may lie down," Nate said. "After today they will need a good sleep. After we unsaddle the horses, you can curry them while I go get them some water and see about putting those stones back in place."

With the horses unsaddled and the saddles hung over the walls dividing the stalls, Nate pulled a grain sack from an iron chest and dumped some grain into each trough. Rowena guessed the iron chest kept the grains from any rodents. That had to mean rodents were here somewhere.

"Do you not need help?" Rowena asked, not certain she wanted to be left alone in the cave.

He shook his head, and after lighting two more candles from the first candle, he set them in the other lanterns and the cave burst into a bright glow, flickering light dancing on the dusty-beige walls. Little nooks and crannies stood out, and several of them had various objects stuck in them or on them, everything from cups and plates to horse combs and scrappers to more metal boxes containing she knew not what, to even jugs of wine. She stared in amazement until Nate looped the rope handle on a wooden bucket over his arm and picked up two of the lanterns. "I must leave one lantern back where we found it," he said, and nodding toward the horse combs, he added, "You start the currying. I will return as quickly as I can but getting those stones back in place will take some time."

Rowena decided she would feel safest if she stayed busy, so she set to work on the horses. She liked being with the large animals. Somehow their nearness comforted her. How the cave, the tunnel, and the waterfall all came to be, she could not imagine, and she was eager to learn more about this well stocked hideout. Nate seemed perfectly comfortable here, so she guessed he had hidden here before. Maybe with some of the other highwaymen.

Looking around, she wondered where they would sleep. Could be one of the other metal boxes held blankets. Did they bunch up some of the straw and throw blankets over it, the ground might not be too hard. The sleeping arrangement sent a tingle racing up Rowena's spine. This would be the first time she had been completely alone with Nate. Would he continue to keep her at arm's length, or might he give in to the passion they were both suppressing.

She was finishing currying the second horse when Nate returned. The second lantern helped brighten up the cave and her mood. How handsome Nate looked when he swept off his hat and brushed his hair off his brow. He was grinning at her. "All done?" he asked.

"Near," she said, returning his smile.

"Well, let me get a couple of ropes out." He stooped over one of the metal boxes, lifted the lid, and pulled out two ropes. "We will get the horses watered and settled then be off to our quarters."

"Our quarters?" They would not be staying in the cave?

"Aye," he said but gave her no other explanation until he had the horses watered, their bridles off, and their long lead ropes secured. He made certain they had plenty of hay in their stalls, not just to lie upon, but to eat once they had finished eating the grain he had fed them. They would spend the night in complete darkness, sleeping and eating.

"They will be fine in the darkness," Nate said after blowing out one of the candles and closing the lantern sides securely around the candle. "Sometimes horses need to be blindfolded, it calms them. Not that these two are high strung, but they will not be alarmed by the darkness."

"I suppose nothing can get inside the cave here to harm them?"

He chuckled. "Did I put the rocks back in place correctly, nothing large enough to hurt these horses can get in. Now come, we have a number of steps to climb." Holding the remaining lantern in one hand, he gestured toward the stone-carved steps with his other hand.

Up and up they went. The steps were narrow, the walls close, and the rock ceiling low. Nate had to keep his head bent, but he held the lantern at an angle so its light fell on the steps. Then the passage turned in two sharp angles, the last one arriving at a heavy oak door with metal plates and a heavy bar across it. Nate handed her the lantern, and using both hands he lifted the bar and set it to the side. Motioning her to step backwards, he did the same and pulled the heavy door open. Taking the lantern from her, he stepped inside another, much smaller cave, and stood aside to let her enter.

She was amazed. This cave was a furnished chamber. It had a drop-leaf table and two ladder-back chairs, a smaller table with a writing desk on it and two more lanterns and a box of candles with flint, steel, and char cloth handy were they needed to light the candles. Another table held a water basin and pitcher and towels hung on bars on the side of the table. And it had a bed – piled high with pillows and warm quilts.

"What is this?" she asked, turning back to face Nate as he closed the door and threw a heavy bolt into place.

Before answering her, he opened a small window at the top of the door. "We need this open for air," he said. "This chamber is so tight, it would not take long to suffocate was it kept totally shut up. Notice, this door can be locked from either side. Because of the turns getting up here, there would be no way to get a battering ram to hit against the door. Plus the door opens onto the steps so it cannot be pushed in from that side. And it would take a mighty fire to set that thick oak door with its metal plates on fire. The smoke in the narrow passage would keep anyone trying to burn the door at a distance. Plus the turns in both the stairway and the tunnel keep light from the caves from filtering out to where it could be seen from the other side of the waterfall."

"But how came this chamber to be here? It would seem it is meant as some kind of hideaway or a defense against invasion, maybe?"

"I will let Rowell Draper explain all to you. I would expect him to be joining us with some food and drink any time."

"Mister Draper is coming here?"

"Considering, we are his guests, yes. And it cannot be too soon for me. I am thirsty and hungry, and I would guess you are, too."

She looked around the chamber again. "There seems to be but one bed."

The smile left Nate's face. Tilting his head to one side, he acknowledged her statement. "Aye, Rowena, there is but one bed." Setting the lantern on the table, he stepped closer to her. "We can share it, or I can bed down on the floor. Draper will be bringing more blankets."

She looked up into those incredible blue-green eyes. He was leaving the decision to her to take their relationship a step further. He would not force himself on her. She licked her lips. "Seems even with blankets, the stone floor would be very hard."

His eyes glued to hers, he nodded. "Aye. Though 'twould not be the first time the ground has served as my bed." Placing his hands on her upper arms, he said, "I know you are married, and I know it is wrong, Rowena, but I have fallen in love with you. I could tell you that I fought hard to resist my growing need for you, but I fear I would be lying. From the moment I pulled you up in front of me on my horse, I knew I was lost. I knew I should find a safe place for you to abide. I should forget about you, but my love for you, my need to have you near me, would not allow me to do what I knew I should. Did I not believe you have feelings for me, I would not now be telling you of my love. I am right, am I not, Rowena? You do have feelings for me."

She placed a hand on his cheek. "Oh, yes, Nate, very deep feelings. Yes, I, too, know it is wrong, but I do love you."

At her words, he clutched her to his chest. "Oh, God, Rowena, what are we to do?"

She remained in his embrace, listening to the pounding of his heart until at last he released her enough that his lips could find hers. Tentative, sweet, his kiss was so gentle. Never had she known such a kiss. Never had her heart felt like it would explode out of her chest. Tingling sensations coursed through her, and she felt a need in her groin she had never before experienced. Oh, and it was a stimulating need. Her arms went up around Nate's neck, and her fingers tangled in his hair. "Oh, my sweet Rowena," he said before deepening his kiss. For her, time stopped. She was lost in a mystical dream. Lord, what she had been missing all these years.

When Nate at last pulled away from her, she felt bereft, and yet he still held her in his arms. "I know I cannot marry you. At least not yet. But I would grow old with you. I will pledge the same marriage vows to you whether we stand before a magistrate or not. I want you for my wife, Rowena, whether 'tis tomorrow or a thousand tomorrows from now. Will you have me?"

"Yes, Nate. I will." She loved the glow in his eyes that her words evoked. "'Tis hard to think our love is a sin. I was but fifteen, barely a year older than Cecily is now, when I married Lindell. I went to him of my own free will. I was not forced to wed him as Cecily was forced to wed Haspel. But though I was old for my age, I was still a child. What did I know of love or of marriage? My father wanted me to marry Lindell, my mother approved of the marriage. I did as my parents expected me to do.

"And I cannot lie. I was happy. I love my children, and I was fond of Lindell. I had no idea I was being denied the kind of true love that can only exist when a man and a woman have a mutual love for each other. The kind of love your sister and her husband have. That Caleb and Sidonie have, and that Dev and Arcadia have found. I was never given the chance to find that kind of love. But now I have found it with you, Nate. And be it right or wrong, sin or no sin, I will pledge those marriage vows to you."

Again his lips found hers. Right or wrong, that night they would become one.

Chapter 34

Hearing the sound of a lock being thrown, Nate pulled away from Rowena, and in a moment, Rowell and Amata Draper entered the chamber. Rowell had blankets dangling over one arm, and he carried a bottle of wine in his other hand. His wife carried a large basket. Both were wearing robes over their bed gowns and had their nightcaps on their heads.

What bits of Rowell's hair showed under his cap was gray. Amata's braided light brown hair was streaked with snowy white strands. They both smiled brightly at their guests. "Sorry if we kept you waiting. I know you must be starved," Rowell said.

Nate chuckled, "That we could do with a meal is for certain. But here let me take that basket, Mistress Draper." He stepped forward and took the basket from Amata and set it on the table. Napkins, plates, and goblets were in evidence along with bread, cheese, slices of ham, and apple tarts. A feast to his rumbling stomach.

"I know you will want to wash up. Let me pour your wine, then I will get you some water" Rowell said, and pulling a cork from the bottle, he soon had their goblets filled.

Rowena and Nate both drank thirstily, and Amata said, "We had to wait until Cook was abed before we could raid his kitchen. Rowell told the scullery lads who sleep on cots in the kitchen to pay us no heed and to make no mention to Cook. We would not want Cook to think he had not served enough at supper. The boys vowed they would breathe not a word."

When Rowell returned with water in their pitcher for their wash basin, Nate said, "I wonder, Draper, would you feel up to telling Rowena how you come by this chamber?"

Both the Drapers laughed, and Rowell said, "You wash and start your meal, and I will bring in a couple more chairs and will tell Lady Crossly the tale of Pine Knoll."

Nate's and Rowena's plates full, and the Drapers seated, Rowell began telling the history of Pine Knoll's caves. "On your previous visit here, Lady Crossly, when you did of necessity pose as Mistress Blucher, my wife told you this castle was built in 1401 in the reign of Henry Bolingbroke. Having usurped the throne, he became Henry IV. He was having trouble with the Welsh, in particular with one Owain Glendower who proclaimed himself Prince of Wales. Henry wanted the border better fortified, and he granted this manor to Sir Reynard Fauchet.

"Fauchet was reconnoitering his manor land, trying to decide where to build his castle – really more a fortified house, having but the one crenelated turret as you have seen – when he heard a beautiful voice singing. Somewhat foolishly bidding his men wait, he dismounted and made his way through the woods, following the voice that held him spellbound."

Nate had heard the tale a couple of times before so he let his mind drift back to the moment his lips first met Rowena's. He had fought his need, his desire for her, albeit not very hard for weeks on end. But now to know she loved him as he loved her left him believing in miracles. This night, he would make her his own. Smiling inwardly, he watched his beautiful love as she sat engrossed in Rowell's tale.

His mellow voice bringing life to his tale, Draper continued, "When Sir Reynard emerged from the woods, he saw the loveliest vision. 'Twas a young woman singing while bathing in the pool at the foot of the waterfall. Her pale skin, glistening with droplets of water, her long blond tresses concealing none of her luscious form, she was perfection. Sir Reynard could do naught but stare until the youthful woman turned and saw him. In an instant, she ducked under the water, disappearing, and though he waited for her to resurface, she failed to do so. He panicked, and tearing off his boots and clothes, he dove into the pond." Rowell harrumphed. "It would seem Sir Reynard, for whatever the reason, was riding about without his armor, here on the border with Wales. At least that is what we must believe, for he would not have been able to rapidly shed his armor. Certainly not without help.

"Anyway, the pool was not deep or murky. It was clear as glass, but he could find no sign of his water nymph. At least not until he heard a tinkling laugh. Following the sound of the laughter, he waded into the waterfall, and on the other side of the falls, there sat the woman in the cave behind the waterfall."

"Apparently still bare as the day she was born," Amata said with a snicker.

"Well, whether she was or not," Rowell said, "she was taken with Sir Reynard, and he with her. She showed him the secret tunnel leading to the large cave where you have left your horses. She pointed to the other passage, and said it led to yet another cave, but the passageway was too narrow and steep to climb. The other cave, this chamber," Rowell swept his arm out, "could only be reached from the top of the knoll, here where our house now sits.

"After learning all this, Sir Reynard decided the knoll would be the perfect place to build his fortified house. Atop the knoll, he found the passage leading to this cave," Rowell pointed to the door where he and Amata had entered, "and he had his bedchamber and a chapel for his wife – oh, he married the lovely siren – built over the entrance to this cave. He also had the passageway leading from this cave to the larger cave enlarged and steps carved into the stone. This gave him the perfect escape tunnel should the Welsh break through the walls surrounding the house and into the house. Though to look at it, you would not know it, but the chapel's alter can be slid forward, and behind it is a short passage leading to this cave."

"How did all these caves come to be here?" Rowena asked.

"You recall my wife's brother, Basil Guildford?" Rowell looked at Rowena.

"Yes, of course. He and his wife were so gracious, so very good to us."

"Well, Basil believes the stream that now empties into the pond once ran a different course, and that it carved out the caves. Then something caused the stream to change its course to what it is now. There is a place south of here where my younger son, Leonius, swears he has found the exact location where the stream used to run before it changed course."

"How fascinating," Rowena said, then gesturing around, asked, "But why is this chamber so grand. Did Sir Reynard hide here?"

Laughing, Rowell said, "Oh, no. 'Twas as bare as the larger cave.

Mayhap more so. Fact is, once Henry VII became King, and the problems with the border subsided, the caves were near forgotten. Might have remained so had not the next generation of Fauchets built and moved to the more modern Fauchet Hall a little west of here. 'Twas a land grant they received from Henry VII. This manor, then, was used as the dowry for their daughter Wannour who married the second Earl of Penhaligon. Generations of Penhaligons had stewards in charge of the manor house and land. Seems one of the stewards found it profitable to do some smuggling. The larger cave was used to store his smuggled goods and to house his henchmen's horses."

"That is why the stalls?" Rowena said.

"Yes, though they have been redone. And appropriate supplies have been left there for those who might need them. Stones that fell from the ledge the waterfall flows over we used to hide the tunnel. Before, it was but assumed no one would discover it. Now, we choose to be more cautious. This small cave we turned into the bedchamber for my older son when he was fighting with Charles I. Gave him a place to visit with his wife once the Roundheads won the battle at Nantwich, and Siward could not safely go home. Of late, we have used it for Nate and his highwaymen. 'Tis little enough we can do to help those who aid our King."

"And your support and generosity is much appreciated," Nate said.

"So what happened to the smuggler?" Rowena asked.

"He made enough so he would never have to work again. Resigned and disappeared. But before he left, he showed the new steward the secret tunnel and told him he could make his fortune was he willing to take the risks. The next steward was not willing to take the risk. He was the one who was here when this manor was given to me by my father, the fourth Earl of Penhaligon. The steward showed me the tunnel and the caves and remained our steward until his sudden death ten years ago. Now, we let my son, Leonius, handle all our accounting as he does for our son-in-law's manors. Lord Shocklach is married to our daughter, Hosanna. They are currently in Europe with King Charles's wandering court. Leonius has managed to pay some of Shocklach's fines, and some of his manors that were confiscated have been bought back."

Rowena smiled. "I thank you for telling me the history of these caves."

"We know not how factual the part with Sir Reynard may be, but it makes a good tale," Rowell said with a chuckle. "But now, you must be exhausted." He looked at Nate. "I have brought blankets that you may bed down upon and so give Lady Crossly the bed. I am that sorry we cannot give each of you your own chamber."

"Oh, never fear," Rowena said, blushing slightly. "Nate and I have shared chambers any number of times, and at a yeoman's home, we even shared a cornhusk mattress in their hall."

"Well, dear," Amata said, "we know you will manage. We wish you a good night's sleep. Sadly, according to Mister Hayward, you will need remain here as our guests for a couple of days until we learn if the search for you has dwindled. When we bring you breakfast tomorrow, we will bring some books and cards that you may entertain yourselves. Also, the larger cave makes for a good place to stretch your legs. Get you out of this tiny chamber. I know Siward said he would have gone mad had he not had the large cave to romp about in."

"We thank you, Mistress Draper," Nate said. "Do you please to give Hayward a message for me. He is to bide close to home, but could he let the Yardleys know that Arcadia is safe."

"So we will," Rowell said. "And a good-night to you."

Once the Drapers exited, Rowena turned to D'Arcy. "How will they know when 'tis safe for us to leave?"

"Tomorrow they will send for Siward, their son. You met him and his wife on our previous visit here."

"Yes, I remember them," Rowena said with a nod to her head.

"Siward will be told our situation. He will visit the Guildfords and inform them. He will also visit their son-in-law, Marvin Bussard in Malpas. You remember Bussard helped us when we freed Yardley."

Again Rowena nodded.

"The Guildfords and the Bussards know people. They have connections. You might even call some of them spies. King Charles might be forced to wander Europe, but he has many loyal followers here in England. Anyway, loyal subjects' tentacles reach out in all directions. They will receive news from Burslem and will learn if my fake identity has been compromised."

"And if it has?"

"I will no longer be able to use the Drummer name, but I already knew I would no longer be able to stay with Ethelinda or keep our prizes in Burslem. 'Tis a loss."

"And 'tis my fault. Had you not helped Cecily and me, neither you nor your cousin would be in jeopardy. I do hope Mistress Tavers will face no drastic consequences."

D'Arcy gathered Rowena into his arms. "Never fear my love. Herman and Ethelinda will be fine. They will never admit, nor will their servants, that I was anyone other than Drummer. Nor will Winnlock Measure. And I would guess, Mistress Pettigrew, my dear friend's widow, will insist she was indeed mistaken about me being D'Arcy. Besides, had I not helped you, I would not have you here in my arms. I would not know the greatest love a man can know." He ducked his head before looking back into her eyes. "I have to admit, Rowena, I chose this particular hideout because I wanted time alone with you. There were other places we could have hidden, but I knew here, I would have the chance to tell you of my love and to learn if you returned my love. That your love equals mine is all I could ask for."

Looking up into his eyes, a tiny smile touching her lips, Rowena whispered, "Oh, Nate. I do love you. And I am so glad you chose to bring me here. I never thought I would know such love. Never knew it truly existed. I thought 'twas but made up stories in books and tales of old. You fill me with wonder."

Her words of love filled his soul, and with his fingertips, he tilted her face up to his and softly kissed her. This night, they would join as husband and wife though no magistrate had joined them in marriage. But to him, she was all he could ever want, ever need, and he meant to spend the rest of his life proving his love to her. And some day, someday, they would be wed.

※ ※ ※ ※

After a night of passion like she never could have imagined, Rowena awoke to gentle kisses on her brow, the tip of her nose, and her lips. She could not see Nate, the candle in the lantern had long since burned out, but she felt his naked body next to hers. Gads, but he had introduced her to magical love-making. Every dream she had ever dreamed had been fulfilled. Yet he had been careful not to empty his seed into her. He wanted to cause her no shame. Nor did he want any child of his not to bear his name.

"I must rise, my love," he said. "Though my need for you is again great, we must ready ourselves before the Drapers arrive with our breakfast. I will get a candle lit."

Reaching up, she pulled his head down that she might claim his lips. His arms went around her, and she reveled in his skin against hers. She had never been completely nude with Lindell. They had both always had their night shifts on. She had a feeling she was going to experience many more delights as she and Nate explored new ways of loving each other. Reluctantly she released him. For now, they would hide their intimacy, but at some point, they would have to announce to the world that they were now and would forever be one.

Working in complete darkness, Nate at first seemed to be having trouble getting a candle lit, though sparks flew as he hit flint to steel. Finally, a piece of the char cloth caught fire, and he was able to light a candle. After putting the candle into the lantern, he lit another candle off the first one. With the chamber aglow, she had a chance to admire Nate's muscled body. He was a fine specimen, and she looked forward to evening when they could again climb into bed together. But now, she had best get dressed, remake the bed, and stack the blankets Nate had not used on the bed.

She had been toasty warm in bed, but upon getting out of bed, chill bumps attacked her arms and legs. She and Nate both hastily dressed. The cave seemed to stay the same temperature no matter was it night or day, winter or summer outside, but it was a slightly chilly temperature. Fine when dressed, and covered with a shawl, but cold on bare skin.

Nate gave Rowena her panniers that she could find her comb and mirror and a fresh shift, but his packs, being near to busting with his plunder, afforded him no extra clothing. His better coat, vest, and breeches were tucked away in Yardley's pack. And Yardley would now be in Nantwich, where he and Rowena had planned to be.

"No reason you cannot make yourself more comfortable, Rowena," he said. "You need not spend your time here in your riding costume."

Changed into a more comfortable gown, she donned an extra petticoat to help against the cold of the cave. She combed out her hair and was just finishing braiding it when the Drapers arrived with their breakfast, several books, a deck of cards, and a backgammon set.

"Mister Hayward and I had a good conversation about turnips," Rowell said. "Could be profitable to over winter more of my herd. We shall see. I will discuss it with Siward. He has been here, he spoke with Mister Hayward, and they set out together for Malpas. The good thing is, no militia have come pounding on my door. They must not suspect you of being in this area. The hope is, they are searching Chester for you. With any luck, you will be able to leave here in a couple of days."

※ ※ ※ ※

By the end of their third day in their tight quarters, Rowena was more than ready to move on. Even with books to read, walks about in the larger cave, and love-making at night with Nate, she felt the cave walls and the darkness closing in on her. That evening when the Drapers brought them their supper, they brought good news.

"I can see no reason you cannot leave tomorrow," Rowell said. "The militia concentrated on Chester and Burslem. We learned they questioned your cousin, Mistress Tavers, and her husband as well as their servants. All swore they have ever only known you as Drummer. They cannot imagine why you would have ignored the militiaman unless you had no way of knowing who he was, and having just left the goldsmith, you might have feared he was a thief.

"The Widow Pettigrew claimed she thought you were an old friend of her husband, a Welshman, by the name of Davis. Luckily, the militiaman had not heard her call you D'Arcy. He only heard you say your name was Drummer. She quickly realized you would still be on the run, and she ably covered her impulsive action."

"So no one suspects Drummer and D'Arcy are one and the same?" Nate said.

"Not to my knowledge, though they did again question your great aunt, Lady Alfreda, and her husband, Sir Dalbert. Mistress Tavers being their daughter, seems the militia had their suspicions Lady Crossly and her daughter might be staying with Lady Alfreda. I understand Lady Alfreda gave them what for. With her husband doing poorly, she claimed she had enough to worry about without having Cromwell's militia disturbing her home for the second time."

Nate chuckled. "Ah, that would be my aunt. Imperious to say the least."

"Well, I would say you need be careful, but I think you run no real threat at this time. When you leave on the morrow, leave the tunnel open. Siward will see it is replenished with oats and hay and candles." He smiled and gave a bark of laughter. "And he will see to the muck."

"That hardly seems fair," Nate said with an answering smile.

Rowell shook his head. "He knows 'tis little enough we do. You and your highwaymen are taking all the risks. He will not mind, I promise you."

"At least, I have it all shoveled into the basket. He will need do naught put pull it out through the tunnel and dump it in the woods."

"Fine. We bid you good-night then. We will bring your breakfast early on the morrow."

"I will have you some bread, cheese, and a couple of crispy chicken legs to gnaw on as well," Amata said before giving Rowena a hug. "I will keep you and your daughter in my prayers, Lady Crossly. You are a brave soul."

"Thank you, Mistress Draper. You and your husband have been so kind."

"'Tis naught, 'tis naught," Rowell said with a wave of his hand. "Until the morrow." With that, he and his wife left, and Rowena could rejoice with the man she loved. They were safe and would soon be leaving the cave. Oh, to see the sun again.

Chapter 35

After leaving the Drapers', Nate had planned a two days stay with the Haywards. "Just to be certain the chase is over," he said. But upon learning Delphine Madigan, wealthy heiress and wife of one of Nate's highwaymen, Torrance Madigan, was sending her personal coach to take Sidonie and Caleb to Arcadia's and Dev's wedding to be held at the Tuftwick manor, Nate decided Rowena would be safer traveling to the wedding with Sidonie and Caleb. With his packs bulging with money and jewelry for the King, Nate preferred not to risk having Rowena with him. Rowena hated saying good-bye to Nate even though she knew he would be joining her again at the Tuftwick Manor.

Planning an early morning leave, Nate expected he could be at the Blucher's by late afternoon. Once there, he would meet up with Chapman, and the two of them would take their prizes to the secret rendezvous with Nate's brother, Ranulf. Ranulf would be responsible for getting their plunder to King Charles. Nate and Chapman would then be free to join their friends for the wedding festivities.

Lord Tuftwick's manor was located in the foothills in the Pennines in Lancashire. The Madigans had purchased land and built their home near Tuftwick Manor. Delphine Madigan and Lady Tuftwick were cousins, and had grown up together like sisters. Their husbands had grown up together like brothers. According to Nate, the two couples were inseparable.

Mistress Madigan's coach was plush beyond anything Rowena had ever imagined. Plus, Mistress Madigan sent two footmen and two outriders to assist them on their journey, and to ensure no highwaymen attempted to rob them. That made Rowena chuckle. Few highwaymen other than Nate's gang would attempt to stop such well-protected equipage.

Sidonie's little son, William, would stay with his grandmother,

Goody Hayward. It was too long a trip for a two-year-old, though when a baby, he had made an even longer trip from Grasmere back to the Haywards' home. Neither the Prestons, Dev's parents, or the Yardleys, Arcadia's parents, were making the trip. Both sets of parents feared they might inadvertently lead the militia to their sons, Dev and Cyril. Cyril would stand as Dev's witness at the wedding. Nor could Dev's sister and her husband attend, Hestia having but recently given birth and being unwilling to travel with her new son. However, both families gave their blessings to the marriage. Rowena could not help but feel for the parents and for Dev and Arcadia that the families could not be together for the grand occasion. Arcadia would at least have her brother, Cyril, and her sister, Sidonie, there. How the Civil War and the Cromwellians had handicapped so many lives.

Caleb Hayward would ride his horse unless the weather turned inclement, but Rowena would ride inside with Sidonie and Sidonie's maid, Clare. Rowena's horse would be tied to the back of the coach. She would need the horse when she again set off with Nate. Winter was coming, and Nate said after a couple more robberies, they would be headed to London. Easy to be one of the multitude in that ever-growing city. Sidonie was hopeful Lady Grasmere would attend the wedding. Did Lady Grasmere attend, then surely Cecily would be with her.

Rowena longed to hold her daughter in her arms. She also hoped to see her sons again before she and Nate went into their winter quarters. She would be seeing London for the first time. And she would be spending three whole months with Nate. Months when they would not be on the run, and he would not be putting his life at risk. They would have the time to truly get to know each other. Time to revel in their new found love.

※ ※ ※ ※

Liverna shook her head as she watched Sir Lindell stumble up the stairs to his bedchamber. He was drinking more and more heavily, and eating less and less. His young sons found him disgusting, and Milo, the older of the two, told his father he stank. "I find you repugnant," the boy said, his lips curling and nostrils flaring. "I am ashamed to call you my father."

Sir Lindell had merely blinked and given his son a wane smile. "Ah, Milo. Ah, Milo," he finally said, and shaking his head he had turned and staggered away.

Rowena's brother, Artus, when stopping in to check on his nephews, had told Sir Lindell did he not stop his drinking he would kill himself. Sir Lindell had answered, "Mayhap 'twould be for the best. Mayhap." He then took another drink of whatever it was he had in his cup.

His eyes bleary, he looked up at Artus. "Have you heard anything from Rowena? Anything? I would know was she alive or dead." He beat his fist against his chest. "I am lost without her. Lost. Can you not see that? Have you no pity?"

His eyes hard, Artus said, "I pity Rowena and Cecily. I have little pity for you, Lindell. Your manor is becoming decrepit in but these few months since you forced my sister to flee that she might save her daughter from that ignoble marriage. Now, Rowena has a bounty on her head. For your sons, you need to stop drinking and see to your manor."

Nodding his head ever so slowly and staring off vacantly, Sir Lindell said, "Yes, yes. I should see to the manor. After all, did I not force my lovely little daughter to marry Haspel that I might save the manor for Milo? Humph. Yes. Despite Rowena's pleas I forced Cecily to marry Haspel. Now Haspel claims he is getting an annulment, and was it not for Rowena's stipend, half the manor would be sold to pay the taxes Haspel levied on me." He looked back up at Artus. "My sons hate me. My wife deserted me." He held up his hand. "Oh, I know in your mind 'twas for good cause. But I am lost without her. Do you hear from her, tell her how I fare. Tell her I regret I failed to heed her pleas. Tell her I need her."

Liverna had stopped Artus when he was leaving and asked, "Is there naught you can do to help here? Mayhap a steward could be found to manage the manor?"

"I will talk to Uncle Gaylord," Artus promised, "but how a steward could be paid is the question."

Another month had come and gone since Artus's confrontation with Sir Lindell, and they yet had no steward. And Sir Lindell continued to drink.

Watching him stumbling up the stairs, Liverna wondered how much longer he could live if he continued to drink the way he was drinking. And if he died, what then? What would become of his sons and the manor? She needed to talk to Artus again.

※ ※ ※ ※

Cecily was so excited. She was going to get to see her mother. Lady Grasmere had decided she would attend Arcadia's and Dev's wedding at Lord Tuftwick's manor. Tuftwick's manor was in Lancashire, not far from the market town of Rochdale, so Lady Grasmere told Cecily, though its location meant nothing to Cecily. She only knew it would mean a journey of at least three days, mayhap longer if the rains persisted. Cecily cared not how long it might take. It would be nothing to all the traveling she had already done since being rescued by her mother and the wonderful highwaymen she had grown to love and respect.

The journey to Knightswood Castle had been tedious by horseback, but the trip from Knightswood to Lady Grasmere's home in Cheshire in the Grasmere coach had been even more tedious, if more comfortable. Lord Grasmere would not be able to accompany them to the wedding. He was confined to the two parishes of his two main residences. He had permission to travel to and from his primary home, Harp's Ridge, to Knightswood each year, but no side excursions were permitted. Lady Grasmere made few trips without her husband. Cecily realized the two hated to be separated. She found the love her foster parents shared ever so romantic. She doubted her mother and her father had ever shared such a love, but she had thought both her parents happy, at least until Haspel had appeared to disrupt their lives.

Cecily felt safe with Lord and Lady Grasmere. They were so very good to her. Lady Grasmere was seeing that she had a whole new wardrobe. And Lady Grasmere was personally seeing to her continued education. She was being given lessons in French and Latin. She was being trained in household management, in delicate sewing, in dance, despite the fact the Puritans frowned on dancing, and in keeping the household accounts. She liked her lessons. They helped keep her mind off her mother, and her brothers, and even her father. Lady Grasmere's five-year-old Timandra also helped keep her loneliness at bay. She and the child had become close in the few months they had been together. Cecily was pleased Timandra was going with them to the wedding.

The day they set out, the sky was drizzling, but the coachman, footmen, and outriders had large hats and woolen capes to help protect them from the rain. All the same, Cecily was glad she was riding in the coach. She hoped she would never again have to take to the roads on horseback, but she worried her mother might yet have many a year to endure such travel. She would hate Haspel until her dying day for accusing her mother of being part of the gang of highwaymen. With a warrant on her head, her mother would never be safe. Not as long as she remained in England, and Cecily could not bear the thought that her mother might someday decide she must leave her home country to find peace.

Pushing such thoughts from her mind, she turned to Timandra and engaged the little girl in a wishing game. They needed something to keep them from absolute boredom in the darkened coach. The shutters being closed to keep out the rain, little light could seep through the cracks between the shutter slats. Did it rain every day, it would be another tedious journey.

※ ※ ※ ※

"Lady Grasmere, do we not stay with the Appletons' tonight?" Phillida's maid, Adah, asked, breaking in on Phillida's reverie. She had been thinking about Sidonie Hayward and looking forward to renewing their friendship.

"Yes, Adah. Have I not already told you that?"

"You did, my lady, but I grow weary, and it does seem we should be there by now. The rain let up near an hour ago to my reckoning, yet we still plod along."

Phillida could not blame her maid for feeling weary. They had rattled around in the dark coach for most of the day. Finally one of the outriders had knocked on the side of the coach to tell them the rain had stopped, did they wish to open the shutters. "No doubt the rain has muddied the highway, making it more difficult to travel. We are all tired, but we must endure until we reach our evening's destination. Be thankful the rain has ceased. Mayhap tomorrow we will have sun, and it will dry out the highway."

"That is what I will wish for, Mother," Timandra said.

Phillida smiled at her daughter. "Ah, then we will all hope your wish will come true."

"Indeed we will, Lady Timandra," Adah said, "indeed we will."

Leaning back against the plush coach cushions, Phillida again let her mind drift. She felt sorry for Lady Crossly, but she was enjoying having Cecily fostered with her. The girl was bright and cheerful and so good with Timandra. And Phillida believed fostering Cecily was good practice for her as she expected to someday foster her oldest brother, Kenrick's, daughter or daughters, Kenrick's wife, Blanche being again with child. Having been fostered herself with her great aunt, Alfreda, she had learned much from the grand old lady, and she hoped to provide as good an education as a foster parent as she had received from her aunt. Luckily, she had not been far from home, so she had never had to spend lengthy periods away from her family as had her brothers Kenrick and Nate who had been fostered with a friend of their father's in Devon.

When Timandra was old enough, Phillida meant to foster her with Berold's sister, Venetia, Lady Tuftwick. That was one reason she insisted upon taking Timandra with her. She wanted her daughter to retain the closeness she had formed with her aunt before her aunt married and moved to her own home. She wondered how she would feel, sending her daughter away from home. Would she be as devastated as Lady Crossly was to leave her daughter? Cecily was such a pretty, sweet girl. Sadly, she and Adah had decided they best continue to use the walnut stain on the girl's silky blond hair. Cecily's hair was just too identifiable. The walnut stain had faded from Cecily's skin as a tan might fade away, arousing no suspicions, and Cecily's creamy-white skin enhanced the girl's beauty. Phillida expected Cecily would one day be a remarkably beautiful woman.

Phillida's greatest hope, though, was that she would arrive at the Tuftwick manor and learn that Nate had fallen so much in love with

Lady Crossly he was willing to give up his highway robberies and take his beloved to the continent where they could both be safe. The question was, would Lady Crossly be willing to go so far away from her children. Somehow, that seemed unlikely.

Her thoughts were abruptly curtailed when the coach made a sharp turn. Phillida heard Adah breathe a sigh of relief. They had turned down the lane that would lead to their night's abode. Phillida, too, sighed. She was oh so ready to be out of the coach.

※ ※ ※ ※

Smiling, Ethelinda watched her daughter and her niece, Jebelle, as they chatted gaily while playing a game of backgammon. Jebelle, having accompanied her father to the Taverses' home, was having a lengthy visit while her father, Ethelinda's brother, Alfgar, visited several of the D'Arcy manors. Alfgar was the high steward for all the D'Arcy and Lotterby manors. He had accepted the position when Nate, previously the steward for both families, had gone off to fight for Charles II and had become a fugitive for breaking his parole.

Ethelinda had not been surprised by Alfgar's visit. Their mother had sent him. She wanted to know why the militia kept invading her home looking for some man named Drummer and some woman named Lady Crossly. Fearing letters would be intercepted, Ethelinda had been afraid to write her mother to explain the situation, but upon hearing the explanation, Alfgar had chuckled and sworn their mother would be delighted by the entire fabrication. She would also look forward to meeting Lady Crossly and would expect Nate to bring the lady to her home.

Nate was often known to visit his great aunt, Alfreda. Her home in Chester, the house Ethelinda had grown up in, made for a wonderful hideout. It was huge. It had a gigantic hall, twenty bedchambers, three dining areas of various sizes, a conservatory, a library, sitting rooms off several of the bedchambers, two parlors, one for family, one formal for entertaining guests, a room Ethelinda's father called his office, two kitchens, one located in the house, one behind the house, and a long gallery housing numerous paintings, busts, and statues. And, to Ethelinda's joy as a child, it had three hidden rooms with a passageway between two of them. What fun hiding in them had been for her and her siblings. Ethelinda could just imagine the militiamen attempting to search her mother's home.

Lady Alfreda Harmon was not one to accept intrusion meekly. She had four burly footmen meant to intimidate anyone who would cross her. No doubt the footmen loomed over the militiamen and allowed no one to venture through Lady Alfreda's rooms without an escort. Even had Nate and Lady Crossly been in his mother's home, Alfgar said, the militiamen would never have found them. Upon telling Alfgar that Nate would no longer be able to stay with her, Ethelinda was pleased Alfgar suggested their mother's home would not only offer Nate and his lady a safe hideaway, his stolen riches could be kept in their father's strongbox which was hidden in a closet off his office. Only problem was, getting word to Nate.

Ethelinda decided she would write a letter to Lady Tuftwick, her cousin Phillida's sister-in-law who was hosting Arcadia Yardley's and Deverette Preston's wedding. Lord Tuftwick was under no suspicion, so a letter to his wife should not be intercepted. Care would still need be taken, but Ethelinda knew she could manage that. She liked the idea that Nate and Lady Crossly could find a comfortable haven with her mother. That Nate and his lady were in love was obvious. That they would consummate that love seemed likely. She but hoped their love would not lead them to do anything reckless that could end in their arrests, or worse.

Chapter 36

Rowena was more than a little glad to once again take to the highway. Had eight months truly passed since she climbed down the ivy to rescue Cecily from Haspel? Spring was in the air, and after three cold winter months in London, she and Nate were again on horseback. They were headed to Chester. She was to stay with his great aunt Alfreda while he visited his family on the Wirral Peninsula. He doubted he ran any risks. Still, he would sneak in and out of his family's home. Besides his mother, his brother, and his brother's wife and young children, few, other than some trusted servants, would know of his visit. He meant to tell his family about Rowena and the love they shared, but he would not risk taking her to his home at Wealdburh. Despite the fact in January, Parliament had refused to continue the decimation tax and the rule of the Major-Generals, the militia could yet be anywhere.

After Arcadia's and Dev's wedding, the two young lovers went to visit their families and revel in their love while the rest of Nate's gang resumed their highway robberies. They swept through Shropshire and into Worcestershire. Rob when they found a good target, then move on. Stay with Royalists when they could to avoid the expense of inns, but visit the inns and taverns to find their prey.

Outside Birmingham in Warwickshire, to Rowena's surprise, they robbed a house. The house had once belonged to a friend of Nate's, and the Cromwellian who had bought the confiscated property and turned out Nate's friend's elderly parents, Nate found particularly loathsome. He knew from the man's drunken bragging that he kept a strongbox in his home. The house servants were no match for Nate's gang, and the contents of the strongbox were soon in Nate's possession. A portion of the take, he meant to later give to his friend's parents. He knew them to be in need. From Warwickshire, they headed to Leicestershire and the highway leading from London to Derby. Being a well-traveled highway, Nate had expected their haul to be lucrative, and it had been.

With winter approaching, the gang disbanded. Tuftwick and Madigan headed for their homes. Chapman and Cyril Yardley were to take the gang's appropriations to Nate's Aunt Alfreda in Chester for safe keeping. As Nate could no longer safely stow the stolen items in Winlock Measure's safe, Rowena understood that Lady Alfreda and her husband, Dalbert Harmon, would now be the trusted keepers of the money and goods plundered for the King. Rowena hoped the King appreciated all that was being done for him, the risks so many people were taking on his behalf.

With the robberies at an end, Rowena had at last been able to again see her sons. Her visit with her sons had been a short, secret visit in her brother Artus's woods. Artus had assured her Milo's inheritance was intact. Rowena's Uncle Gaylord had arranged to use Rowena's stipend left to her by her grandfather to pay the taxes. But the best news was, Haspel had filed for an annulment. Rowena had no doubt the annulment would be granted. The marriage had not been consummated, and despite the reward Haspel had offered for the return of his bride, thanks to Nate and his highwaymen, the militia had been unable to find Cecily. Rowena prayed her daughter would soon be free of Haspel.

Rowena had also learned her husband was in poor health. Liverna said she feared Sir Lindell might not live out the year. Rowena wished she could feel some sympathy for the man, but when she looked at her two sons and saw the sorrow in their eyes when Nate said she and he had to be going, she could find no compassion in her heart for her sons' father.

After Rowena's visit with her sons, she and Nate had headed for London. Chapman's home was in Chester so he would spend the winter with his sister and her family, but Cyril, like Arcadia and Dev, had joined Rowena and Nate in London. Nate had taken rooms in a house in a quiet area, and he and Rowena lived together as husband and wife. Rowena had at first been embarrassed by the arrangement, but Arcadia had been so supportive and understanding, Rowena had soon come to think of herself as truly being married to Nate.

Now, though, she would be staying with Nate's aunt. Despite Nate's assurances that his Aunt Alfreda would be accepting of their love,

Rowena could not help feeling abashed. She wished Arcadia would be with her, but Arcadia and Dev were to again visit their families before joining Nate and Rowena and the other members of the gang in Manchester. King Charles would be running short on funds. Time to resume their banditry to replenish the King's purse.

After Nate's visit to his family, he and Rowena were to head for Harp's Ridge that Rowena could visit with Cecily. Rowena had not seen her daughter since Arcadia's and Dev's wedding. That had been a wonderful occasion. Lady Tuftwick had assigned her and Cecily to share a bedchamber, so when alone at night, the two could talk freely. Rowena was pleased Cecily was happy with Lady Grasmere, though she missed her mother. But all too soon, the wedding celebration was ended, and Cecily had to return with Lady Grasmere to Harp's Ridge.

Rowena had found little about London to her liking other than the fact they were not constantly traveling. And Nate and his gang were not putting their lives at risk. Almost all forms of entertainment had been closed by the Puritans. Rowena would have liked to see a play, but she was not sorry the cock-fighting and bull-baiting games had been banned. She had never understood the fun in seeing animals being tortured.

She and Arcadia liked the shops. They had marveled at some of the fabrics for sale. Not that they could afford them, but they had been delicious to goggle and to touch. The busy, smelly lanes, the constantly dingy, smoky air, and the never-ending noise soon had Rowena and Arcadia ready to leave London. "I wonder you can stay here winter after winter," Rowena said to Nate one evening after a particularly noisome day. It had rained, and the street gutters were afloat with all manner of noxious refuse.

Chuckling, Nate said, "I enjoy the freedom I have here. And, I learn much. Much that will help me know where and when to plan our springtime robberies. Many of these Cromwell supporters are getting wealthy off the spoils they have taken from Royalists and the King. I learn who they are, where they live, and what gains they mean to carry home with them. As you already know, the highway from Derby to London is our most fruitful resource, but we must ever be wary. We dare not raid too often in the same places. Traps could be set for us. 'Tis best we never stay in any shire too long."

Both Rowena and Arcadia had missed the Christmas celebrating. London might be crawling with Puritans and Cromwellians, but the merchants liked their Christmas and few opened their doors on Christmas Day despite Parliaments' orders to the London mayor to keep the shops open. Celebrations were held quietly in private homes. In their rooms, Rowena and Arcadia had been able to do little more than bring in some holly to brighten up their chambers. The landlord and his wife might not be Puritans, but they were not willing to risk the wrath of the militia, so they held no celebration, had no feast, no goose or turkey or special Christmas ale.

Rowena missed the large yule log her husband had always had drug into the hall. She missed the holy and ivy and evergreen boughs that had decorated her home. How the children had loved the special little treats the cook prepared, and they had always attended a Christmas service at the local parish church. She wondered if any celebration of Christ's birth had been held at Crossly Oaks this year. Mayhap her brother, Artus, had seen Milo and Godwin were treated to some type of celebration.

And so Christmas had come and gone with little notice, and December had faded into January and January into February. Bitter cold had often kept Rowena and Arcadia wrapped in their cloaks and sitting before a coal fire in the parlor they shared with the landlord and his wife. The landlord claimed coal was pricy, and he used it sparingly. Rowena missed the wood fires that had burned brightly in the Crossly Oaks hall before the war, before Crossly Oaks had been confiscated and Sir Lindell had needed to sell off a large portion of his woods to buy back his manor. She hoped her sons were being kept warm enough. Godwin was often subject to colds.

While in London, she and Nate were again the Bluchers, Arcadia and Dev were the Jamiesons, and Cyril Yardley was Roy Chambers. They might be known by any number of names once they were again robbing Cromwellians. They would assume any number of disguises. More often than not, she would be wearing the blond wig. Arcadia might be dressed as a male servant, or she might be dressed as a bereaved widow with a veil covering her face. The young woman could play almost any part. She was a born actress. And she seemed to thrive on the adventures. Rowena had to admit to a certain thrill herself when she had played her part well. At the same time, her nerves were always tied in knots until Nate and his gang rejoined her and Arcadia with their booty in hand and no one injured.

Nate's sister, Phillida, had more than once begged Nate to give up what she termed his precarious game of hide and seek – hide from the militia, seek out the wealthy Cromwellians – but Nate only hugged Phillida and promised her he would be mindful of her suggestion. Rowena doubted Nate ever considered giving up the robberies. He had committed himself and his gang to helping support his King. She admired his honor, but she could not help but fear that at some point something would go wrong. While in London, she had learned of other highwaymen who had been caught and hanged.

She learned that in 1652, James Hind, a Royalist who had fought with Charles II and had, like Nate, robbed only Cromwellians, and had often given money to poor Royalists, had been caught and had been charged with treason rather than robbery which meant he had been hanged, drawn, and quartered. At times Rowena had a hard time keeping that horrid image from her mind. She knew that image must be what Nate's sister feared. And mayhap the wives of the other highwaymen could not avoid envisioning such a fate for their husbands. If Arcadia ever had that fear, she never mentioned it to Rowena, and Rowena had never spoken of her fears to Arcadia. Somehow, it seemed if she broached the subject, it would be an ill omen and might even cause the fearful event to come to pass.

At least they would have a couple more weeks before they renewed their banditry. Time for Arcadia and Dev to visit their families. Time for Cyril to see his wife and daughters, although they would have to visit him at the Haywards'. All believed 'twas too risky for Cyril to visit his own home, but no one would be suspicious of Tamar and her daughters visiting the Haywards' for they did so a couple of times a week.

There was time for Nate to visit his family, and eventually, time for Rowena to see her daughter, to hold Cecily in her arms, and to assure her all would be well. She would not be able to see her sons or learn the condition of her husband until Nate and his highwaymen worked their way back into Derbyshire. When that would be, she could not guess. Once all the highwaymen met up in Manchester, only then would decisions be made about where they would next strike. Until then, they were all living in Limbo.

※ ※ ※ ※

With an arm around each of Rowena's sons, Liverna stood with the boys in the March wind and watched the boys' father's casket being lowered slowly into the open pit that had been dug in the Crossly Oaks consecrated cemetery that was home to four generations of Crossly Oaks ancestors. The old, if not particularly distinguished family, now had a new head. Milo, aged but eleven, was now, Sir Milo Crossly, Baronet of Crossly Oaks.

Rowena's brother, Artus, and his wife, Dorisande, and Gaylord Doggett, Rowena's uncle, as well as the Crossly Oaks tenants and servants were also present for the final ceremony. Liverna saw Godwin had tears in his eye, but Milo stood stiff and straight, and not even his lips trembled. Sir Lindell had died peacefully in his bed. His man servant had found him when he came in to help him dress in the morning. For the last month before he died, Sir Lindell had given up drink, had set his servants to cleaning up the house, and had begun working with the steward Gaylord Doggett had hired to manage the manor grounds.

Liverna had no idea what had caused Sir Lindell's sudden change. What had returned him to his senses? He again took an interest in his sons, and though they still resented him for causing their mother to flee that she might save their sister, they had begun to warm to him. Sir Lindell had made a grave mistake in selling Cecily to Haspel, but other than that foolhardy and life-changing flaw, he was at his core, a good man. She hoped he would rest peacefully in his grave. At least he had gone to his maker knowing his daughter would be freed from the man he had forced her to marry.

After the burial, Liverna would return to the house to supervise the packing. She, the boys, and the boys' tutor were to live with Artus and his wife. The steward Gaylord Doggett had hired to manage the manor grounds would continue on as steward. The cook and a maid would remain at the manor house to keep it ever ready for the return of its mistress, God willing that should happen. The old house steward was pensioned off, and the other house servants were released from their contracts and given references and a month's pay. The shepherd and one stableman would be kept on. They and the tenants would report to the steward who would report to Artus and Doggett.

Rowena was now a widow. Liverna wondered if Rowena had formed an attachment to the handsome man who accompanied her each time she visited her sons. Rowena had been a good and faithful wife to Sir Lindell, and a loving mother to her children, but now she was a widow, what would her future hold for her? How would she react on her next visit when she learned she was a widow? Had she any loving feelings left in her heart for Sir Lindell, or had she buried all of them as Sir Lindell was now being buried?

With Haspel no longer offering a reward to have Cecily returned to him, that meant Cecily and Rowena would be safer. The militia would have no great zeal to search for them. Mayhap Cecily could even return home. But with a warrant on her head, Rowena might never be able to return home. Tears rose to Liverna's eyes. That her beloved child might ever need be on the run was breaking her heart. Please God, she prayed, keep the dear child safe.

Chapter 37

Rowena had ended up thoroughly enjoying her visit with Nate's great aunt Alfreda. Though in her mid-seventies, she was a vibrant entity with seemingly boundless energy. Her husband, Sir Dalbert, soon to be turning eighty spent much of his time in a cushioned chair in his library, a book propped on his lap and glasses propped on the end of his nose. Lady Alfreda kept a blanket wrapped around his legs, a cap on the tuft of white hair still remaining on his head, and a mug of warm ale or cider on a small table beside his chair.

Rowena had been surprised Lady Alfreda's eyes were not the distinctive blue-green eyes she had come to expect in the D'Arcys. Her eyes were an incredible sea-green. And she said her snowy-white hair had once been a flame-kissed auburn. The combination which dated back to a distant Celtic ancestor popped up ever so often in the family. None of her five children bore her coloring, but two grandchildren did.

With her ever-ready smile, Lady Alfreda showed Rowena around her huge house. "This house has been added on to as the family grew. Two of my sons live here with their families, but they have their own quarters. We mainly see them when they choose to dine with us. My oldest son, Oswin, named for my father, carries on my husband's business. And please ask me nothing about the business. I told Dalbert when I agreed to marry him that I wanted to know nothing about the business, I but wanted to spend the money he made." She laughed at her sally and Rowena joined her. The woman was a delight.

Rowena met Lady Alfreda's two sons and their wives and the children that were at home during her visit. The entire family seemed to have Lady Alfreda's joy in living. But why should they not? They lacked for nothing. They had love, a beautiful home, wonderful food to eat, coaches and riding horses, warm and fashionable clothes, servants to do their bidding, and the children had promising futures ahead of them. None would be forced into unwanted marriages. Lady Alfreda was adamant about that, having herself at sixteen been forced into an unwanted marriage. But her first husband had died, and she had then been able to marry for love, her dear Sir Dalbert. "He bought the baronetcy so my father would be more willing to let me marry him. Afterall, he was but a merchant's son. A very wealthy merchant's son, but still, but a commoner."

Though Rowena and Nate, the couple of nights Nate stayed at Lady Alfreda's, had been given separate rooms, they were adjoining rooms. Lady Alfreda recognized they shared a love. She never mentioned nor judged their relationship, she but gave them the opportunity to sleep together did they so choose to do so. And they had chosen to spend those lovely nights wrapped in each other's arms, expressing their love and their need for one another.

When Nate returned from his visit to his family with love to Lady Alfreda and her family from his older brother and family, he sent word to Chapman that 'twas time to head for their rendezvous with his younger brother. They collected the money and jewelry they had left with the Harmons, and after many thanks to Lady Alfreda and Sir Dalbert, they set off for Harp's Ridge.

※ ※ ※ ※

Time with Cecily at the Lotterbys' Harp's Ridge flew by. Each day with her daughter was so precious, but Rowena knew all too soon Nate and Chapman would return, and they would be off to Manchester to meet up with the other highwaymen. One evening in Phillida's sitting room, after Cecily and Timandra had gone to their beds, Phillida again asked Rowena if she could not convince Nate to give up his dangerous highway robberies.

"I cannot ask him to stop," Rowena said. "I can wish it and pray for it, but had Nate not been involved in these robberies that he may help support the King, Cecily and I would not now be here safe with you. I cannot say to him, Nate, my daughter and I are now safe, you need no longer support the King."

Shaking her head, Phillida said, "All I know is he loves you. Could anyone convince him to give up these robberies, 'tis you. I fear for him. I love my brother."

Rowena gnawed her lower lip and looked down. "I love him more than I love myself," she finally said, "and I, too, am in constant fear, but I cannot do what you ask." She looked back up at her hostess. "We have pledged our love to one another. And though we know not what our future will be, we know we will be together for whatever it brings.

"I never dreamed I would know the kind of love I know with Nate. I thought such love was only to be found in romantic fables. I have seen enough of the love you and Lord Grasmere share to know you have been gifted with the kind of love Nate and I have found. Now that I have shared such a love, I know not how I could live without it. Yes, I believe were I to ask Nate to stop the robberies, he would do so, but it might destroy a piece of him. Slight though that piece might be, I cannot ask him to give up this obligation he feels and is committed to."

Phillida sighed. "I suppose you cannot ask him. But I can. And I will."

And she had. But as usual Nate had merely said he would pay heed to her words. He gave her tidings from her brother, Ranulf, who collected the moneys and jewels to be given to the King, and the next day, Nate, Rowena, and Chapman set off for Manchester.

※ ※ ※ ※

Arcadia was thrilled to again be masquerading as a young boy. She had an important part to play for the gang of highwaymen. Upon leaving Manchester, they had rapidly traversed Cheshire into Shropshire, headed for Shrewsbury. The market town was prosperous due to its woolen trade with Wales. It had been a Royalist town during the war, but had been betrayed and defeated. Now it hosted many Puritans busy in various trades, but the richest were the woolen merchants of the Drapers Guild. One merchant in particular was the highwaymen's prey. Arcadia's job was to venture into Turner Lott's shop and discover when he might be planning his spring trip into Wales.

She was to enter Lott's shop and ask the scrivener or clerk a simple question, "Is your master still planning to leave on the morrow, or is he to leave next week?"

"Master Lott leaves next Monday as planned," said a clerk looking up from his customer who was judging a sample of woolen fabrics. "Who would be asking?"

Arcadia chuckled. "That I am sworn not to tell. But the lady be pretty, 'tis all I will say." With that she turned on her heel and hurried out, leaving the clerk and his customer mystified and no doubt wondering if Lott had a mistress.

Arcadia then hurried back to the inn where she and Dev and Rowena and D'Arcy were staying. She gave her report to D'Arcy, then snuck up to her room, and changed back into a young woman. At some point during the evening, her brother, Cyril, would join them to tell them what the other highwaymen had discovered and to learn what she had discovered. Everyone had their parts to play. Cyril and Caleb Hayward and Chapman were staying with a Royalist family. People Chapman knew from his days on the road with his father. Tuftwick and Madigan were staying in another inn. Best they not all be seen together. Plus, different inns offered more possible prey.

What fun, Arcadia thought as she squiggled out of her male's coat and shirt, and donned her petticoats and gown. What fun!

※ ※ ※ ※

D'Arcy was pleased he had not missed his chance to rob Turner Lott. He had learned of Lott while in London. A member of the Drapers Guild, Lott was one of the wealthiest men in Shrewsbury. Besides having his hand in the woolen trade, each spring he journeyed into Wales and dealt personally with the weavers. By getting to the weavers before they brought their cloths to Shrewsbury, he had an advantage over other merchants. But he had to carry a good deal of coins with him to seal his bargains. He traveled on horseback with his pack train following behind him.

Caleb and Cyril had been able to find out from the Royalist family housing them that Lott traveled with a couple of guards. And they said Lott was known to be armed and a good shot himself. D'Arcy had never been forced to kill anyone during his robberies, but he would not feel too guilty was he forced to kill Lott. The man was suspected of being in league with the Parliamentarian sympathizer who in 1645 had opened St. Mary's Water Gate to the Cromwellian forces so they had been able to enter Shrewsbury and defeat the Royalists. Because of the no quarter given, prisoners had been forced to draw lots and twelve had been killed. To D'Arcy, their deaths were partially on Lott's head.

Chapter 38

Clutching the horse's reins, Rowena waited beside Arcadia and strained her ears to hear shots fired. Please let no shots be fired, she prayed. Please let all go smoothly. This was the first time she and Arcadia were participating in a robbery. Both were dressed as men, and their job was to bring up Tuftwick's and Madigan's horses once the prey had been subdued. Tuftwick and Madigan were hidden in a stand of woods bordering the trace leading into Wales that Turner Lott and his pack train were following.

Nate and Cyril Yardley were waiting up ahead for Lott and his train to come into view. Chapman, his hat brim tipped low on one side to conceal his face, was riding casually past the train to determine the fire power they would be up against. Dev and Caleb Hayward were riding along a little ways behind the train but considerably ahead of Arcadia and Rowena. The plan was that Lott and his guards would be so intent on the riders coming toward them, and those following them, that they would pay no heed to the wooded area they were passing beside. Tuftwick and Madigan should be able to jump out and get the drop on them.

Please let it all go as planned, Rowena prayed. Please let no shots be fired.

※ ※ ※ ※

"Lott has three heavily armed guards," Chapman told D'Arcy, "and I would say the two men leading his pack horses are also armed. I am thinking Lott will not let go of his coins without a fight."

"Did they look wary of you when you road past them?" D'Arcy asked.

"Aye. One of the guards kept his pistol pointed at me. I nodded and said good-day, but I received no response other than a grunt. They are indeed wary."

"Is it worth the risk?" Cyril asked.

D'Arcy rubbed his chin. After a moment, he said, "This may be one time we have to shoot to kill. I cannot say I like it. Still, I think we hold the better hand."

"Well," Chapman said, "here they come. Let us go."

Even as he urged his horse forward, D'Arcy wondered if he had made the right decision. There could be a lot of gun play, possibly even some sword play, but he trusted Madigan and Tuftwick to deal with any needed swordsmanship. Madigan was one of the best with a sword that he had ever seen.

"No sooner do they see we wear masks, expect them to fire," D'Arcy said, and he was right. Almost a moment later a shot rang out and D'Arcy heard the ball whiz past his head. A wasted shot. That was good, one pistol barrel emptied.

Lott and his train stopped right next to the woods. The guard at the rear had just loosed a shot at Dev and Caleb. Their faces now masked, they were coming up from behind. At the same instant, Tuftwick and Madigan sprang from the woods, and with pistols in both hands, they ordered Lott and his men to drop their weapons. One guard turned to shoot at Tuftwick, but Tuftwick shot him first. The man yelped and fell from his horse. The second guard and the two men leading the pack horses raised their hands, but the rear guard spurred his horse forward and tried to run Madigan down. Madigan was forced to jump aside and shoot at the guard. He missed, and the guard sprang from his horse and onto Madigan.

Lott fired again at D'Arcy, but Lott's horse, excited by all that was happening, was prancing around and Lott's shot went wild. D'Arcy was then upon Lott and with one well-aimed punch, knocked him from his horse. Dev and Caleb arrived from the rear, and Dev jumped from his horse and brought his pistol butt down on the head of the guard who had jumped Madigan.

While Caleb was keeping his gun on the guard and the two men with the pack horses who had raised their hands, Cyril and Chapman relieved them of their weapons. They were then bound with ropes from the backs of the frightened pack horses. The guard who had been shot was not dead, but he was bleeding profusely. D'Arcy feared he might not survive. He hated that. Still, he and Chapman worked hard to staunch the bleeding. Did the bleeding stop, he might live.

Lott, the breath knocked out of him from his fall off his horse, lay on the ground gasping and moaning. Tuftwick had picked up his pistols and tossed them into the woods. All the other weapons were also tossed into the woods. The guard Dev had hit over the head was coming around. He groaned, but he was not badly injured.

When Rowena and Arcadia arrived leading Tuftwick's and Madigan's horses, D'Arcy could see the worry in Rowena's eyes. He gave her a little wave to assure her all was well with him and his men. Though masked, Rowena and Arcadia knew they were to keep quiet and stay mounted. They could do naught but watch the proceedings.

With Chapman continuing to hold a rag against the injured guard's wound, D'Arcy turned to searching the now flailing about Lott. "You will never get away with this," Lott was hissing between gasps for air. "I will have you hunted down."

When Lott attempted to reach up and pull off D'Arcy's kerchief, D'Arcy flipped him over on his stomach and bound his hands behind. He then resumed checking Lott's pockets and his purse. He had a goodly sum of coins on his person, but D'Arcy knew that could not be near enough to buy the woolen cloths he was going into Wales to purchase. "We will have to check the pack horses," he said. "They are carrying supplies for the journey. Could be the coins are concealed in the supplies."

He had been right. Buried in the grain sacks ostensibly being carried to feed the horses was a treasure trove of coins. "I do think we have it all. If not, we will leave whatever else might be hidden to Lott," D'Arcy said with a chuckle.

Propped up in a sitting position against a tree, Lott was again railing and calling down all forms of evil on the highwaymen's heads.

"Let us mount up," D'Arcy said. "Get that guard onto his horse, and we will leave him at the first house we come across. The bleeding is stopped, he might live does he receive care. He is lucky, the ball went right on through him. He will need his wound cleaned well, though. Any cloth from his shirt extracted. Give a slap to the rear of the other horses so they head on down the trail a ways. It will take Lott and his men a time to recover their mounts once they have worked their way free of their bounds and found their arms in the woods."

A few well-placed slaps to the rear ends of the still frightened horses, and the poor beasts took off at a gallop. Tuftwick and Madigan mounted the horses Rowena and Arcadia had brought for them, and with the injured guard tied securely onto his mount, and Chapman leading the horse, D'Arcy and his gang headed back toward Shrewsbury. Their horses were rested, but because of the injured guard, they had to slow their pace. Within a couple of miles, though, they spotted a lone croft with the farmer out in his field. No doubt the man could use the coin they would leave with him and his wife to care for the guard.

The farmer and his wife and children were at first afraid when Chapman and D'Arcy rode up to their home with their kerchiefs still covering their faces. But when D'Arcy tossed the man a handful of coins and bade him and his goodwife see to the guard's care, the man bobbed his head and promised his wife would do her best to care for the man. "She is a healer," the farmer claimed. "She is known to all around for her skills in caring for the ill. She will do her best to see he lives."

"Does he not, use a coin to see he is decently buried," D'Arcy said. "The rest are to pay you for your care of him."

"Thank you, sir, and God speed to you."

Behind his mask, D'Arcy smiled. The farmer and his wife had no idea why the man was shot or why he and Chapman wore masks, but with needed coins in the palm of his hand, the man was ready to wish them well on their journey.

Rejoining the others on the trace, D'Arcy said, "'Tis time we remove the masks. And this haul is so large, I think we must immediately get it to my aunt's. Jack, I dare not trust this to you alone. 'Tis too much for you to carry. You might tempt robbers. I think Maddy and Tuftwick should go with you. With the pouches divided between the three of you, you should not raise any suspicions."

"When we have left this haul with the Harmons, where do we rejoin you?" Tuftwick asked.

D'Arcy smiled at Tuftwick. The man was a happy soul, more so since he had married Lady Venetia Lotterby. "I do think with this haul, you and Maddy should go home to your wives once you have seen this treasure deposited with my Aunt Alfreda."

His blue eyes alight, a winsome grin spreading across his face, Tuftwick nodded. "Aye, now that is a grand plan, Nate. I have no doubt Venetia and Delphine will both be more than pleased and surprised to see us return home so soon."

"And 'tis good cover, too" D'Arcy said with an answering grin. "Being gone away from your homes for long periods too often could arouse suspicion even among loyal servants. So we will find a safe place to distribute the coins, then you three need be on your way at a good clip. Cover as much ground as you can before nightfall. Jack, try to stay away from inns. Any Royalists you feel you can trust, stay with them."

Chapman nodded. "Aye, the sooner we get these coins divided up into our pouches and can be on our way, the better I will like it. I have in mind a home I would like to reach before it grows dark. Good people."

"Then let us get going," D'Arcy said. "I have no mind for any of us to stay the night in Shrewsbury. I am of a mind to make it to Upton Magna tonight. 'Tis a small town, but it has one inn Caleb and Cyril can stay in. The rest of us will stay with the Murdocks."

"Fine plan," Chapman said. "The Murdocks will give you a hearty welcome."

"Agreed," Nate said, and with that, he put his heels to his horse and soon they were all racing back the way they had come earlier that morning.

※ ※ ※ ※

Racing along behind Nate, Rowena felt her heart swell with joy. Nate and none of his gang had been injured. She knew Nate hated that one of Lott's men had been seriously injured, but she liked that he had done his best to see to the man's care. With three of the gang being sent away, Rowena wondered if Nate would make fewer robberies. She hoped so. At the same time, she had to admit she had felt a certain thrill being part of the robbery. She knew for certain Arcadia had been exuberate. The girl only wished she could have played a larger role. Rowena was quite satisfied with the small role she had played.

Where they were headed next, she had no idea. She had a feeling

Nate meant to distance them as quickly as possible from the Shrewsbury area. They would pass through Shrewsbury on their way to their night's abode. Anyone tracking them would have no idea which direction they had gone once they left Shrewsbury, so many roads led out of that prosperous town. She had little worry that they would be caught, but the militia in the area would be on high alert, so best to move on to another shire. But which shire? She would just have to be patient and trust Nate would keep them all safe.

Chapter 39

Spring melded into summer and Rowena could not believe how much of England she was seeing. After racing through Shropshire, they had dashed through Worcester into Warwick then into Oxfordshire where they pulled off a couple of lucrative robberies. From Oxfordshire, they swept into Northampton, and from there into Lincoln. Nate seemed to know families he trusted in every shire. How many were members of his large extended family, she could only guess, but all homes made them welcome. Some of their hosts were well-off like the Tavers, Prestons, and Guildfords. Some were poor like the Nadlers where cornhusk mattresses on the floor served as their beds, but the families were ready to share what they could. Nate always left a few greatly appreciated coins with them. Other hosts were in nice homes, but they were scraping by after paying fines to regain their confiscated lands or high taxes just for being known Royalists. Nate often left a little something with them, too.

Nate's gang being smaller with Chapman, Tuftwick, and Madigan returned to their homes, Nate was even more careful about his prey selection. They would pull only one robbery in any area before fleeing. Rowena felt relieved when they finally headed back to Leicester where they were to meet up with Chapman. A couple of robberies on the road between Derby and London, always prosperous, and Nate promised they would then visit her sons.

'Twas August, and one full year since she, thanks to Nate and his highwaymen, had rescued Cecily from Haspel. She had not seen her daughter since April, but she trusted Cecily was being well cared for my Lady Grasmere. She but hoped her sweet daughter was happy. She almost felt guilty because she was so happy. Her love for Nate and his for her was continuing to grow. They had been living as man and wife since the end of November. Sometimes they were the Bluchers, and

Dev and Arcadia were the Jamiesons. Other times they all had different names. Sometimes all Nate's gang stayed in one home, sometimes some stayed in an inn or they all stayed in inns. No matter, they were always on the move within a day or two.

Rowena no longer felt any embarrassment at posing as Nate's wife, or sharing his bed. How could she when their love seemed so right. Besides, none of their hosts knew whether they were or were not married anymore than they knew that Dev and Arcadia truly were married. Nate had once said they were destined to be together. She had to believe he was right.

※ ※ ※ ※

August zipped by, and true to his promise, after two robberies in Leicestershire, Nate sent Chapman and Caleb to call on Artus and arrange a meeting in the woods for Rowena and her sons. Clasping both her sons in her arms, Rowena could not get enough of them. The warm September sun was beaming down, and a soft breeze had the trees' burnished leaves whispering. "You are truly well?" she asked her sons. "You are happy with your Uncle Artus?"

"Yes, Mother. Aunt Dorisande is ever spoiling us, but we do miss you and Cecily so much," Milo said.

"When can you come home to stay, Mother?" Godwin asked.

Rowena shook her head. "I know not. If I could come home tomorrow, I would, but I fear it would not be safe. Not for me or for Cecily."

"I know," Milo said, his face taking on an angry look. "'Tis Haspel's doing. Him claiming you were in league with those highwaymen and having a warrant put on your head is what keeps you from being able to come home. Were I older, I would challenge him to a duel, I would. The no-good blackheart."

Rowena rubbed her son's hair. "Yes, Haspel is a blackheart. That is for certain, but I would not like you to be fighting any duels now or when you are older. But tell me, boys, how do you without your father? Do you miss him? At least a little?"

"I cannot say I miss him much," Godwin said. "I miss how he was before Haspel came. Before Father made Cecily marry Haspel. I miss how we were all a family. But when you and Cecily left, Father changed so much." He grew quiet.

"'Twas his drinking made it all worse," Milo said, taking up when his brother broke off. "But about a month before he died, he stopped drinking, and he was easier to be around. Still, I resented him for what he did to you and Cecily." He looked down then back up. "Had I known he was going to die, I think I would have been kinder to him."

Rowena gave him a smile. "Yes, but you must not feel bad, my dear. I have no doubt he understood your feelings. Mayhap that was the reason he stopped drinking. Mayhap he wanted to prove to you that he was sorry and would try again to win your love and trust. That is what I would like to believe."

"I think you may be right, Mother," Godwin said, his young voice bright. "I think Father may have been trying to think what he might do to bring you and Cecily home."

Milo shrugged. "Could be. 'Twould be nice to believe 'twas his plan. But what will you do now, Mother? Must you ever continue to live in hiding?"

Rowena glanced at Nate. When they had first met Artus, Liverna, and Rowena's sons in the woods, Liverna had embraced Rowena, and with tears in her eyes, said, "My dear Lady Crossly, I fear I must tell you that Sir Lindell has died. You are now a widow."

Milo asked what was in her future. What must she answer him?

"Rowena, might I speak with you a moment?" Nate said. "In private."

She nodded, and they stepped a little way apart. With his back to Rowena's family and her maid, Nate took Rowena's hands. "Near ten months ago, I did pledge my love to you. And you did pledge yours to me. If you are still of the same mind, I would like to tell your sons that you have agreed to be my wife."

Looking up into Nate's wonderous eyes, Rowena smiled. "Oh, yes, Nate. I am indeed still of the same mind. Yes, let us tell my dear ones of our love."

A wide grin spread across Nate's face, and he raised her hands to his lips. "I know I must be the luckiest, the happiest man in all of England." With that, he turned with her to tell her sons, brother, and maid that they were to be married.

All were at first silent. They but stared at Rowena, then Liverna stepped forward and grasped Rowena in her arms. "My dear one, I thought mayhap you had found in this man a true love. 'Tis only right you should at last know such a love." She released Rowena and took one of Nate's hands. "I cannot help but think you must love her very much. You have protected her. You have brought her here that she might visit her sons. Yes, I entrust her to your care."

"Thank you, Liverna," Nate said before looking down at Rowena's sons. "Have I your blessings, Milo and Godwin? I do swear to you my love for your mother knows no bounds. And can we some day manage it, I would hope to again unite you with your mother and sister."

The boys continued to stare at Nate and their mother. Rowena was beginning to fear the announcement had been too soon after their father's death, but Artus stepped forward, grabbed Nate's hand, and said, "Congratulations. You have done much to win our favor in bringing Rowena to visit us. And in sending Mister Hayward to tell me of the new farming ideas. I did as he suggested. I planted clover rather than leave my fields fallow. My soil is now more fertile. I am considering his recommendation on the turnips that I might over winter more of my cows. Your Mister Chapman I also like. My wife ordered several fabrics from his pack samples. To have such good friends, friends willing to help arrange these meetings with Rowena and her sons, must mean you are a man to be trusted. And so I do give my sister into your hands."

From Nate, he turned to Rowena and gave her a kiss on the cheek before looking at Milo and Godwin. "What say you to your mother and Mister Blucher, her future husband."

Rowena wished she could tell her family Nate's real name, but that would be too dangerous. Should anyone slip and it become known Nate was in England, not on the continent with his brother and the King, 'twould place him and her at risk. She looked to her sons. Finally, Milo stepped forward with his hand outstretched. "I congratulate you, Mister Blucher. Does my mother consent to marry you, you must be a good man."

"Thank you, Sir Milo," Nate said. "I do promise you, I will do my best to be a good husband to your mother."

Copying his brother, Godwin reached out his hand. "Congratulations, sir. If you could bring Mother to visit more often, we would appreciate it."

"Then that I must do, Master Godwin. I know that will also make your mother happy, and making her happy will ever be my greatest desire."

Rowena stretched out her arms, and both her sons eagerly accepted her embrace. She looked with shining eyes at Nate. She was to marry the man she loved so dearly, and he had also promised he would bring her to see her sons more often. She could ask for little more.

※ ※ ※ ※

Arcadia was thrilled. She was to stand as witness when Rowena and D'Arcy were married. But what a great distance they had to travel to the place D'Arcy considered was safe for them to be married. She knew D'Arcy had considered Tuftwick Manor where she and Dev were married, but the D'Arcy name made even that secluded area risky to stick around for the three weeks needed for the banns to be posted and read. D'Arcy and Dev had discussed taking a boat over to Ireland, but Chapman stated he believed the militia in Ireland was ever on alert, and it could be even more risky. The militia could well wonder why an Englishman would travel to Ireland to be wed.

Finally, D'Arcy settled on his older brother's manor, Tyneford Hall, outside Hexham, Northumberland. According to D'Arcy, the manor had been granted to Halvor D'Arcy when Henry VII made him an Earl in 1490. It was in thanks for Halvor's support of Henry during the War of Roses. Also Henry wanted a forceful presence on the border to help protect against raids from Scotland. Halvor had a strong defensive keep built, and his younger brother, Lovell, was made the steward. Lovell's descendants had continued on as stewards for seven generations, and numerous D'Arcys populated the region.

"Consequently," D'Arcy said, "marriage banns being posted for a D'Arcy will not be that unusual." They were all sitting around a table in a private dining chamber at an inn in Nottingham. They were to make one more robbery, then Chapman and Caleb were to take their gleanings to D'Arcy's aunt in Chester.

"I went to the manor once with my father when I was still quite young," D'Arcy continued. "And once when I was acting as high steward for my brother when he was in prison and then confined to Wealdburh and could not visit his other manors. I cannot say I found Tyneford Hall a pleasant abode, but my cousin and his family seem happy. Tyneford Hall manor is the most lucrative of my brother's manors. There never has been much arable land on the manor. They grow some barley and oats, and have their kitchen gardens, but 'tis the cattle and sheep that are profitable. My father used to go there once a year to check on things. When I was steward for my brother, I was scheduled to go a second time, but then King Charles II decided to make a try for his crown." He chuckled. "So here we sit instead."

"Well, does all go as planned on the morrow," Chapman said, "you and Lady Crossly and Dev and Arcadia and Cyril will be headed north. 'Tis wishing I could be there for your wedding, but I know Caleb and I must transport our goods to safe keeping."

"I, too, wish you could be there to celebrate with us, Jack, dear friend. Mayhap we can have a celebration in the late spring at Knightswood when Phillida and Berold go to Grasmere. Phillida would like hosting such an event I am thinking."

"I would not like to cause your sister any trouble," Rowena said. "She is already doing so much. That she is giving Cecily a safe home is all I could ask of her."

"Nonsense," D'Arcy said. "She has been after me for years to get married. She will be delighted."

Rowena was shaking her head, but Arcadia believed D'Arcy was right. She had little doubt but what Lady Grasmere would want to have a celebration for her brother. "Where do we go after you and Rowena are married?" she asked D'Arcy.

"We go to Carlisle. From there, you, your husband, and your brother will take passage to Liverpool. 'Tis not far from Liverpool to Harp's Ridge. You may visit my sister, then visit your families. We will of necessity need to winter again in London."

"Do you say we are to do no more robberies before winter?" Dev asked, and Arcadia placed her hand over her husband's. She could hear the hope in his voice.

"Aye. That is exactly what I am saying," D'Arcy answered, putting an arm around Rowena and pulling her against him. "I intend to cater to my soon to be wife. After Carlisle, she and I will go to Knightswood. It will be closed up but for the couple who live there year-round, but they will make us welcome. We will then visit my sister at Harp's Ridge that Rowena my see her daughter." He gave Rowena a kiss on her head. "Then back once more to see her sons before we meet you in London. I will send word to Caleb where we will be staying. We never stay in the same abode one year to the next," he informed Arcadia and Rowena.

"Dear Nate," Rowena said. "Thank you. But are you not afraid if you rob no more Cromwellians this autumn, the King will fall short of funds and may find himself in rags?"

Arcadia laughed at Rowena's sally. "Is the King in rags," she said, "'twill not be on our heads. 'Twill be because he keeps too large a court following him about."

"Or so our father says," piped up her brother, and she gave him a playful punch on the arm. Their father was very much against his two children, especially his daughter, being highway robbers. He was loyal to King Charles, but all had heard tell of Charles's dallying and dancing. Cromwell's followers loved reporting on all the scandals in Charles's court.

"Does the King need tighten his breeches, then that he must do. As a married man, I will see to my wife first," D'Arcy said, and the way he was looking at Rowena made Arcadia sigh. Such love.

Chapter 40

Everything went smoothly. The coach driver pulled up and never attempted to reach for a gun. The two footmen hopped down and raised their hands. The merchant and his frightened wife climbed out of the coach when ordered to do so that D'Arcy might search the interior. He found a money bag and a box of jewelry. The woman cried when she saw the box in D'Arcy's hands. As always, he felt sympathy for the women.

"Choose your favorite items," he told the small woman with tears in her large gray eyes. Her eyes widened even more in surprise, but she hastily chose several items from the box. More than D'Arcy had meant to allow her, but he made no protest. He simply dumped the remainder of the jewels into the money bag and handed the box back to the woman.

"You should be ashamed," the merchant said. "Robbing a woman's jewels."

"Aye, and you should be ashamed you give so little to those in need."

"Riders coming and fast!" Chapman said, and D'Arcy looked down the road. Four maybe five. Probably militia on patrol, and having spotted the holdup in progress, they were driving their horses hard.

Thrusting the bag into Chapman's hand, D'Arcy said, "Take this." He looked back at the merchant and his wife. "Back in the coach, now!" he ordered sharply. "You, too," he told the two footmen. "And you, coachman, do you value your life, turn this coach sideways on the road."

While the merchant and his wife, with the help of the footmen, scurried back into the coach, the driver cracked his whip, and with a yank on the reins, he began maneuvering the coach so it crossed the road. At the same time the two footmen clambered into the coach and rapidly closed the door.

"Put the brake on and climb down," D'Arcy ordered the coachman.

"Then hide yourself in the woods." The coachman hastily obeyed as D'Arcy turned again to Jack. "You and Caleb go. Get the women and take them to the Brewsters. Tell the Brewsters we were delayed on business but should arrive shortly. Then you and Caleb head for my aunt's. You have all the bounty in your bags. I want the militia on my trail, not yours."

"Are you certain you can hold them off?" Chapman asked.

"Look to them." D'Arcy nodded toward the horsemen. "Since we turned the coach, they have slowed. They know they are in for a fight, and that has made them cautious. That bodes well for us. Now, go."

"Good luck to you," Chapman said, and he and Hayward mounted their horses and raced away. D'Arcy was left with Yardley and Preston to hold off what looked to be five militiamen.

The merchants querulous voice rose from inside the coach. "What do you mean to do with us?" he said.

"Just keep your heads down so you will not be shot," D'Arcy said. "Does all go well, you will soon again be on your way."

This would not be the first time a militia patrol had come upon them, but it was the first time since Rowena and Arcadia had been traveling with them. Sad it was the last venture of the season. He wished he had been satisfied with the take they had already accumulated and had proceeded on to Tyneford Hall. He knew Rowena and Arcadia would be worried. He was a little worried himself. He would have liked to have Tuftwick and Madigan with him. Well, nothing for it but to hold off the militia long enough for Chapman and Hayward to get the women to safety and themselves on the road to Chester.

Holding their horses to a trot, the militiamen were advancing on the coach blocking the highway. "Give yourselves up," hollered one man, standing up in his stirrups. "You may yet avoid the rope."

"Let go the blunderbuss," D'Arcy told Preston, but be careful not to hit him.

A loud kaboom had the coach horses neighing and prancing and making the coach rock and the merchant's wife scream. It also halted the militia's advance. Several drew their flintlocks and fired. D'Arcy saw the flames burst from the nozzles and the sound of the shots ripped through the air, but the balls landed short and did nothing but splatter dirt.

"When you have reloaded fire again," D'Arcy told Preston, "then ready the horses." Taking aim at a militiaman's hat, D'Arcy fired a shot from his long-barreled flintlock. The hat went flying, and the militiaman almost fell from his horse. Hastily reloading, D'Arcy saw Yardley aim and fire with his double-barreled flintlock. First one shot, then the other, both hitting just shy of the horses. It splattered up dust and set the militiamen's horses to prancing. The militiamen dared not advance any closer, but D'Arcy could tell they were discussing how they might sweep around in a pincer movement. That is what he would do was he attempting an attack. Well, he and his men would soon be gone.

Another kaboom from the blunderbuss, more neighing and prancing horses, and Preston and Yardley were on their horses and racing away. D'Arcy swung up on his horse. With a glance behind him, he saw the militiamen were wary at first, but on spotting him astride his horse, they whipped their horses and raced toward the coach. They would have to maneuver around the coach before they could give chase. That gave D'Arcy, Yardley, and Preston all the time they needed to outdistance their pursuers. He knew they had by far the better horses.

Racing up beside Preston and Yardley, D'Arcy signaled to Preston to split off once they rounded a wooded bend. Preston would head up over a low hill that would hide him from the militia. He would then make his way across any number of fields until he reached the Brewsters. D'Arcy and Yardley would lead the militia on a merry chase until night fell, and the militia would have to give up the quest. With the hunt ended, he and Yardley would rest themselves and their horses, but once the moon came up, they would set off for Sheffield in Yorkshire. There, they would wait for Preston and Rowena and Arcadia to join them.

After spending the night at the Brewsters', Preston would be responsible for getting the two women to their rendezvous in Sheffield. Having once had one of his men injured when the militia had closed on them too rapidly, D'Arcy made certain the gang's future holdups had a backup plan. There always had to be a safe place to meet up when the gang needed to scatter. Early on, he had made Rowena and Arcadia aware of these plans, but as over the past year, no problems had arisen, he imagined Rowena would be in a near panic. Well, Preston would soon be with them, and he should be able to calm their fears. He but hated to be causing Rowena any grief. Could be he might need heed his sister's advice and give up being a highwayman.

❈ ❈ ❈ ❈

Waiting in a wooded area just off the highway, Rowena and Arcadia watched the road. This was to be the last robbery of the season, and they would then head to Northumberland and the D'Arcy Tyneford Hall. It was a long journey, but Rowena could not be bothered about that. Had they not already covered what seemed like half of England as they went from one robbery to another. All she wanted was to have this robbery over and have Nate back at her side.

Had she heard shots?

"Look," Arcadia said. "'Tis Chapman and Caleb and they are riding hard."

Rowena saw the two men racing up the highway. Something was wrong! What was wrong! Fear gripped Rowena's heart. Chapman and Hayward pulled up sharply as they reached Rowena and Arcadia, and Chapman said, "We are to take you to tonight's destination. We were spotted by a militia patrol. Nate, Dev, and Cyril are holding them off long enough for us to get off this highway. Follow me, we will have to take to the fields."

"Caleb!" Arcadia cried, "what can you mean my husband must hold off the militia," but neither Hayward nor Chapman answered her, they but spurred their horses and sprinted down the highway. Rowena and Arcadia had no choice but to follow. They had been told they must never question D'Arcy's decisions or someone could end up dead or injured. So they rode, and when Chapman and Hayward jumped their horses over a low rock fence into a field of grazing sheep, Rowena, with Arcadia right behind her, urged her horse up and over. The sheep looked up, but seeing no threat as the riders raced by, resumed eating.

After crossing several fields, Chapman led them onto a narrow lane that meandered around other fields. At this point, he slowed his mount to let Rowena and Arcadia catch up. "Mister Chapman," Rowena said, "can you not tell us more? You must know we are worried."

"Yes, Caleb, are my husband and brother in any danger?" Arcadia having grown up with Hayward, and Hayward being married to her sister, she stood on no formality with him.

"Cadia, whenever we pull a holdup," Caleb said, "you know there will be some risk. You knew that when you chose to marry Dev. Tamar knew it when she married your brother. Only my dear wife had no way of knowing her husband would end up being a highwayman. However, Nate will let no harm come to your loved ones." He looked at Rowena. "Nor will he let any harm come to himself. Now, we are to take both of you to the Brewsters where you will spend the night. At some point, Nate and the others will join you. On the morrow, you should be on your way to Northumberland. Jack and I are to but leave you with the Brewsters. Considering we have all the bounty we have collected over the past four months, we dare not dawdle. We must set out to Nate's aunt in Chester."

"So let us be on our way," Chapman said, and with a shake of the bridle his horse bobbed his head and started galloping down the lane. Everyone else followed.

It was late-afternoon before they reached the Brewsters, and they had had nothing to eat but some bread and cheese from Chapman's pack. Dear man was never without some form of sustenance in his pack, but 'twas usually naught but bread and cheese. The Brewsters' home was no great manor house, but it was a substantial stone house with a newly thatched roof. Rowena guessed Mister Brewster, a tall man, neatly dressed with gray-streaked shoulder-length hair, and wide blue eyes, to be somewhere between a gentleman and a yeoman farmer. Rather like Caleb's father she guessed. Brewster, upon learning that Rowena was Nate's betrothed, hurried to help Rowena down from her horse. His friendly face showed the wrinkles and creases that come from a life in the sun and the wind, but he had a youthful laugh and strong arms.

His wife was as gracious, eagerly urging Rowena and Arcadia to enter the house. What a treat to have guests. Chapman, as usual, had gone ahead to prepare their hosts for visitors. Rowena had to wonder how much a treat it really was to have two strangers appear at their door that they were expected to house and feed.

The Brewsters' hall had been partitioned into rooms. The front hall functioned more as a parlor than as an age-old hall. The Brewsters tried to get Chapman and Hayward to stay and partake of supper, but the two insisted they had to be on their way.

"Had we not been asked by Mister Blucher and Mister Jamieson to escort the women here, we would already be on our way," Chapman said. "Hayward has a lecture to give on the morrow in Derby, and we dare not linger."

"Ah, I can well understand," Brewster said. "Have I not profited from all he has taught me. I cannot in all conscience hold you up when others may profit from learning of the new techniques, but I hope the both of you will join us again soon."

"Oh, before you go, Mister Chapman," Mistress Brewster said, "might you have any steel sewing needles. I would dearly love to have a second one. My daughter is ever borrowing mine."

"Happens I do have one," Chapman said, and taking his pack from his back, he dug carefully through it until he came to a securely bound bundle. He unwrapped the bundle which contained numerous small items from thread to thimbles to the pins to the prized steel needle.

"How much would that be," Mistress Brewster asked, picking up the needle and holding it carefully in her palm.

"I give it to you for being so kind to give shelter to Mister Blucher's betrothed and Mister Jamieson's wife."

"Nay," Mister Brewster said. "'Tis our pleasure to have the ladies as our guests."

"Indeed it is," Mistress Brewster affirmed.

"All the same, 'tis a gift for all the times you have housed us on our numerous journeys."

"Now we must be going," Hayward said.

And with a few more good-byes and well wishes, Hayward and Chapman departed and Mistress Brewster took Rowena and Arcadia up to their room that they might refresh themselves before supper. They were to share a chamber as Mistress Brewster had been told Nate and Rowena were but betrothed, not married, so Rowena and Nate could not share a room. Nate and Dev would share a chamber, and as the house had but four bedchambers, Mistress Brewster said, "Your brother, Mistress Jamieson, can share our son Aubrey's bedchamber. Now have yourselves a nice rest, and I will call you when supper is to be served."

Left alone, Rowena and Arcadia hugged each other. "Of course they are safe," Arcadia said, and Rowena agreed, but her fear for Nate had not lessened. She felt half of her was missing and she would not feel whole until Nate was back with her, but to her dismay, as they were just sitting down to supper, only Dev arrived.

He was warmly welcomed by the Brewsters, and Arcadia threw her arms around him and showered his face with kisses, but Rowena stood with her hands clutched to her heart and tried to staunch the panic rising in her chest.

Dev was laughing. "Now, Arcadia, what is all this fuss about. So our business kept us a little late. 'Tis naught to cause such a commotion. I do fear, though, that our business has sent Blucher and Chambers on up the highway. We will head out in the morning, and by the time we meet up with them, they will have finished with their business."

"Of course, let us all resume our seats," Mistress Brewster said. She turned to the young maid who had shown Dev into the dining chamber, "Molly, do bring Mister Jamieson a plate and mug. And Mister Jamieson, you eat your fill before you try to tell us anything else. I know you must be starved after such a busy day."

Once supper was ended and they all removed to the parlor where a crackling fire had been stoked up, Aubrey Brewster, a younger version of his father, said, "Where do you need travel to on the morrow, Mister Jamieson?"

"We go to Sheffield. Do we leave early, we should make it before the night falls."

"You will need ride hard. 'Tis more than twenty miles from here. I think mayhap, would be best do I ride with you. At least as far as Chesterfield. I am known to the militia. They will be patrolling the highway. They would be less likely to trouble you am I with you. They know I often have cases in Chesterfield."

Rowena had learned Aubrey was a country lawyer who practiced in the small village near their home as well as in Nottingham and other surrounding towns and villages. He did conveyancing of various kinds, drew up deeds and marriage settlements as well as land transfers. And he often appeared before borough courts. He defended petty criminals or took cases for local tradesmen, farmers, and even landed family gentlemen who might have a grievance.

The following day, they were glad Aubrey Brewster was with them. They were stopped by the militia. They were warned that highwaymen were in the area. They had robbed one merchant the previous day, and the militia suspected they might well try to hit again, but they planned to be ready for them. Being with Aubrey, the militia never questioned what business Dev might be on with the two women. They were treated courteously and were soon again on their way. But Rowena's heart was soaring. That the militia were still seeking Nate and Cyril Yardley meant they were safe. Nothing else mattered to her.

Aubrey left them in Chesterfield, after a brief meal at an inn he recommended. Then they were on their way to Sheffield. From there they would journey to Tyneford Hall. For the time being there would be no more holdups. Rowena could relax and revel in the knowledge she would soon be married to Nathaniel D'Arcy. 'Twas a dream come true.

Chapter 41

Rowena could not help laughing as Nate's cousin's wife, Meriall, and Arcadia fussed over her and decked her out in a shimmering bed rail made for her in Hexham. For the past three weeks, she and Nate had been made to sleep in separate rooms. She had been given the prize room. The room the Earl of Tyneford was always given when he visited Tyneford Hall.

Tyneford Hall was a large square stone keep. It had no turrets, but it was four floors high, and her room was on the top floor. The room had large windows, and an incredible view out to the River Tyne and beyond. The keep was surrounded by a thick, high stone wall with rounded towers at each corner. There was no outer curtain wall and no moat, but there were two gatehouses. Both well-fortified.

There was no entrance to the keep at the ground floor. Wooden staircases at the side and the back of the keep that could be drawn up inside should an enemy breech the wall were the only way in or out. The first floor was a huge hall with a dais at one end, and a screen hiding the buttery and a small kitchen at the other. Like at Nate's Aunt Alfreda's home, a larger kitchen was outside the keep. A massive curtain behind the dais concealed a small chapel. The second floor housed the D'Arcy steward and his family, and the top floor had the rooms for guests.

Stables, barracks, a brew house, laundry shed, animal pens, and a variety of other buildings and sheds were situated against the back wall and one side wall. The steward no longer needed to keep a huge garrison, but he still had a number of men he could call on did reports of Scottish reivers come in from his tenants. The theft of livestock was still prevalent enough that the steward needed to be vigilant. Sweet grasses on the low hills fattened sheep and cattle, and come late fall, when the cattle were fat, was when they were most vulnerable. Little grain farming was done on the manor other than some rye and barley, but a large herb and vegetable garden was in evidence near the kitchen.

During the three weeks Rowena and Nate waited for their banns to be posted and read, Rowena learned much about Tyneford Hall and the surrounding area. Nate took her, Dev, Arcadia, and Cyril to view the Roman ruins at the nearby town of Corbridge. They had done some shopping in Hexham, and Arcadia had helped Rowena pick out the fabric for her wedding night rail. She had also insisted Rowena must have a new gown made for her wedding day. Nate's cousin's diminutive wife, Meriall, her brown eyes bright and shining, her generous mouth spread in a delighted smile, had agreed with Arcadia, and a seamstress had been set to work fashioning Rowena a soft red woolen gown with a gold flower-brocaded petticoat.

"How am I to pay for this?" Rowena had protested, but Meriall pooh-poohed her.

"You are marrying Nathaniel D'Arcy," Meriall said. "The Earl of Tyneford would want nothing less for his brother's future wife."

As Nate had agreed with Meriall, and had even had a tailor make him a new coat and breeches, Rowena had acquiesced. And she had to admit she loved the gown and the night rail. What she would hate would be stuffing them into her panniers when they must leave Tyneford Hall and again take to the road.

"You look lovely," Meriall said, breaking in on Rowena's reverie. She had finished combing out Rowena's hair and was arranging it around her shoulders.

"Indeed you do," Arcadia said, and she gave Rowena a kiss on the cheek. "I am so very happy for you and for Mister D'Arcy. Oh, I mean Nate."

"After a year on the road together," Nate had told Arcadia one afternoon when they were touring the manor, "I do believe we can be less formal. Call me Nate."

Rowena smiled at Arcadia then turned to Meriall. "I cannot thank you and your husband and his many cousins enough for all you have done for us."

"We were delighted to have you and Nate and your dear friends here." She glanced over at Arcadia. "And 'tis always great fun to have a wedding celebration. 'Tis a chance for Saul to see his cousins and for me to get to see my two daughters and my grandchildren. Now the girls are married and one lives in Prudhoe and the other in Brampton, I seldom get to see them. Your wedding gave them a good excuse to get their husbands to bring them to visit."

"How many cousins does your husband have?" Arcadia asked.

"I could not honestly say," Meriall said with a chuckle.

Certainly the hall had been packed. Extra help had been brought in from Hexham and Corbridge to help cook and serve for the gathering. The marriage ceremony had been quietly administered by the Hexham justice of the peace as was required by law. Only Nate's cousin, Saul, Meriall, Cyril, and Dev and Arcadia as witnesses had been present for the ceremony. Then they had all hastened back to Tyneford Hall for the wedding celebration. The justice of the peace, being a D'Arcy, and his wife and children had joined them. It had been a merry trip back to the manor.

Rowena had felt her heart bursting with joy. She and Nate were married. She could not think when she had ever known such happiness. Now, she only needed Nate to join her in the richly furnished bedchamber with the tapestries on the walls, the highly polished oak chest and the tables beside the bed, and the wax candles in silver holders. As if he could read her thoughts, Nate knocked soundly on the door. "Have I a wife in this chamber?" he demanded. "If so, I mean to enter."

Giggling, Arcadia opened the door to him. Cyril, Dev, and Saul stood behind him, but Rowena had eyes only for her husband. The chamber was aglow with candles, and Rowena sat in the rather large bed with her back propped up against several pillows, a light woolen blanket covering her legs.

"My God, you look so beautiful," Nate said, slowly entering the room.

"Does she not," Arcadia said.

Dev had started to follow Nate into the room, but Nate turned and said, "Oh, no, you may think to serenade us as was done to you and Arcadia after your wedding, but I will not be having it. Out! Out all of you. I mean to be alone with my wife."

The men protested, but Meriall, tiny though she was, flapped her hands at the three large men and said, "Shoo, shoo, the lot of you."

Grabbing Arcadia's hand, she tugged her along while pushing the men out. At the door, she looked back and smiled that generous smile, then softly closed the door. Nate immediately bolted the door after her.

※ ※ ※ ※

"Tis hard for me to believe anyone as beautiful as you would consent to marry me." D'Arcy shook his head. "Here I stand before you, a man with no future. No way to provide you a home. And yet, here you are, my wife. Could any man be more lucky than I am?"

"Oh, Nate," Rowena said. "I am the lucky one. You are the ideal of any dream I ever dreamed. And I have not had you in my bed or held you naked in my arms for three weeks. Do stop your foolish blathering and come prove to me how much you love me."

D'Arcy needed no further enticement. In an instant he had his polished boots off and was stripping out of his new coat and breeches. They were tossed over a chair and his stockings and shirt soon joined them. Naked and already aroused, he slid into the bed and took Rowena into his arms. His hands roamed up and down her back as he pressed her to his chest.

"Help me remove this shift," she whispered.

"Soon," he said, "but I want to feel your body all silky and shimmery first. I cannot tell you how luscious you look and feel." His hands moved to her legs, up to hips, and then to her breasts. "Gads," he groaned. "This, our wedding night, I want to make slow, sublime love with you, but I am already in such need of you, I fear I will be a poor lover."

Rowena chuckled softly in his ear. "I, too, am in need of you, my husband."

God how he loved hearing her call him her husband.

"We have the whole night," she said. "Let us tend our needs now. Later we can take more time with our love-making."

"How wise you are, my wife. I do love calling you my wife," he said, his hand working up under the silky shift to caress her. Finding her ready for him, he helped her slip down in the bed, and pushing her shift up around her hips, he moved on top of her. For the first time since they had become as one, he could loose his seed in her. Never had he felt a greater thrill. Never had he been so fulfilled. She gave him new life. Made his world complete.

When they had both found their release, he helped Rowena strip off her shift that he might feel her naked body next to his. Skin against skin. Nestled in his arms, she gave him a kiss on his cheek. "That might not have been slow, my love, but it was certainly sublime," she said.

"I would have to agree with you. Would you nap a bit, or would you rather talk? We have things we must discuss now we are wed."

She pulled away from him enough that she might look into his eyes. "You have me curious. Do we have things to discuss, I say, let us discuss them."

"Very well," he said, "but first I will put out the candles before they begin to sputter." Hating to leave her side for even a moment, he forced himself out of bed, and with a cupped hand about the flames, he blew out the half dozen candles situated about the chamber.

※ ※ ※ ※

Rowena loved looking at Nate's body, his muscled legs and firm buttocks. And when he returned to the bed before blowing out the candle on the table next to the bed, she admired his strong arms and broad chest. His member was, for the moment, limp, but she knew that would change ere long. All was dark when he blew out the last candle and crawled back in beside her, but a half-moon was lighting up the sky, and soon their eyes adjusted to the dimly lit room.

"So what are we to discuss, my wonderful husband?" Rowena asked, placing her hand on his cheek then running her fingers up into his dark hair.

"Our future."

"Our future?"

"Yes. When I was racing away from the militia after our last robbery, I knew I could not go to you. I had to go on to Sheffield. I knew you would be worried. And I wondered was it fair to you to have you worried and wondering what was happening to me. I began to think mayhap I might need give up this occupation."

"You are right. I was terribly frightened. Not until we were on the road to Sheffield did I learn the militia had not caught you. Only then did my heart resume its normal beat. But do you give up these robberies, what would we do? Where could we live? I tell you now, I will not go to the continent and leave my children behind."

"Aye, that I would not expect you to do."

"Nor will I live year-round in London. 'Tis bad enough living there through the winter."

He chuckled. "That I understand, also. The only place I know we could be truly safe is with a friend in Cornwall. His manor is small and isolated, and none of his servants know me. We could be the Bluchers and no one would ever be the wiser."

"Oh, but Cornwall. That is so far from my children. Near as bad as going to the continent. And what of Dev and Arcadia and Cyril? What would they do?"

"To be honest, my dear wife, I had not thought what they might do. I was but thinking how happy all the wives would be were their husbands no longer putting themselves at risk. 'Tis possible Cyril and Dev could turn themselves in to authorities in London. Possible they would spend but little time in prison. Neither broke paroles as Ranulf and I did. Their fathers would pay their fines, but they would be taking a chance. Could be some judge might want to make an example of them. 'Tis possible they might be sentenced to spend several years as indentured servants somewhere in the colonies, or they might be made to prove their loyalty to the Puritan government by serving in the militia in Ireland." He shook his head. "Could be Cyril, to gain his freedom, would be told he would have to name those who helped him escape the Malpas prison. That could be bad for all."

"Indeed. Yet, do they not turn themselves in, what is to become of them? Where could they live? How would they support themselves? How would we support ourselves? Surely we could not forever live off your friend in Cornwall."

"At present, I receive some funds from my older brother. Cyril and Dev also get some funding from their fathers, but we also must use some of the moneys we take in our robberies, especially if we need replace any horses. As you have learned this past year, we have many

Royalist friends who offer us sustenance and shelter. We make do. But is this anyway for us to begin our lives together? What if you get with child? It would be wonderful, but you could not very well travel around in such a condition. Does Arcadia get with child, much as she would miss having Dev at her side, she can go home to her parents. But you cannot go home with that warrant hanging over your head."

"I can think of nothing more wonderful than should I get with child. Was that the case, we could go to your friend in Cornwall or come back here. But we need not face that at present. I say we enjoy these days you have planned for us. We enjoy our time together. Then when I have visited my children, and you and Mister Chapman have given this summer and autumn's take to your brother to give to the King, we go to London as planned. Dev and Arcadia and Cyril will be depending on you. Come spring, am I not with child, we resume the highway robberies. 'Tis not how I would wish to spend our lives, but I cannot see where we have any other choice. At least not for now. We must wait and see what the future may hold for us."

"You are a remarkable woman."

"No more so than the other wives who suffer their husbands to ride off with you. I am but lucky that I get to ride with you. I am not separated from you as the other wives, other than Arcadia, must be separated from their husbands. I am not remarkable. I am but practical. For the present, this game of hide and seek, as your sister does term it, is what keeps us and Cyril and Dev and Arcadia safe. It allows me to occasionally see my children and Cyril to see his wife and children and Dev to see his family. I think for now that is all we can ask for."

"As you say, 'tis what we must accept for the time being, but I do swear to you, Rowena, this will not be forever. I have been proud that I could help the King. But this game cannot continue forever. The people tire of Cromwell and his Puritans who suppress their fun, have taken away their Christmas and their Sunday games. Surely these Puritans cannot remain in power that much longer. I hear mumblings and complaints in every inn and tavern. I see revolution on the horizon. But is there to be no change, at some point, we will have to give up this game and find us a better way to live our lives."

"And we will," Rowena said, giving him a kiss. "I know we will.

But in the meantime, I do believe I recall you saying something about making slow, sublime love to me."

"Mmmm, you have a good memory," he said and his lips found hers.

They would again make love, and she would capture him deep inside her and claim him as her own. What their future held, she could not guess, but she intended to fully revel in the present. Little more than a year had passed since she climbed down the ivy, bent on rescuing her daughter. Never could she have guessed that in saving her daughter, she would find her true love. The future would be what it would be. But now, she had her husband in her arms, his lips and hands were caressing her. For the moment she could ask for nothing more.

The End

Look for my Next Novel!

Excerpt from
Fate Takes A Hand

Chapter One

England 1681

Amaryllis Bowdon set her portmanteau down and shifted her young brother to a better position on her hip. She lodged the canvas bag she carried on her shoulder more securely and squatted to retrieve the portmanteau. It was heavy, and she debated discarding some of the items she had stuffed into it but decided all the articles were needed.

A crackling noise in the woods to her left made her start and her heart jumped into her throat. A squirrel raced up a nearby tree then sat on a branch to chatter at her. "Irksome creature," she hissed when her heart resumed its proper pace in her chest.

"Ryllis, I am tired," came her six-year-old sister's plaintive little voice. "Can we not rest for a bit? This bag handle hurts my hand."

"No, Tabitha." She looked down at the sweet face turned up to hers. "We must reach the inn before they close their doors for the night. We must not bring undo attention to ourselves. They will be curious enough about us arriving at this hour of the night."

"Well, could you carry my bag for a while?"

"Oh, really Tabitha, how can I carry your bag. 'Tis all I can do to carry Charlie and his bag and this portmanteau. Now do start walking. We must hurry on."

Tabitha set off, her bag knocking against her leg. "They will not catch us will they?"

"No dear, they will not catch us. With the potion Cook gave Nurse Palmer, she will sleep into the morning. We will be on the stage bound for Leicester before we will e'er be missed."

Amaryllis looked down the moonlit path and prayed she was right. Did the children's nanny arise at her normal hour, the carefully laid plans could go awry, and they must not go awry. Charlie's life depended on their clandestine escape.

☙ ☙ ☙ ☙

Reginald D'Arcy shifted on his saddle, arched his back, craned his neck, and waggled his shoulders. He was tired. He should not still be in the saddle this late in the evening. He glanced up at the full moon that brightened the night sky before he glared over his shoulder at his sister. She appeared as fresh as she had when they set out that morning. Yet the delay that kept them from reaching their evening's destination in a timely fashion was entirely her fault. He had known when they left on this journey that traveling with Selena would mean trouble, but the first two days had gone smoothly enough, despite being held up on their second day out by a brief but torrential downpour, which in all fairness, could not be blamed on Selena. Foolishly, he had dropped his guard. But today, naught but their third day out, her delaying tactics had begun. That Selena would do anything to postpone her arrival at her final destination was a given. But get her there he would, then the devil take her. He shook his head. Nay. She was his sister and he loved her. Besides, he doubted even the devil would be a match for Selena.

Spoiled, that was what she was, spoiled. 'Twas his father's fault. The Earl of Rygate doted on his only daughter. After their mother's accident that left her paralyzed from the hips down, Selena had had no one to curb her antics. Having four brothers, she copied them and expected to do whatever they did. Proud of Selena's prowess on horseback and her near preternatural way with animals, their father seldom attempted to discipline her. When she took to wearing her brother's clothes when she went riding, he condoned the action saying, "'Tis safer to ride astride. I cannot think the side-saddle, combined with the cumbersome riding costumes women are expected to wear, are at all practical." As long as Selena appeared appropriately gowned at the dinner table, or when they made occasional trips to London, he had no objections to her indecorous conduct within the confines of their estate or the nearby village.

To be honest, Reginald admitted, he had no objections to his sister's brazen behavior. Only two years separated them in age, and she had been a much more satisfactory playmate than had his older brother, Giles, heir to their father's earldom. No, he but wished he had not been the one selected to escort Selena to their Uncle Nathaniel's. Uncle Nathaniel's wife, their Aunt Rowena, was to turn Selena into a lady that Selena might find a husband. Reginald wished his aunt luck. In truth, he doubted the task could be accomplished.

"Master Reginald, I do think I see the lights of Albertine ahead."

Reginald's valet, Bernard Nye, brought Reginald's attention back to the present, and he peered into the darkness. Indeed, he did see the dim twinkling of lights, no doubt betokening a few townsmen not yet in their beds or tradesmen working late, and the inn where, God willing, they would reside for the night. The innkeeper should be expecting them. Word had been sent ahead to reserve accommodations, but they were arriving so late. Could be their lodging had been given to other travelers. Good inns were hard come by. In the village down the road where they stopped to refresh themselves, he had thought they might spend the night, but Selena's maid maintained in adamant terms, did they stay in that inn, they would all leave the next morning with a number of tiny vagabonds accompanying them.

"Sir, would you have me ride ahead and insure all is in readiness?" Nye asked.

"I think that a fine idea. How I might fare without you, I want never to discover." Reginald meant what he said. Ten years Reginald's senior, Nye had been with Reginald since he went off to Oxford. Nye had been his mainstay when he traveled through Europe on his grand tour, and now he was seeing to their comforts on their journey to Whimbrel,

Uncle Nathaniel's estate in the north of Leicestershire. When possible they would stay the night with friends of the family, but the occasional stopover at an inn was unavoidable. This was one of those nights.

Riding up beside Reginald, Selena said, "Does Mister Nye go to secure us a meal? I am near to starving."

Reginald turned to his sister. She offered him a bright smile, her teeth gleaming in the moonlight. Her face devoid of embellishments, her near black hair tied behind her head, and her slim figure clothed in a man's apparel, she could easily pass for a youth. No one would suspect she was Lady Selena D'Arcy. Still angry at their long delay, Reginald did not return her smile.

"You deserve to be hungry," he snapped. "I yet cannot believe you have kept us from our supper and our beds for that mangy whelp."

Selena laughed, the sound tinkling out into the night air. "Fate is no longer mangy. You know well Esmeralda would never allow him to ride in the coach with her did he have so much as one flee left on his poor little body. Poor dear has been scrubbed until his skin looks pink beneath his hair. And that splint the surgeon put on his leg will keep him from being a nuisance."

"So you have named him have you? I suppose that means you are set on keeping him." Selena had found the small black and white dog by the roadside. His left hind leg broken, he looked as if he had been run over by a cart and left by the side of the road to die. Cold, hungry, and whimpering, the dog had wrung Selena's heart. Naught would do but she must take him up, find a doctor to set his leg, have him bathed, then deposit him on a blanket on the floor of the coach. Selena's maid, after years of service in the D'Arcy household, knew better than to complain. 'Twould do no good and would but delay their journey even longer.

"I shall keep him unless I find him a good home before we arrive at Whimbrel," Selena said. "We have several days travel ahead of us. Who knows what will transpire."

Who indeed could know, Reginald thought. With Selena, anything was possible. Setting his heals to his horse, he urged the animal into a trot. He could see the inn at the edge of the town. All would be bustling as the innkeeper and his minions prepared to greet their guests.

Biography

Celia Martin is a former Social Studies/English teacher. Her love of history dates back to her earliest memories when she sat enthralled as her grandparents recounted tales of their past. As a child, she delighted in the make-believe games that she played with her siblings and friends, but as she grew up and had to put aside the games, she found she could not set aside her imagination. So, Celia took up writing stories for her own entertainment.

She is an avid reader. She loves getting lost in a romance, but also enjoys good mysteries, exciting adventure stories, and fact-loaded historical documentaries. When her husband retired and they moved from California to the glorious Kitsap Peninsula in the state of Washington, she was able to begin a full-fledged writing career. And has never been happier.

When not engaged in writing, Celia enjoys travel, keeping fit, and listening to a variety of different music styles.

Visit my web site at:
cmartinbooks.kitsappublishing.com